FAITH AND SCIENCE
IN A
SKEPTICAL AGE

Faith and Science in a Skeptical Age

Edited by
Jesse Yow

CONCORDIA PUBLISHING HOUSE • SAINT LOUIS

Manufactured in the United States of America

Library of Congress Cataloging-in-Publication Data

Faith and science in a skeptical age / edited by Jesse Yow ; WRITERS, Norbert Becker, Adam Francisco, Christopher Halbert, Angus Menuge, Robert Weise.

    pages cm

  Text derived from the Faith on the Edge Bible study series copyrights 2002, 2003, 2004 Concordia Publishing House.

  ISBN 978-0-7586-4413-8

1. Religion and science. I. Yow, Jesse.

  BL240.3.S3487 2014

  261.5'5--dc23

2013047258

1 2 3 4 5 6 7 8 9 10   23 22 21 20 19 18 17 16 15 14

CONTENTS

PREFACE

Truth is, in the minds of many, the Everest of human achievement. I was reminded of this recently while reading a massive text on human physiology in which the author sought to sort out just what was going on in human beings, while dismissing earlier theories and proposing his own new one. This is an ongoing task for research scientists who collect facts and find themselves dissatisfied with earlier conclusions. The author stated in a matter of fact way that the goal of science is to discover truth. Yet it is relatively easy to pull together facts, pile them high in a supporting arrangement, climb to the top, and declare, "I have found it!" while falling woefully short of Everest-like truth. Scientists achieve many great things, but summiting truth is a complicated matter—that Everest is strewn with the corpses of those who never made it or who did not live to tell about it. What is more, scientists now tell us that Olympus Mons, the tallest mountain on Mars, is nearly three times the height of Everest! Truth be told, it seems there is always a bigger hill.

The age of reason (seventeenth to eighteenth centuries) gave modern science its lofty ideals, the pursuit of truth being among them. Now in the twenty-first century, we discover an important truth about scientific learning. It is not, as many hoped, as solid as Everest and not nearly as lasting. We observe how often one fact is replaced by another. Today's plausible theory becomes yesterday's groundless assertion. One scientist doggedly hunts another in an effort to be first, to be right, to go farther and higher. Truth attained, like the summit of Everest, is cold. From that summit, one is driven to look down again and crave the warmth of baser climes. In the end, the scientist must confess that having the truth is hardly enough.

This is why religious faith—the supposed nemesis of the age of reason—continues to flourish despite predictions that science made it passé. *Faith and Science in a Skeptical Age* helps scientists and the scientifically minded explore this truth while grasping truths that are both higher and baser than those attained by science. For no scientist attempts Everest without first experiencing the warmth of human embrace, the nurture of love and kindness. No one takes his first steps alone. The Creator made it so. And as Paul observed before the learned men of Athens, "He is actually not far from each one of us, for 'In Him we live and move and have our being'" (Acts 17:27–28).

Edward A. Engelbrecht
Senior Editor of Bible Resources
Concordia Publishing House

INTRODUCTION

In the past, science served as a stepchild of alchemy, a handmaiden of theology, and a tool of industry. As the twentieth century began, science took on a new role. For many, science became the answer to all of humankind's problems. Scientists pulled on their white lab coats, prophesied through their theories, and consecrated each discovery or invention. Humans marveled.

In response to these accomplishments, a new type of literature arose— science fiction, which sometimes warned us about the maddening pace of technology: The robot would replace the human worker. Nuclear fallout would devastate life on Earth. Man would merge with machine. Civilization would restart on another planet. Science would solve all our problems by doing away with people or at least by doing away with their humanity.

Today, people remain thankful for science, but they also recognize that science does not hold all the answers. In fact, they see that science often raises more questions than it answers, driving people further in quest of understanding, truth, fulfillment, and contentment.

This book considers the intersections of the progress of science, people's fascinations and fears about science, and the human yearnings beneath these intersections. Editor Jesse Yow adapted and updated the text from the popular *Faith on the Edge* Bible study series (CPH):

Off the Edge: Faith, Science, and the Future

The Quest for Spirituality
> by Adam Francisco

The Unexplained: Miracles, Mysteries, and More
> by Christopher Halbert

Heaven and Hell: The Edge of Eternity
> by Norbert Becker

Playing God: Redesigning Life
> by Robert Weise

Science and the Savior: The Calling of a Scientist
> by Angus Menuge

Each section introduces a contemporary topic(s), summarizes what science has to say about it in popular perceptions, and then provides biblical answers and guidance so that you can face the future with the wisdom and confidence that only God can provide.

Off the Edge
Faith, Science, and the Future

On July 20, 1969, Edwin poured a small cup of wine and set out a wafer of bread. He silently repeated the words of a Communion service given to him by his pastor. Then, like millions of other people across the centuries, he ate and drank and prayed.

But Edwin's altar was a shelf in the lunar module *Eagle*. His "sanctuary" was 240,000 miles from the Earth on the surface of the moon. Edwin "Buzz" Aldrin had a Communion experience unlike any other.

Since its beginnings, Christianity's skeptics and critics have asserted that Christianity's days are numbered. They have reasoned that if and when humans leave Earth's atmosphere, they must also, inevitably, leave behind the earthly superstitions of religious faith. However, Aldrin's faith in Christ and his desire to commune with Christ traveled with him (even if "self-Communion" is a contradiction in terms). Faith crossed the boundary of Earth's atmosphere as easily as your eyes run across this page.

The skeptics and critics have not understood the persistence of Christianity because they have not understood the person of Jesus Christ. They have assumed that advances in science have narrowed or limited Christ's teaching. They have failed to see the Earth and the heavens as Aldrin did, as the work of Christ the Creator. As a human, Aldrin could peer down at the Earth and see his natural environment. As a Christian, he could look out into the vastness of the heavens and feel at home.

Writers such as Robert Zubrin, author of *The Case for Mars*, have argued for a "spacefaring civilization." More space travel seems to be in our future, if not coordinated by the United States then perhaps by another country. With Christ, you can face that future with optimism. You can see the compatibility of genuine science and faith.

This section will help you understand key questions and issues about science, the Bible, and your life. It will help you embrace the future in faith because Christ faithfully embraces you by His grace.

1

Faith in the Age of Science

"I have been told that you wrote this large book on the universe and have not even mentioned its Creator."

"Sir, I have no need of that hypothesis."

Religious belief characterized the Western world for centuries. However, the above conversation between Napoleon Bonaparte and the mathematician/scientist Pierre-Simon Laplace (1749–1827) marked the emergence of a new standard of truth.

- In the Age of Reason, some scientists explained the universe apart from traditional biblical teachings.
- By the late nineteenth century, many people viewed science and Christianity as enemies. (See John Draper's *A History of the Conflict between Religion and Science* [1874] and Andrew Dickson White's *A History of the Warfare of Science with Theology and Christendom* [1896].) They pitted science and religion against each other, with science emerging victorious.
- The twentieth century witnessed tremendous scientific advances. Laboratory experiments increased in precision. Powerful telescopes enabled astronomers to peer into the expanding universe, and particle accelerators probed the nature of matter at a subatomic scale. Rockets transported men to the moon and enabled scientists to take pictures of Mars.
- This century will likely see the first manned landing on Mars and perhaps on other planets and moons.

In light of the vast advances in scientific knowledge of the universe, a prolific author of scientific literature, Isaac Asimov, remarked that for people to attribute the existence and sustenance of the universe to God has always been and will always be premature. He warns us not to bury scientific knowledge under folly and ignorant superstition (that is, religious belief).

Many people assume that religion and science are enemies, or at least unrelated. We can probably find examples in news stories and articles that cross over from one area into another without recognizing or properly reflecting the other area (for example, describing scientific discoveries while dismissing their moral implications). We might also find examples in the attitudes of friends, family members, co-workers, and so on.

Some scientists (e.g., Isaac Asimov and, more recently, Stephen Hawking) are hostile toward religious faith. Certain religious groups also show animosity toward science. Meanwhile, some media presentations dwell on one side or the other to highlight the conflict and use sensational stories and facts to sell to their audience. Hence, much of their coverage presents only the extremes in both religious and scientific groups.

Often it becomes tempting to view science as working against religious faith, but this reflects a narrow picture of science, faith, or both. If we consider the rich value of knowledge, wisdom, and understanding portrayed in Proverbs 8:1–11, we realize that the roles religion and science should play in relation to each other are broad, rich, and worth exploring.

Science is vital to progress in improving health and human welfare (e.g., discovery of vaccines, weather prediction, and energy production all depend on science). Without it, life would be tremendously different. It is difficult to think of anything in the secular realm that does not rely in some way on science.

Religion plays an essential role in life as well. Christianity presents a worldview that does not limit the role of legitimate science in public life. Christianity first and foremost concerns itself with the Gospel of Jesus Christ.

The vocation of scientist does not necessarily lead to a conflict with Christianity; it is just as God-pleasing in its proper function as the vocation of pastor. Just as a pastor or priest can abuse his vocation, so can a scientist. *Bad* science is not an enemy to religion alone. It is an enemy to science as well. Our Maker calls us to live in wisdom, to grow in our understanding of the spiritual and physical aspects of life. *All* truth is of interest to God's people.

However, scientific and religious truths often appear in conflict with each other or segregated into two separate realms of knowledge. Distracted from the most valuable matters, discussion often focuses on side issues instead of coming to grips with what we think of the Christ. Fortunately, after years of conflict, scientists and theologians are beginning to engage one another in better dialogue. In fact, many capable scientists contribute to religious life and practice as well. Various scientists even find that their research offers indication and, in some cases, confirmation of religious belief.

The relationship between religion and science is dynamic and continually in flux. Until modern times, those who engaged in scientific inquiry were trained theologically as well. Typically, the role of scientist was seen as investigating the wonders of God's creation. Some of the greatest scientists over the course of the Middle Ages and the early modern era were clerics—Blaise

Pascal, Johannes Kepler, and Nicolaus Copernicus. Isaac Newton trained formally in theology while engaging in scientific research.

At present, scientists and theologians are in constant dialogue. For example, Oxford University and other high-profile universities have entire academic programs dedicated to dialogue and mutual interest in the disciplines of science and religion. Some of the dialogues are marked by compromise (typically from the side of theologians). However, if the proper limits of each discipline are clearly defined, no compromise need take place.

Science: Methods and Limits

At the foundation of modern science lies the scientific method. The scientific method lays ground rules for research and enables scientists to reliably discover the wonders of the universe. As technology advances and experiments continue to support scientific theories, writers report the findings, teachers educate their students, and knowledge of the universe increases. This in itself is wonderful!

A realistic and reasonable view of the methods and limits of science enables scientists as well as the general public to distinguish science fact from fiction. Science that is aware of its limits and proper methods in no way militates against religious faith. In fact, there are some similarities between scientific and theological methods.

The scientific method establishes the foundation of scientific research. Simply put, it approaches the knowledge of facts (science) in a systematic and experimental manner with logical steps. The following steps help maintain the reliability of science:

- Observations or measurements are made of the thing or event under investigation.
- A hypothesis is proposed to explain observations.
- The hypothesis helps to predict the results of new or additional observations.
- The hypothesis is then tested against further observations or experiments and is modified if necessary to fit the new data. (It must fit the old data too!)
- Steps 3 and 4 are repeated until the hypothesis no longer needs improvement. (Either it fits all the data and proves true, or one abandons the hypothesis.)

These rules distinguish good science from bad science. Fake observations can be uncovered if similar experiments by other scientists fail to produce the same results. Hence, the scientific method carries implications of honesty and integrity.

As useful as the scientific method is, it also has some important (and sometimes unappreciated) shortcomings, such as these:

- The scientific method is better suited for methodical research than it is for unexpected discoveries, although it may still be useful to verify discoveries. It implies systematic progress rather than a flash of inspiration from creativity.
- The scientific method does not address unique events (events that cannot be reproduced), such as miracles or anomalies.
- Even though the scientific method requires integrity, it cannot command it. Scientific hoaxes come and go. One can find hosts of websites and books devoted to describing hoaxes throughout the history of science.
- The scientific method can become an excuse for elitism or resistance to new theories. Over the course of but a few decades in the twentieth century, plate tectonics went from a questioned theory to an accepted fact among geologists. Once it became "fact," any theory that deviated from it met the same kind of scorn that plate tectonics had received only a few decades earlier.
- The scientific method can also become an excuse for avoiding issues. Research may explain how something happens but have trouble with questions of why something happens. For example, physicists attempt to tell how the universe began but cannot deal with the question of why it exists.

As long as scientists follow the methods of science and recognize its unavoidable shortcomings, scientific and religious truths avoid conflict. Facts are facts, and observations are observations. However, a distinction must always be recognized between facts bound by time and space (scientific truths) and eternal, immutable facts (theological truths).

Scientific truth *describes* the universe through observation of particular things or events. Its scope is limited by what is observed. Claims made beyond what has been observed remain speculation until confirmed by observation. Even then, better measurements may later change our understanding of what we observe. Scientific truth may suggest what we should look for and how to observe it, but it does not *prescribe* what we will observe or find in our research.

What about theological truths? Theology derives from the roots *theos* (referring to God) and *logos* (meaning "word," or a "message" or "teaching"). A theological truth is a teaching made about God that is accurate. As science is a *descriptive* discipline, theology certainly is *descriptive* as well. Theology describes God and His relationship to His creation. However, theologians are limited in scope by what the Bible says of God and the world He made. Theological claims beyond what the Bible says are mere speculation. Theology is also *prescriptive*. It does not simply describe God and leave it at that. Rather, it prescribes what one should believe about God and humanity as well as the relationship between the two.

Put simply, the scientific method begins with an idea that a certain thing acts in a certain way. Scientists test this idea. If it passes carefully scrutinized experiments, then it can be considered accurate. The theological method is not much different. Theological statements must be tested against relevant passages of Scripture. However, the Bible is not bound by what we consider established rules of logic. Because of the supernatural element in the Scriptures, unexplainable events should be expected and accepted.

Many theologians have offered "systems" of theology. Some, in their desire to establish a coherent, logically consistent system, used nonbiblical standards of truth in their theological claims. However, theologians of the sixteenth century, drawing on the best theological traditions, put together documents informed by the Scriptures alone (e.g., Luther's Small Catechism and the Book of Concord).

Attacks from science on religious belief often claim that religion requires a blind leap of faith, but scientific research requires faith too. At a fundamental level, scientists exercise faith or trust in their senses and their reason. They trust their perception of the events that occur in experiments and the conclusions they draw from them. Though this element of faith appears to be "common sense," it still qualifies as faith. Attacks on religion because of its faith element are unwarranted. When scientists make claims beyond what they have observed, *they* make a blind leap of faith. The saying "Where reason ends, faith begins" points out the necessity for faith in all human endeavors.

HUMAN LIMITATIONS

The very fact that we are able to reason testifies to a purpose behind creation. Increases in knowledge about our world testify to the special place of human beings as creatures endowed by God with reason and senses.

God "experimented" with Adam's curiosity in Genesis 2:19. He invited Adam to choose names for the animals and birds. This demonstrates the freedom and creativity of both God and human beings living in a parent/child or teacher/student relationship. The "scientific" notion of a purposeless creation by chance, taken to its logical conclusion, leaves no room for human choice and creativity guided by human reason—it leaves only humans guided by seemingly random chemical processes.

Scientific thirst for knowledge can get us into trouble. We can ignore the facts or information God gives us—eternal, unchanging facts. It seems quite obvious (or at least it should be obvious) that if God tells us something, then it is true. However, our intellect fails to grasp this. By taking human reason as the bar of truth, we judge God's timeless truth by our limited experiences. In other words, science and reason become the master, and we try to box God in. Though this is an intellectual problem, its roots lie deep within the human will—a will inclined to question and doubt what God says. In fact, we would like to judge God.

Proverbs 1:7 says, "The fear of the LORD is the beginning of knowledge; fools despise wisdom and instruction." After reading this, a Christian student told her friends that since her professor was not a Christian, he must be a fool. (The professor was a reputable scientist but was also an atheist.) But does a scientist have to be a Christian to be a good scientist? No. An atheist can be a good scientist. On the other hand, fools despise spiritual wisdom. In particular, they despise that which makes us wise for salvation (2 Timothy 3:15). Fools despise the eternal wisdom that God gives, which only faith can grasp. When others see this behavior, it raises questions about how we could see things so differently. Certainly there are intellectual obstacles to faith, because God's ways are not our ways. However, all rejections of the Gospel stem from humanity's inherently sinful condition. This condition impels us to rebel against God. Anticipating these kinds of contrasts and questions, Peter exhorts us to be prepared to answer inquiries about the reason for our Christian hope (1 Peter 3:15).

The fact that a scientist happens to be a Christian does not necessarily affect how that scientist engages in scientific work. Recognizing the proper roles and limits of science enables scientists to engage in science while maintaining their religious commitment, and the scientific method does not dictate against matters of faith.

Theologians speak of reason and science as *servants* of religion and theology. This is because reason and science should be subject to the Creator's Word, and sound reason and science should support theological truths. In broader terms, the Bible presents a worldview that remains open to God's intervention. The word *servant* implies a hierarchy of authority that is logical only when we realize that we are finite beings investigating things made by an infinite God. Science and reason help us determine how things work within the world that God made.

You may ask what role the Bible's teachings about events such as creation and the end times play in scientific research and findings. The Bible's central theme is the history of God's revelation within His creation. In particular, it tells God's story of how He redeemed His fallen creatures. At the center of it all is the crucifixion and resurrection of Jesus Christ. However, the Bible is not a science textbook! It does not claim to explain all the intricacies of the universe. Nevertheless, as God's revelation to humankind, the Bible does tell us the origin of the universe and the basis for understanding it. God is in a position to give us undisputed knowledge, whereas scientific knowledge is limited by time and human abilities.

Science works from within the created order. The Bible gives us the words of the Creator. Where the Scriptures are clear about the nature of the universe (e.g., creation and the end times), science remains subject to these truths. However, science can offer many insights on matters the Bible does not address, provided that science does not contradict the bigger picture offered by Scripture.

Christians should not fear science. In fact, a host of serious scientists remain confessing Christians. Even when the popular scientific notions of the day *appear* to contradict belief in God and His authority over creation, these scientists maintain their faith in Christ.

Nevertheless, we may find ourselves doubting, in light of scientific claims, what God has revealed in the Scriptures. Sometimes we hold certain scientific claims as truth, and we change or alter God's Word to fit what science purports to be true. Not only is this unreasonable, but it is also sinful. Doubting God and His Word yields dreadful consequences.

Consider Eve's conversation with the serpent (Satan) in the Garden of Eden (Genesis 3:1–7). Eve's sin was rooted in doubting and then defying God's Word. Because she doubted God's provision and grace, she took the fruit and ate it. So which should we question—God's Word or human science and reason? God's Word does not change, but science and reason do change with new discoveries and new information. God is unchanging and can be trusted more than any human being, so if science and Scripture are at odds, we should question any scientific claims that contradict Scripture.

Romans 1:18–32 lays out the consequences of suppressing God's truth. These consequences include foolishness, idolatry, sexual impurity, homosexuality, greed, arrogance, depraved minds, and so on. Doubting God also has eternal consequences. Notice that all it took was one seed of doubt to take root in Eve's mind for Adam and Eve to find themselves separated from God. The same attitude that raises doubts lies in each of us. We doubt God and find our mind and heart inclined to our own will. Instead of trusting God and His Word, we trust ourselves. This is but a symptom of the disease inherent in all human beings—the sickness of sin and its inevitable consequence of death.

DIVINE INTERVENTION

Our situation looks bleak. Seemingly, we live only to die (Ecclesiastes 2:15–16). Our attempts to gain wisdom appear futile. Yet grasping this truth is the beginning of wisdom.

When the Holy Spirit leads us to see the truth of the human situation—our inherent sinfulness and distrust of God—true repentance can begin. *Repentance* means "a change of mind." When faced with the truth of our corruption, we turn to God for help. Yet what kind of God do we find? We cannot see Him. We cannot find Him by our own reason or strength. We are still left without hope.

Theologians call the God whom we cannot "see" *the hidden God*. Apart from divine revelation, we cannot be sure of *the hidden God's* attitude toward us. The only way for us to know God and His attitude toward us is for God to make Himself known. This remains problematic from our perspective. Where do we look for God? How can we be sure of our perception of Him? For us to know God and be certain of His love, God had to speak to us.

Read John 1:1–5, 14 and consider who "the Word" is and what "the Word" has done. "The Word" is Jesus; "the Word" is the One who was with God and equal with God. "The Word" took part in the creation of the world. "The Word" became flesh and lived among human beings within the realm of human history. The same Word who took part in creation lived visibly *within* His creation. By doing so, He brought light to the darkness that prevailed in human hearts.

Jesus was and is the eternal Word of God. He came and lived in the midst of space and time. The eternal became finite (while retaining His eternality). The Creator no longer remains hidden from human eyes. God is made known in and through Jesus Christ. If we want to know God, we must look to Jesus Christ.

John 1:14 speaks of the Word made flesh as the One sent from the Father. The Father is the First *Person* of the Trinity. The Son, sent by the Father, is the Second *Person* of the Trinity. The Holy Spirit is the Third *Person*. All three persons are united in one divine essence. That is, they are all equally God yet distinct persons. Analogies fall short of conveying the true concept of the Trinity. The only way the Trinity can be known and understood is through the One who was sent from all eternity. Jesus went forth from God the Father. He refers to Himself as God's Son. In John 14–16, Jesus speaks of the Holy Spirit as One who *proceeds* ("goes out") from the Father.

At a specific point in time, during the reign of Caesar Augustus (about 2 BC), God took to Himself human flesh and lived among His human creatures. In the person of Jesus, God is no longer hidden from our eyes. He appeared with flesh and blood (John 1:18).

What does Jesus reveal to us about God and humankind? Though all the evidence points to our birth as leading only to death, Jesus reveals a different plan, and God chose us to fit in this plan. Jesus did not offer a theory or "ten steps" on how to achieve eternal life. He offered another way. He knew His children had gone terribly awry in choosing rebellion and arrogance. There was no way for them to reverse the effect and result of sin—death. So the Creator came down in order to restore His creation, and He did this visibly for all to see (Hebrews 1:1–3).

The One sent by God, the One who created us, bore the punishment for sin. This did not take place in the abstract. Rather, this took place on a Roman cross. Jesus suffered extreme humiliation and the judgment of hell for all people. On the cross, God's love for His dear ones was revealed for all to see (Romans 5:6–8). One of the last things Jesus said from the cross was "It is finished" (John 19:30). The work of redemption was complete. Though Jesus was perfectly righteous and deserved no punishment, the righteous judgment of God on sinful people was borne entirely by Him. Jesus exchanged His righteousness for our sinfulness.

The Good News is that we need do nothing to have the righteousness of Jesus and to be right with God (see Romans 3:21–28). Nothing! The righteousness of Jesus is *given* to us as our own. Apart from any good deeds, prayers of acceptance, or changes in lifestyle, we receive the righteousness of Jesus Christ and faith through the work of the Spirit on our behalf. As Paul states, "We hold that one is justified by faith apart from works of the law" (Romans 3:28). This truth is the center of Christian theology. Without it there is no Christian faith.

Christ's death paid for our sins. However, there is more! Three days after His death, He rose from the grave. Not only did Jesus pay the price for sin, but He also conquered death. So we need not fear death or futility in life. Christ has won the victory for us!

POINTS TO PONDER

Think about the sources of scientific knowledge and the sources of religious knowledge. How is our body of knowledge limited by our finite capabilities and understanding, and what has God done to help us with our limitations?

WORDS TO REMEMBER

You have been acquainted with the sacred writings, which are able to make you wise for salvation through faith in Christ Jesus. All Scripture is breathed out by God and profitable for teaching, for reproof, for correction, and for training in righteousness, that the man of God may be complete, equipped for every good work. (2 Timothy 3:15–17)

2

FROM SOUP TO SCIENCE (COSMOLOGY)

A humanistic view of the universe holds that roughly fifteen billion years ago all that existed was "soup." This was no ordinary soup; it contained the potential for matter. In a sort of bubble (some speculators prefer the term *quantum fluctuation*) emerged a small, seedlike thing. This thing contained all the mass and energy of our present universe. Voila . . . the Big Bang! And the rest is history.

Thinkers throughout the history of the world have developed and studied theories about the origin and continuation of the universe (cosmology). Theories proposed by ancient philosophers and astronomers (Aristotle and Ptolemy, in particular) viewed the universe as *static,* set in place with definite boundaries.

However, after measuring the change of color in starlight from distant galaxies (known as the *red shift*), American astronomer Edwin Hubble discovered that the universe is expanding (1929). In 1965, radio astronomers Robert Wilson and Arno Penzias, along with some Princeton physicists, discovered what was thought to be the echo of the Big Bang. Everywhere they turned their radio antennae they heard *cosmic background radiation* (the Big Bang's "echo"). Wilson and Penzias received the Nobel Prize. About the same time as their discovery, various scientists calculated how much hydrogen and helium would have been produced a few minutes after the Big Bang. Their theoretical calculations matched well with the presently observable amounts of hydrogen and helium in the universe.

Hubble's observations, the abundance of hydrogen and helium throughout the universe, and the 1965 discovery of background radiation provide the basis for Big Bang cosmology. Though a few other cosmologies have popped up over the last forty years (e.g., the steady-state theory and the oscillating-universe theory), most scientists work with a Big Bang cosmology.

Regardless of whether the Big Bang idea accurately describes how the universe began, what does this theory fail to explain? The Big Bang theory fails in at least two ways. (1) It does not answer why the so-called Big Bang occurred as opposed to why it did not. Some theologians attempt to explain that God used the Big Bang as His method of creating the universe, but a "how" question is not the same as a "why" question. (2) It fails to explain where any preexisting "stuff" came from. Some thinkers claim that the primordial soup ("stuff") existed from all eternity. Yet this begs the question: How do they know that? It also fails to explain how the soup existed from all eternity, since the laws of thermodynamics state that over a long enough amount of time, energy equalizes and "freezes" (entropy).

Recalling the scientific method from our previous discussion, we realize that the Big Bang theory does not fit the scientific method because scientists cannot repeat what supposedly occurred. Scientists have been able to replicate small-scale "Big Bangs" but nothing with the potential of forming an entire universe. Even if they were somehow able to demonstrate the universe-building potential of a "Big Bang laboratory," they would have to acknowledge that they had designed this Big Bang—implying that a Designer or a Mind/Will was the cause of the Big Bang itself.

Soup without a Chef?

Views on the cause and appearance of matter after the Big Bang have varied. Some persons, such as science writer Isaac Asimov, claimed that matter always existed but that at one point in time the universe began to take shape. Rather than explaining how scientists know that matter has always existed, Asimov simply asserts that it *just has.* This attitude is hardly scientific, and it deflects rather than answers fundamental questions of what, how, and why. The *philosophy* of science seeks to do just the opposite by minimizing such assumptions of content. More recently, some scientific thinkers tried to explain how the universe could begin without any previously existing matter since they see no evidence that matter always existed.

(Please note: For sake of discussion, the following theories are presented in summary form. Readers who wish to learn the details should consult the appropriate science texts.)

Lawyer, theologian, and philosopher John Warwick Montgomery distinguishes between "assumptions of method" in science and "assumptions of content" in science. Perceiving the assumptions of any claims, scientific or otherwise, is an invaluable skill, and the distinction presented here is an important one.

Assumptions of method deal with commonsense skills such as the use of inductive and deductive reasoning and basic rules of logic (e.g., the law of noncontradiction, the law of identity, the law of the excluded middle). For example, if we are to cross a street at a busy corner, we use inductive reasoning by observing the color of the signals to determine whether oncoming traffic threatens our safety. We use basic rules of logic (as well as inductive/deductive inferences) to determine the meaning of the traffic signal. This mental activity *assumes* intuition and decision-making skills, which set the basis for the scientific *method.*

Assumptions of content are unwarranted assumptions in scientific theorizing. The scientist assumes that certain unproven things are true before any investigation. For example, believing that God could not have created the universe and then developing a theory around this idea assumes content—the absence of a divine Creator.

Such grand assumptions of content are characteristic of what Montgomery calls *the religion of science.* These assumptions provide a conclusion before investigation begins. If a scientist begins with the assumption that God either does not exist or had no part in creation, then, *regardless of the evidence*, his or her conclusion cannot acknowledge a divine Creator responsible for creation.

Scientific evidence points to a beginning for time, which was followed by matter and eventually life. Scientists believe they must explain how matter sprang from nothing. For thousands of years, philosophers, theologians, and scientists have worked with the following idea: from nothing, nothing comes (*ex nihilo, nihil fit*). You can't get something from nothing. Historically, scientists, philosophers, and of course theologians have taught that God is the cause of matter appearing at a certain time. That is, since nothing comes from nothing, things must come from *something.* Most people believed that the initial something was actually someone—God.

But since the 1970s, scientists have attempted to explain how something (matter) could come from nothing *apart from* divine causes. Using theories from quantum mechanics, Edward Tryon explained that just as particle/antiparticle pairs (or electrons and positrons) appear spontaneously, so the matter involved in the Big Bang must have arisen spontaneously. Tryon explained the Big Bang as one of those things that just happen from time to time.

Though Tryon's theory appears sound, it rests on an assumption of content, just as Asimov's theory does (that matter has just always existed). Tryon's explanation draws on evidence from laboratory experimentation that demonstrates the spontaneous appearance of subatomic particles. However, this implies that an environment similar to the one in his laboratory (a space-time manifold or energy field) existed before the alleged Big Bang, which is a bit of a stretch.

Until the late-twentieth century, no one put forward any true *ex-nihilo* models or explanations for how something came from nothing. In 1983, the famous University of Cambridge scientist Stephen W. Hawking and his associate J. B. Hartle proposed that the universe is self-contained and self-existing. This model is recognized as a possible answer to how the universe could have begun from nothing. The Hawking-Hartle model attempts to explain the existence of the universe without positing any previously existing *things* or environments. Some analysts regard this model as espousing a truly spontaneous, or *ex-nihilo,* beginning. That is, it proposes that something did in fact come from nothing. In his popular book *A Brief History of Time,* Hawking concludes that there is no need to appeal to a Creator in order to explain the ultimate origin or cause of the universe. On account of this, John Gribbon, author of *In Search of the Big Bang: Quantum Physics and Cosmology,* triumphantly states that we are finally able to answer the question of the universe's origin without appealing to God.

Psalms 10:4 and 14:1–3 start from the "assumption of content" that fools assume there is no God. As a result, they are corrupt and vile and their boasting reveals their shame. The Hawking-Hartle proposal does offer a possible explanation for the beginning of the universe. Nevertheless, it has received substantial criticism within the scientific community.

First, J. V. Narliker, author of *Introduction to Cosmology,* stated that the proposal is highly speculative. The math equations may add up, and the proposal may offer a definitive proof on paper. But it lacks any observational evidence (recall the scientific method!). The Hawking-Hartle proposal offers an explanation for the cause of the Big Bang by "examining" the conditions of the universe in the first ten seconds after the Big Bang. Here is the problem: the beginning of this universe occurred only once. So the Hawking-Hartle proposal cannot be repeated—a necessary condition in the scientific method.

A second criticism came from Heinz R. Pagels, the author of *Perfect Symmetry: The Search for the Beginning of Time.* He stated that the Hawking-Hartle model is nothing more than an imaginative guess. This model works as a theory, but scientists should not substitute theory for factual knowledge derived from experiments and observation. Also, to test the Hawking-Hartle model, scientists would need a massive particle accelerator. According to Pagels, the production of such a machine is beyond the scope of present-day invention. Scientific philosopher and theologian John Jefferson Davis noted that the machine required to test the Hawking-Hartle theory would need to be a thousand light-years in circumference, whereas the size of the solar system is only one light-day around.

At the end of the day, all the Hawking-Hartle model gives us is advanced math applied to more theories, with no way to check the numbers. On a positive note, scientific research such as Hawking and Hartle's work and the work of others concludes that the universe did have a beginning and that the "stuff" of the universe came from nothing. Theologians have been saying this all along! Regardless of scientific explanations for how the universe began, however, the question of *why* something such as the universe exists remains unanswerable by the scientific method. The most advanced scientists are reduced to the position of a child, continually repeating the question "Why?"— unless, of course, they acknowledge a Creator.

Some scientists have argued that appealing to a Creator means giving up on finding a natural explanation for the origin of the universe, but of course this depends on what you assume is natural. If the Hawking-Hartle model is taken to be fact, it exhibits a prime example of the religion of science. That is, it holds to something as fact in the absence of evidence. As a matter of faith, it assumes from the beginning that there is no Creator.

In Psalm 139, David describes the futility of trying to escape the Creator. His journey shows similarity to that of scientists who spin out theory after theory only to end up back where they started. But the psalmist finally has the answer to *his* problem—there is *no* escaping God, who is present everywhere.

The idea of the Big Bang might raise questions about God's existence, but sometimes the best approach to modern unbelief is to ask the right question. So much of unbelief is characterized by grand assumptions, and the right questions help pull back the curtain and reveal those assumptions.

In considering the Big Bang and other theories about the origin of the universe, some probative questions could include the following: (1) Why is there anything at all as opposed to nothing but chaos? (2) Where did the primordial soup come from in the first place? (3) Does the Big Bang necessarily rule out a Creator? (4) Why is there order instead of chaos?

If opportunities arise to discuss this with others, whether Christian or not, you could lighten up the conversation by offering proof for the existence of a chef (or at least a cook) from a bowl of soup. Then you could draw a comparison to the cosmological argument for God's existence. For example, imagine that you were served a bowl of soup at a fine restaurant. It would be absurd for you to think that the soup appeared out of nowhere and ended up in the bowl. Hence, someone had to make the soup.

To assume that all the things of the world came from nowhere and in such splendid order would be absurd. Hence, someone had to bring the things into existence. That someone is the Creator.

From Something to Nothing

Before philosophy became an academic discipline, men and women who sought out truth were called philosophers. The very title *philosopher* means loving (*philos*) wisdom (*sophia*). It wasn't until modern times that distinctions were made between philosophers and scientists, and to this day someone earning a doctorate in science is often awarded a doctor of philosophy degree, or PhD. Both scientists and philosophers purport to seek truth.

However, those who claim to seek the truth often do the opposite. When they are not chasing philosophical novelties, they seek only to affirm their worldview. Before they investigate facts, they already assume that what they want or think is truth (see Genesis 6:5). Then they find half-truths and make them fit their claims. This makes the truth manageable. In a sense, this makes truth an idol.

The apostle Paul wrote that many who profess to be wise have become fools (Romans 1:22). When they twist the eternal truths of God revealed in the Scriptures, they make their own idols. This can be our foolishness too! We sometimes ignore and disregard the truth God gives us in exchange for a self-concocted lie masquerading under the guise of truth. Romans 1:18–25 describes how this process of self-delusion affects humanity. Worship not directed toward the triune God is directed toward created things. In Romans 1:23, Paul describes these as idols that resemble human beings and/or birds and animals.

Idolatry extends beyond images of birds or half-human, half-animal objects. Today some people believe in or "worship" abstract idols, such as fate or the process of life; others worship ideal sensations, such as pleasure or contentment. Though these beliefs may seem more sophisticated, they share the weaknesses of ancient idolatry. They focus on the creation rather than the Creator.

Christians, too, become guilty of exalting earthly things above God. Rather than serving God, we seek money, worldly knowledge, fame, and other earthly treasures. These things are not bad in and of themselves. However, when they take precedence over worship of God through Jesus Christ, they become idols to us.

We may turn up our noses at the thought of worshiping graven images. However, we often form and worship our own idols. Just as the pagans of Paul's time formed their own images of God and truth, so we form our own ideas of what God is like and what the truth is. At our best (relatively speaking), we *appear* to follow God's Law. At our worst, we worship a self-created god rather than the God who created us and revealed Himself to us through Jesus Christ.

Further, we may inadvertently diminish God's Law to trivial moral principles, such as avoiding smoking, drinking, "cussing," and movie watching. The list varies from person to person. Such list making, or moralizing, avoids the real issue: our relationship with God. These lists become our attempt to reduce God's Law to something we are able to keep.

The fact is that we cannot keep God's Law. We cannot even grasp the depths of His commandments. Jesus explained all God's commandments simply: love of God and love of our neighbor.

We find it easy to point out problems and inconsistencies in science. Yet sometimes we adopt scientific ideas inconsistent with biblical teaching. What is even more serious is when we live in a manner inconsistent with our Christian principles. Even if we acknowledge the truth about God, we fail to live up to His Law. Jesus interprets the Law of the Old Testament in a dramatically new way. He shows the full application of the Law, demonstrating tha we break God's commands in many subtle ways not previously understood.

We may think we understand Christianity. Nevertheless, we find ourselves continuously disregarding God's Law. In fact, we delight in our sin. We even plan it. This does not spring from a lapse in judgment. Rather, we sin because we are sinners. There is no way around it. Just as a child born with a physical deformity is unable to change it on his or her own, we are unable to change our inherently sinful condition. It is as hereditary as green eyes or male-pattern baldness.

Early in the twentieth century, many theologians started to doubt and even teach against the biblical truth of inherited sinfulness (original sin). Surrounded by major scientific advances, they reduced Christianity to moral or ethical principles. They taught that one could become a better person by following the example of Jesus. Better science coupled with the idea of better people gave birth to a great deal of optimism. But then two world wars occurred, and the "old" biblical picture of humankind became dreadfully clear. Despite attempts to bury the concept of sin under human optimism, the Bible's description of wayward human beings proved accurate.

The horrors and atrocities of war exemplify humanity's propensity toward evil. Psalm 14:1–3 and Romans 5:12 explain that our inherited nature is sinful and, in addition to war, there are plenty of other examples of humanity's depraved nature (e.g., murder, violence). Beginning with Adam and Eve and extending throughout human history, we see a perpetual inclination against God and toward selfish desires. Paul writes succinctly in Romans 3:10, "None is righteous, no, not one," and in the Psalms, David describes the inherited condition of human beings in similar terms.

Falsifying evidence and faulty experiments have ruined some scientists' careers, but falsifying or weakening God's Law carries even worse consequences, as indicated in Matthew 5:18–20. The consequences of falsifying or weakening God's Law are grave. When we weaken God's Law, we do so in order to make it manageable for us to keep. However, this is self-deceiving. Not only are we unable to keep the laws we make for ourselves (under the guise of God's Law), we also fail miserably to measure up to God's original Law. Concerning this Law, Paul writes, "Now we know that whatever the law says it speaks to those who are under the law, so that every mouth may be stopped, and the whole world may be held accountable to God. For by works of the law no human being will be justified in his sight, since through the law comes knowledge of sin" (Romans 3:19–20). The Law makes us conscious of our sinful nature and shows us our need for Christ.

Repentance isn't simply turning to God's Law and attempting to keep it. Rather, it is getting a whole new mind. When we experience a heartfelt sor-

...w for our sin, the Gospel points us to Christ as the One who put our sinful nature to death with Himself on the cross.

FROM NOTHING TO NEW CREATION

The reality of sin makes us painfully aware of the human situation. Consistent with the old philosophical truth, our attempts to make something of ourselves come to nothing. From a sinner come only sinful deeds. The consequences of sin stare us down until we despair. Yet in the stages from having *original* sin to being *doers* of sin to being *damned* by sin, something outside the bounds of logic occurred. The Maker of heaven and earth addressed the chaos of our lives with the goal of making a new creation. This new creation did not begin with a bang but with a birth.

Romans 8:19–23 portrays the effects of sin in causing chaos throughout the physical creation. The creation is frustrated. It groans as if in pain, awaiting the revelation of God's children. We can look forward in hope for the liberation of all creation from frustration and decay and into glorious freedom.

John 1:10–14 shows us God's hand in bringing about the new creation. Transforming into a new creation is not something we do for ourselves. It is something God does for us through His Son, Jesus. In His mercy, we are born to new life and become a new creation. Pause to reflect on your personal status. Are you part of the new creation? Everyone who trusts in Jesus Christ for forgiveness is part of the new creation. Through Baptism, the heavenly Father adopts us as His dear children.

Earlier we saw that many philosophers and physicists overlook the question of why the universe was created. We need to address the same question, but with the new creation in view. Reading 2 Corinthians 5:17–21 and Ephesians 4:20–24, we see that the Creator desired the new creation because He wanted to be reconciled to us. Therefore, He placed our sins upon His Son and gave us His righteousness. Along with this, He gave us a new status: ambassadors of Christ who appeal to others to be reconciled to God (2 Corinthians 5:20). He also desires that we live in holiness.

In Genesis 1:1–2, creation begins with the presence of God's Holy Spirit hovering over the waters. John 3:3–5 and Romans 6:1–4 describe a new creation, our re-creation, through water and the Spirit. In Baptism, God puts to death our sinful nature and brings forth new life. Just as He breathed His Spirit into the newly formed Adam (Genesis 2:7), He gives us His Holy Spirit to bring about our birth.

Because our relationship with God remains hidden during our sojourn on earth, God established concrete, visible elements by which we receive assurance that we are part of His new creation. Christ Himself instituted the Sacraments of Holy Communion and Baptism. Just as the wonders of heaven and earth testify that God created the universe, the Sacraments testify that

God renews His creation. These Means of Grace assure us of God's gracious favor through the forgiveness of sins.

In our Baptism, we are baptized into the death of Christ. That is, our sinful nature is put to death in Baptism. We emerge as new creatures who are marked as God's children and coheirs of His kingdom (Romans 6:1–4). God works in and through the water and the Word at Baptism, regenerating us for eternal life with Him (1 Peter 3:21).

Throughout our sojourn on earth as the baptized people of God, we receive another gift. God graciously provides the Sacrament of Holy Communion. In this Sacrament, we are offered the body and blood of Christ. As we eat and drink the bread and wine, coupled with Jesus' true body and blood (according to Jesus' own words), we experience true communion with the risen Christ. This experience is quite different from other "religious experiences." Holy Communion bestows forgiveness of sins and newness of life. Other "religious experiences" fizzle and fade and remain suspect of authenticity. In the Lord's Supper, we are *guaranteed* the presence of Christ. Here we know for certain that we encounter and remember God in Christ as He would have us remember Him—in the forgiveness of sins.

All these benefits are given to us on account of God's eternal plan of redemption carried out for us by Jesus Christ. We can live in the certainty that when time winds down, we will go on living forever with the Lord.

POINTS TO PONDER

At one time or another, early in life as a child, in a midlife crisis, or late in life when death lies just ahead, we wonder about the really big questions. Where did we come from, and where are we going? Where did the universe come from, and why are we here? What has God done for you to give you answers, peace of mind, and hope for the future?

WORDS TO REMEMBER

For by grace you have been saved through faith. And this is not your own doing; it is the gift of God, not a result of works, so that no one may boast. For we are His workmanship, created in Christ Jesus for good works, which God prepared beforehand, that we should walk in them. (Ephesians 2:8–10)

3

ORIGINS OF LIFE

Early in the twentieth century, the Swedish chemist Svante Arrhenius suggested the possibility of bacteria or microbes traveling through space from planet to planet. Other scientists proposed the likelihood of these microbes seeding hospitable planets with life. Though most scientists turn to physics and chemistry to explain the emergence of life on the planet Earth, this so-called *panspermia hypothesis* still receives attention from contemporary scientists.

Attempting to explain how life began (apart from supernatural intervention), naturalistic scientists generally appeal to *biological determinism.* British theoretical physicist Paul Davies has claimed that biological determinism is the predominant biological philosophy among the general populace, from NASA scientists to schoolchildren.

Hard (or strong) biological determinism explains life's existence on the basis of the laws of physics. Under just the right chemical conditions and suitable physical environments, life will inevitably result. Soft (or weak) biological determinism holds that the laws of physics *encourage* the beginnings of biological entities. Whereas hard biological determinism holds to the *certainty* or *necessity* of life resulting from particular chemical and physical environments, soft biological determinism maintains that, given the right chemical and physical conditions, life will *probably* develop. In both views, the laws of physics are responsible for the genesis of life. Once life takes hold, the evolutionary process is thought to take over.

The idea that life on Earth came from other planets (panspermia hypothesis) raises a new set of questions: Where did that life on other planets originate? How did it get here and survive the trip? Cosmologists such as Fred Hoyle, who coined the term "Big Bang," speculated over the mode and the cause of travel of these microbes. He suggested that the possibility of life emerging spontaneously on Earth is so improbable that "seeds" of life must have arrived here on a comet or a meteorite. Francis Crick, Nobel laureate and co-discoverer of DNA structure (in *Life Itself: Its Origin and Nature*), and Leslie Orgel assert that life spread throughout the galaxy by the will and means of extraterrestrial intelligence. In 1971, Carl Sagan, famous cosmologist, spoke at the first international conference on communicating with extraterrestrial civilizations. Sagan stated that life on Earth may have originated from extraterrestrial microorganisms, but admitted that this possibility does not explain how life ultimately began. The panspermia hypothesis fails to answer this question.

Naturalistic discussions of the origins of life usually spin around two separate hubs: (1) the evolution of single-celled organisms and (2) the evolution of human beings. Though both these hubs have important implications for how people view life, discussion of human origins usually gets more press and sparks hotter debate.

For example, evolutionary anthropologists recently discovered the "Toumai" skull. Many of them consider it one of the most important fossil finds in the last hundred years. According to Harvard biological anthropologist Daniel Lieberman (*Time*, July 22, 2002), the "Toumai" skull alters how scientists view human origins. Rather than seeing human ancestry as a "tree," wherein humans evolved directly from a walking, primitive ape, many paleontologists now see human evolution from primates as a sort of "bush," where a host of potential missing links died off or stopped their evolutionary progress. For these scientists, the "Toumai" skull could prove to be one of the many potential links in human ancestry.

It may matter to you whether you see yourself as descending from an apelike creature or as starting from the creative act of a personal God. The study of human origins deeply affects views of morality and the meaning of life. If you owe your existence to impersonal chance or fate, then how you live has little meaning in the grand scheme of things. However, if you owe your existence to a personal Creator, then what you do with your life has implications for a relationship with that Creator. It's the difference between nihilism (nothing really matters) and personal religion.

The subtitle of Darwin's *The Origin of Species* reveals the dark side of his theory of evolution: *The Preservation of Favored Races in the Struggle for Life.* Darwin spoke out against slavery. However, Social Darwinists used his biological theory as the basis for racism and class stratification. The best races could oppress all other races of people—in fact, in their view, it must be morally right for them to do so. The practice of slavery was natural for the Social Darwinist. The extinction of Aborigines in Tasmania, Jews in Europe, or the bourgeois class in the Soviet Union could be justified by Darwin's theory. Some Darwinists hunted the "primitives" of Africa, Asia, and Australia. Darwin himself collected some of their skulls to measure their brain capacity and determine how low they ranked on the evolutionary scale.

Charles Darwin published *The Descent of Man* in 1871. Since then, debate about the origins of human life has been heated between creationists and evolutionists. But it has also been heated among the evolutionists themselves. Each time a human jawbone, pelvis, or skull emerges from the dust in Africa, someone seeks to redesign the theory of human evolution. Scientific reputations and grant money are frequently at stake. However, the shifting character of a naturalistic interpretation of human life tells you something about the strength of the theory. A shifting theory is an unstable theory; it lacks significant evidence to stabilize it. Each major new fossil discovery jerks the theory of evolution in a new direction.

A HOSPITABLE PLANET

Can the existence of intelligent life be explained by an appeal to the laws of physics alone? Or does the existence of life require further explanation? Scientists and philosophers have argued over this for decades and even centuries.

In 1974, British astronomer Brandon Carter coined the phrase *anthropic principle.* Simply put, the anthropic principle states that the existence of life depends on special conditions not otherwise required for the existence of the universe. In other words, the matter of the universe could exist under harsh conditions where life would inevitably die off or never begin. Hence, one philosopher stated that the universe must have "known we were coming" because certain unique conditions exist that make life on Earth sustainable, whereas these conditions have not been found elsewhere. Such conditions show a universe that is fine-tuned to sustain life on Earth.

Much evidence supports this anthropic principle. For example, the nuclear force that holds protons and neutrons together needs to be at a certain level to support the fusion of hydrogen to release energy from the sun. A slightly stronger nuclear force would make hydrogen rare within the universe. But hydrogen is necessary for the solar energy required to sustain life. Moreover, if the sun's consumption rate of hydrogen were too rapid, the sun, which "burns" hydrogen, would burn itself out. If the nuclear force were a bit weaker, hydrogen would not burn at all. Then the sun would never have begun to burn. The nuclear force is just right to support the continued burn rate of the sun that sustains life on Earth.

Life on our particular planet requires a solar system with planets called *special gas giants.* These planets, such as Jupiter and Saturn, act as cosmic vacuum sweepers. George Wetherill of the Carnegie Institution of Washington showed that without Jupiter, Earth would be struck by comets and asteroids 100 to 10,000 times more frequently. If this were to occur over a sustained period, human life would end.

Another condition required for life within our solar system is a *double-planet system* orbiting at the right distance from the sun. The Earth's moon stabilizes our planet. This keeps it from tilting either too close to the sun or too close to Jupiter, which would result in either an increasing greenhouse effect or a permanent ice age. Fred Heeren, author of *Show Me God—What the Message of Space Is Telling Us about God,* describes the probability of the Earth-Moon relationship developing by chance as one in a million.

Further evidence supporting what has been dubbed the *Rare-Earth Equation* comes from the composition of the Earth's crust. A planet needs a certain combination of elements to produce a magnetic field that protects it from high levels of cosmic radiation. These elements are made available by just the right conditions of the Earth's crust and core. This is something found, thus far, only on Earth.

Yet another piece of evidence comes from the naturalists. Stephen Jay Gould, a Harvard paleontologist, claimed that the development of only one intelligent species on Earth shows the rarity of intelligent life forms. Leading evolutionary biologists and paleontologists, including George Gaylord Simpson, Theodosius Dobzhansky, Francois Jacob, and Francisco Ayala, agree that the information-processing ability of humans is extremely rare. It is so rare that it is highly improbable to assume it has occurred on another planet.

Even the chemical makeup of humans is highly improbable, left to chance alone. The probability of one single molecule of DNA developing by chance is 1 in 10 with 415 zeros behind it, says Dr. Frank Salisbury of Utah State University.

Big Bang cosmologists, such as Stephen Hawking, admit that the beginning of the universe was delicate. At only one second following the Big Bang, if the expansion of the universe had been one in a hundred thousand million times smaller, the universe would have collapsed on itself. If it had expanded one part in a million more than what it did, then it would have expanded too rapidly for the stars and planets to form. The existence of the universe and of life on Earth depends on some very precise conditions.

What conclusions can we draw from all this evidence, and what are some other options for explaining the universe's design? Many scientists agree that the universe has an intricate design. The variables are simply too restrictive for it to have occurred as a matter of chance. Hence, there must be a Designer who is (on the basis of the previous chapter) also the Creator.

However, many alternative explanations for the apparent design of the universe have been offered throughout history. Some speculators have suggested that there is a sort of Divine Mind behind the ordering of the universe. Others suggest that the present arrangement of the universe is the planned result of a First Cause, an event meant to set the creation of our universe in motion, but without any external influence since then.

Science can take all this evidence and interpret its cause in two different ways. Either the precise conditions for life just happened by chance, or a Designer is behind the ordering of the universe, its physical laws, and the existing life within it.

Which of these explanations do you think requires the lesser amount of faith? If you were asked to explain why belief in God is more consistent with the facts than belief in chance, how would you answer? Both explanations require a measure of faith. Even so, deciding on an answer just because it allegedly takes less faith does not make the answer correct. The question should not be what requires less faith but what is more consistent with the facts. In this case, a purposeful Creator is more consistent.

Oxford philosopher Richard Swinburne uses the evidence that establishes the anthropic principle to argue that God's existence is the best explanation for the facts of apparent design or purpose in the universe. Historically, this argument has been called the *teleological argument* or the *argument from design*. Until recent decades, it received a host of criticisms, but today many able Christian philosophers and scientists support it. The argument simply states that the universe exhibits design—therefore it is more probable than not that a Designer exists.

A consistent objection to the design argument is that we posit the design of the universe only because it appears designed for *us*. As more highly developed organisms, we have lived with the hospitable elements of our universe. If we did not fit in with our environment so well, perhaps the universe would not look so intricate. Some persons add that all the extinct species certainly would not have thought the universe appears designed.

The concept that some species did not fit in well with their environment may be a legitimate challenge to the design argument. However, what are the options? How would someone who objects to the design argument explain the absence of chaos in a universe brought into being by random chemical and physical processes? Pressed to offer facts that show the universe is *not* orderly, objectors to the design argument fail to offer alternatives. The fact remains that most of the universe is inhospitable to life. We have to ask why Earth alone hosts an abundance of life.

After passing a pond full of scum, a particularly observant man remarked that the fact that life arises practically everywhere on Earth testifies to a Creator who loves life and sustains it. Earth seems to be particularly suited for life. We could push a bit further and ask why the universe acts in accordance with laws of nature. Are these laws just a product of random chance? The best explanation—the only *real* explanation—continues to be that a Designer created the universe. The Designer is God, the Father of our Lord Jesus Christ.

Straying from God

The self-righteous religious person sneers at those who attempt to explain life's origin apart from God. The self-confident naturalist mocks the religious person for his naiveté. Though they view the origin of life differently, these two types of people share the same false god.

In the end, both the self-righteous religious person and the self-confident naturalist find themselves looking inward. However, authentic science pushes one to look outside personal opinions and feelings about the universe to what the empirical evidence says about the external world. Likewise, true religion and worship drives people to look outside themselves for an explanation of life's meaning and humanity's relationship with its Creator. Religion remains authentic only when it thrives on truths revealed by God in the Scriptures. Unfortunately, whether it is justification of particular scientific theories or justification of our wrongdoings, we run away from truth that stands outside and independent of us. But what do we really see when we take a hard look around us?

Imagine for a moment that you have grown up in a small village in a rain forest. You have never seen people from other villages or other parts of the world. You have never been exposed to the Bible or any Christian missionaries. By thinking hard, what could you know about God, and what could you say about His relationship with you and/or His attitude toward you?

It is quite conceivable that someone who never had exposure to the Bible or to Christians could conclude that a Creator exists. Many cultures throughout the history of the world have arrived at this conclusion. Building from there, these cultures each developed their own account of creation. Evidence of the existence and design of the universe begs the question of how it got its design, but people have an innate sense of curiosity that is not easily dismissed. Also, people have an innate sense of right and wrong. If we ask ourselves where the moral law comes from, we might conclude that there must be some sort of moral lawgiver.

People have an innate knowledge that God exists. The medieval theologian Anselm concluded that it would be absurd to think of a universe where God did not exist. For him and many other theologians and philosophers, God's existence is necessary for anything to exist. Thomas Aquinas wrote that our existence was not an accident. He reasoned that there must be a cause for the existence of all things, adding that a necessary being must have set in motion the creation of all things. This necessary being he identified as God.

The apostle Paul affirmed our innate knowledge of God as well as the evidence of a Creator found in creation (Romans 1:18–20; Acts 14:15–17; 17:24–28). He used these arguments of natural theology to point to our need, indeed our hunger, for a clear revelation from God concerning right worship and fuller knowledge of God.

The psalmist rhetorically asked, "What is man that You are mindful of him?" (Psalm 8:4), driven by a keen awareness of the status of human beings in the universe. Human beings were given a position of power and authority over creation. The psalmist (David) says, "Yet You have made him a little lower than the heavenly beings and crowned him with glory and honor" (v. 5). We were made to rule God's creation.

However, we fail miserably at fulfilling this role. We wage war. We ravage the environment. We hunt animals and races of people to extinction. Much of what we do points to our horrible misuse of our authority and responsibility. The Bible tells us unequivocally that we are products of God's creative work. We bear the mark of the divine image and are given the privilege to be stewards over God's creation (Genesis 1:26). Nevertheless, we often turn this privilege into a task. Even worse, we often fail miserably at it.

Trying to find our identity as humans, we may choose as animals choose, following our own instincts and emotions. However, God holds humans accountable for their actions. Trying to escape the Law of God, people begin to doubt that the Bible's picture of them is true.

Ironically, strict naturalists take comfort in the belief that there is no God looking over their shoulders. Yet they fail to realize where this leaves them—fully subject to their own vices. In their view, humanity's only hope is to breed and to trust that the next generation will likewise stay one step ahead of inevitable extinction. The cheery optimism of biological determinism tears off its mask, revealing biological fatalism: Life is an accident. Survival is in part determined by successful breeding. But statistics and reality warn us that another "accident" must come. We cannot escape, for whether by plague or fireball we must die.

Each death you witness is a glimpse of the unmasked fatalism behind the theory of evolution. In contrast, Paul describes death (1 Corinthians 15:26) as defeated and the future for believers in Christ (vv. 53–57) as victorious. He views death as an enemy to be destroyed. He sees victory over death for believers through the resurrection of Jesus. For Paul, death is not natural. Our Creator designed us for life.

Some people allege that the Bible is obscure, whereas science appears precise and offers clear conclusions. The concept of evolution seems logical. After all, scientific evidence supposedly supports it. So we may try to synthesize our religious convictions and evolutionary science. We may come up with the idea that God created by using the process of evolution, or we may retain religious practices while believing popular scientific theories. We may even find occasion to reduce Christianity to a set of moral principles designed to help us reach our full potential.

Where do all these ideas and practices come from? From the human mind! We sometimes exchange the truth of our position in the universe for a cheap imitation. Rather than living as repentant servants of God, we may place ourselves in the judgment seat over God and His Word.

If we try to place ourselves above God and His Word, we find ourselves living in defiance of God's Law and fighting God. The consequences are that God will give us what we want. If we want self-rule, God will grant us our desire. However, our self-rule in the here and now is self-deception. All people will be held accountable to God's Law. The final consequence of failing to meet the standards of the Law will be an eternity under the wrath of God.

RETURNED TO GOD

Some assert that Jesus became man in order that we could become divine. However, the reverse is closer to biblical teaching: Jesus was born and gave His life in order that we might be more human. Considering the position of human beings in God's creation, what might this mean?

Adam and Eve's original position within the created order was one of authority and blessing. God created them to oversee the rest of creation. When they ruled, they enjoyed a personal relationship with God. God spoke with them, and they obeyed God's will. When Adam and Eve decided to turn their backs on God's command to stay away from the fruit of the tree in the middle of the Garden of Eden, their personal relationship with God ceased. Their position as the authority over creation was severely marred. God banished them from His presence in the garden.

Christ's work of redemption reversed humanity's separation from God. Not only did God take to Himself human flesh, but He also lived and died in the midst of people. He did the things people do. This has profound implications for humanity and for all of creation.

God and His Law bring fear. However, through Jesus we have access to God. We have peace and a loving relationship with God. Paul wrote, "Since we have been justified by faith, we have peace with God through our Lord Jesus Christ" (Romans 5:1). Having peace with God, we are restored to our original identity of man and woman—creatures in personal communion with their Creator.

The Declaration of Independence rightfully declares, "All men are created equal." However, at one time slave ownership was quite common throughout the Southern states. Slaves were bought and sold as if they were livestock. This horrible period in United States history saw many attempts at freeing slaves. Not until the enactment of the Thirteenth and Fourteenth Amendments did slaves receive their rightful position as American citizens.

Like the slaves in early America, all humans have been given over to slavery—the slavery of sin. Yet this slavery is something we choose (unlike the American slaves, who were unwillingly torn from family and country). People reduce themselves to the status of slaves under their chosen master—sin!

We have been emancipated from this master. This freedom did not come about after years of attempts and the death of thousands upon thousands of persons (as in the Civil War in the United States). Rather, this emancipation was secured by the death of God's own Son. Unlike the slaves in America, we do not deserve our freedom. We willfully and continually disobey God, yet in mercy God still declares us free from the curse of the Law.

Colossians 1:13–14, 21–23 summarizes the redemption of human beings from the mastery of sin. Because of God's good favor, He took the initiative to rescue us. Because God loved us, He sent His Son to die for us. He looks on us with unmerited mercy and sent His Son solely on the basis of His good favor, not because of any quality in us. The death of Jesus was the one thing necessary to redeem us and reconcile us to God. He exchanged His righteousness for our sin. Just as Adam brought sin into the world, Jesus reversed the effects of sin on the world. It is faith that grasps this truth. A simple trust in the merits of Christ connects us to the freedom given in the Gospel.

It is too easy to forget or get confused about the freedom won for us by Christ. Although we are free from bondage to sin and its consequences, we still find ourselves returning to our old sinful habits. It seems that the more we grow in God's grace, the more we become aware of the depth of our sinful condition. However, God continues to remind us of our freedom.

Each week in the Divine Service, we hear God's Word of forgiveness. Our freedom is proclaimed in Holy Absolution. After the confession of sins, the presiding pastor announces our forgiveness and consequent freedom from bondage to sin. When the pastor announces forgiveness, it is not a human proclamation that we hear. Rather, we hear the very words of Christ. God Himself declares, "Your sins are forgiven!"

This freedom gives us status as real human beings, no longer self-imposed slaves. We are free in our relationship with God. We are coheirs of the kingdom of God, returned to Him. All this comes through the death and resurrection of Jesus.

Hebrews 2:5–18 describes Jesus' work of redemption and some of the effects of Jesus' person and work on all human beings. The work of redemption began when God became human in the person of Jesus Christ. Jesus experienced all the temptations, sorrows, and emotions to which we are subject. In a few words, Jesus' work can be characterized as *substitution* and *representation*. He became human in order that he might *represent* all human beings. In His life, death, and resurrection, He *substituted* His righteousness for our unrighteousness. His death took the place of our death. His resurrection is the guarantee of the resurrection to eternal life of all believers in Christ. Throughout the Book of Hebrews, the author compares Jesus to a high priest. Jesus is our High Priest, ensuring and certifying our ability to stand before God in righteousness by His sacrificial death.

POINTS TO PONDER

Many people believe that humans evolved from unknown or speculative origins and that we are basically animals, relatives of the great apes. God tells us that He made us in His image, that we have souls, and that His Son, Jesus, came to redeem us. What difference does it make in your worldview and outlook on life to know that God created you and sends Jesus to bring you home?

WORDS TO REMEMBER

Therefore [Christ] is the mediator of a new covenant, so that those who are called may receive the promised eternal inheritance, since a death has occurred that redeems them from the transgressions committed under the first covenant. (Hebrews 9:15)

4

EXTRATERRESTRIAL LIFE

During the late-sixteenth century, the Dominican monk Giordano Bruno suggested the probability of numerous worlds inhabited by various extraterrestrial beings. On February 17, 1600, the Inquisition saw fit to burn him at the stake. Over four hundred years later, many scientists now agree with Bruno. What would it mean to our understanding of God, creation, and humanity if life, even in simple forms, exists on other planets? From a scientific point of view, what would constitute enough proof to establish the fact of extraterrestrial life?

Many people are fascinated with the idea of extraterrestrial life. For example, Carl Sagan remarked that it would be a great waste of space if life existed only on Earth. The 1997 film *Contact*, based on a fictional account of contact between humans and an advanced extraterrestrial civilization, included the same assertion. When *Entertainment Tonight* interviewed filmmaker M. Night Shyamalan concerning his film *Signs,* Shyamalan stated that it is highly improbable for Earth to be the only planet supporting life. Even Microsoft founder Bill Gates once remarked in the *New York Times* (February 10, 1999) that the universe quite likely teems with life.

Interest in extraterrestrial life as a scientific issue began during the seventeenth and eighteenth centuries. For example, in 1794, the American author and revolutionist Thomas Paine (1737–1809) wrote in *The Age of Reason* that the existence of extraterrestrial beings inhabiting other worlds or planets would render Christianity ridiculous and unbelievable. (It was thought that scientific interest in extraterrestrial life would raise serious questions concerning the significance of Christian ideas about God, human beings, sin, and Christ.)

Reasserting Thomas Paine's charge, Roland Puccetti (in his 1968 book *Persons: A Study of Possible Moral Agents in the Universe*) argued that roughly 10^{18} (1,000,000,000,000,000,000) sites of possible extraterrestrial life exist in the galaxy. On account of this, he said, the ideas of sin and redemption are absurd since, obviously, God in Jesus Christ could not have redeemed all existing creatures, earthly and extra-earthly. Puccetti concludes that modern scientific research into extraterrestrial life decisively shows the inadequacy of Christianity.

How Christians should deal with the question of extraterrestrial life will be investigated in some detail later on. Meanwhile, we should realize that Christians have wrestled with a similar problem before. When explorers in the fifteenth and sixteenth centuries discovered new varieties of human life on other continents, they had to ask themselves whether the Bible applied to these newly discovered beings.

We need to consider how Paine's or Puccetti's arguments, presented very briefly above, might be flawed either in their logic or in their underlying assumptions. An argument's validity rests on its assumptions. If its assumptions are true, then the argument can lead to true conclusions, although such an outcome is not assured. If the assumptions are false, then the conclusions will be false.

Typically, arguments against Christianity regarding extraterrestrial life follow these lines: (1) The Bible does not speak of life on other planets. (2) The Bible informs us that sin affects the Earth, not other planets. (3) The restoration brought about by Jesus is valid only for humans, other earthly creatures, and the Earth itself. Hence, the Earth-centered worldview of the Bible does not accommodate modern scientific knowledge of the universe, and Christianity must be found irrelevant in light of modern scientific knowledge. But there are problems with this line of reasoning!

Here are some of the fallacies with this kind of science versus Christianity approach: (1) That the Bible does not speak of extraterrestrial life does not mean that the Bible asserts that it does not exist. The Bible is not a zoological or biological textbook! (2) The Bible informs us that *all* of creation is under a curse since the fall of Adam and Eve. "*All* of creation" has *universal* implications. (3) Likewise, Jesus' work of reconciliation was for the entire cosmos, or universe (see 2 Corinthians 5:19, where the Greek word *kosmos* is usually translated as *world*).

POSSIBLE BUT NOT PROBABLE

Discovery of extraterrestrial life would certainly be highly significant. However, the imagination of science fiction authors and our fascination with discovering new things should not outweigh careful and factual investigation. This sort of careful investigation should also characterize our thinking about how the discovery of extraterrestrial life would affect Christian theology.

As you consider various arguments about whether life exists on other planets, recognize that these arguments are based on *calculations* and not on *data*. Though calculations and theoretical models can be helpful for setting up an experiment, they are not scientific data. Remember: science depends on observation, not speculation.

Because calculations about the possibility of life on other planets are so popular, let's review a few of the arguments. Assumptions about extraterrestrial life rest on the idea that conditions to sustain life exist elsewhere within the universe. Life somehow, either through space travel or through the process of evolution, took hold and thrived in extra-earthly habitats. (Notice that this neglects the question of where or how life originated in the first place!)

The delicate nature of life presents difficulties for this opinion. Astronomer Hugh Ross determined a numerical figure for the probability of life outside Earth. Taking into account about forty conditions necessary to sustain life, such as chemical composition and physical conditions, Dr. Ross calculated the probability of all these conditions occurring on a single planet. He ended up with the following figure: one in $1,000,000,000,000$ (10^{12}) planets in the universe contain the biological requirements necessary to sustain life. Hence, the possibility that life exists on other planets remains very slim.

The father of SETI (Search for ExtraTerrestrial Intelligence) science, Frank Drake, developed a mathematical formula that allegedly measures the potential number of intelligent alien civilizations: $N = R^* \times Fp \times Ne \times Fl \times Fi \times Fc \times L$. The problem with the Drake equation is that each variable remains speculative at best. In spite of the weight of mathematical and biological evidence against the probability of extraterrestrial life, Roland Puccetti argues that roughly ten sites within the universe *may* contain extraterrestrial life, basing his figure of ten sites for possible extraterrestrial life on Drake's formula. Yet the formula itself is based on huge assumptions. You see the problem—piling assumption on top of assumption can never reach the level of fact.

The calculations show the improbability of extraterrestrial life, but this does not mean there are no extraterrestrial creatures. It does mean, though, that conclusions in support of the existence of extraterrestrial life are presumptuous. We cannot state that such life exists. Likewise, we cannot say that it does not exist.

Our attitude toward methods of discovering extraterrestrial life should remain critical. We can affirm, like Carl Sagan, that there appears to be a lot of potential for life because of the sheer size of the universe. However, because life itself is rare, we should not jump to conclusions. Sagan himself, who authored the novel on which the movie *Contact* was based, states that the best of our critical thinking skills and a healthy skepticism should guide the search for extraterrestrial life. This from a huge proponent for the possibility of extraterrestrial life!

Just as the search for extraterrestrial life must employ a careful and reasonable method of investigation, Christian reflection on the possible discovery of extraterrestrials should be carefully and biblically informed.

When Thomas Paine and modern scientific authors (e.g., Roland Puccetti) state that theologians largely ignore extraterrestrial issues and that Christianity fails to incorporate extraterrestrial life into its worldview, they speak without investigating the evidence. To begin with, theologians and philosophers throughout Christian history have wrestled with the idea of extraterrestrial life and its implications for Christian teaching. For example, Steven Dick has written an informative book that surveys the debates concerning extraterrestrial life—*Plurality of Worlds: The Origins of the Extraterrestrial Life Debate from Democritus to Kant.*

Those who argue that Christian theology fails to treat the question of extraterrestrial life, as well as those who claim that the Bible does not speak at all to this issue, fail to thoroughly comprehend Christian theology and the Scriptures. The following sections examine the relationship between the Bible (and Christian theology) and the potential discovery of extraterrestrial life.

It is important that Christians adopt careful attitudes about the search for extraterrestrial life. Christians must read the Scriptures correctly and understand the full implications of the Bible's teachings. In other words, the Scriptures must inform our worldview. We should not impose our worldview on the Bible.

The Bible teaches that God fills all things. It describes angels as coming and going from heaven. (This does not mean that we should regard God or the angels as extraterrestrial life, as that phrase is typically used.) Otherwise, we would be hard-pressed to find a biblical passage that supports belief in life outside the planet Earth. This does not mean that the Bible denies the existence of such life. It is silent on this entire issue of our understanding the universe. (Mormons and perhaps others would cite John 10.16. However, the "other sheep" whom Jesus refers to in this verse are Gentiles, not extraterrestrials.)

THE PROBLEM OF DOUBT

Thomas Paine's and Roland Puccetti's arguments provide an amazing example of how science sometimes gets used against a caricature of Christian theology. Paine and Puccetti failed to understand Christian teaching drawn from the Bible.

However, Christians themselves often fail to understand the Bible. Like scientists who misuse facts to promote the validity of a certain worldview, Christians often misuse the Bible. Instead of relying on the Bible as the basis for what we believe or do not believe, we draw conclusions from the Bible to fill in blanks where it remains silent or to affirm our preconceived worldview.

The Scriptures tell the story of human beings' fall into sin and their redemption by the Lord. The entire Bible points to one particular event—the death and resurrection of Jesus. Here lies the intent of the Bible and the proof of the Christian worldview. The chief intent is to disclose the message of salvation. The historical events of Jesus' life, death, and resurrection prove that God has redeemed His children.

In our attempts to answer the unanswerable, we may draw unverifiable conclusions from the Scriptures. Sometimes we even use the Bible to justify our errors. For example, we may quote the Bible to support our condemnation of others. Or we may quote the Bible out of context to prove an irrelevant point. The more we fail to see the thrust of the Bible, the more we use it apart from its intent.

If we take Scripture at face value, as we must, there are a number of "unanswerables" in the Bible. For example, we do not know exactly what is meant by "The sun stopped in the midst of heaven and did not hurry to set for about a whole day" (Joshua 10:13), *how* Jesus' body and blood are present in bread and wine, how Samson's strength was connected to the length of his hair, or who the Nephilim were (Genesis 6:4).

We can attempt to offer answers, but alternative explanations always remain. The Bible is not a book of philosophy or science. It is chiefly a record of God's dealings with His people in the course of human history, culminating in God the Son's taking to Himself human flesh and dwelling among His people. This is the one thing that *must* be maintained and remembered in our reading of the Scriptures.

After Jesus' death and resurrection, He appeared on a road outside Jerusalem. Two of His followers did not recognize Him but accepted His company as they walked to Emmaus. Jesus showed them how all the Scriptures testified to His appearance on earth and His death and resurrection (Luke 24:25–27, 44–46). This organizing principle should guide our reading and interpretation of the Bible.

When Christians misuse or misapply the Bible, they expose the Christian faith to ridicule. For example, some well-meaning Christians argue that the Bible's silence on the issue of extraterrestrial life means that extraterrestrial life does not exist. So they disregard the possible relevance of the search for extraterrestrial life. In misguided zeal, they argue for a geocentric view of the universe. Misinterpreting the Scriptures gives the impression to the public that the Bible is a book with a particular scientific worldview—when, in fact, the Bible's worldview is centered on a person: Jesus Christ.

So really, the scriptural worldview is not one of a closed universe where all the answers to questions about the natural world can be found in the verses of the Bible. Rather, the biblical worldview is open to investigation of God's creation, on Earth and throughout the universe. The question of whether extraterrestrials exist lies in the realm of empirical science. Their discovery would not invalidate the Bible.

Such openness has other implications. Scientific findings should not cause doubt about God in the Christian's mind. Doubt about God, as well as its consequent unbelief, is sinful.

On the other hand, asking questions and probing for greater understanding does not offend the Creator of the universe. A great God can put up with a great many questions. But this great God also calls us to great faith. Here is the heart of the matter! Honest inquiry honors the Maker of the human mind. Self-righteous pride and mistrust dishonor Him.

Consider the questions raised by Ethan the Ezrahite in Psalm 89:46–52. How does Ethan, a believer in the Lord, receive resolution of these issues, and what does this teach you about questioning God? Ethan prays that the Lord would remember his suffering. If it's all right for the psalmist to question God, it's all right for you to question Him. However, ask your questions in humility and trust.

Read Job 31:24–37. This is the end of a long speech by Job, beginning in chapter 26. Job indirectly accused God of injustice and then defended himself as righteous. And God apparently listened patiently, just as He is willing to listen to us patiently. Now read 38:1–11 to see how the Lord responded to Job's assertions. Notice that God never tells Job not to ask questions. He does, though, remind Job of his place in creation. The Almighty answers Job's self-righteous assertions with a series of questions for Job that he cannot possibly answer. Our self-righteous assertions can anticipate sharp rebuke from the Lord.

Form a personal answer for the Lord's question in Job 40:1–2 with help from 42:1–6. Job responded to God's challenge by repenting. In contrast, the sin of Adam and Eve was not that they raised questions about their Maker and His plan for their lives, but that they sinned when they knowingly, self-righteously "sank their teeth" into something He had explicitly forbidden.

As a consequence of the fall into sin, we find ourselves doubting God's faithfulness. God proves that He cares for us in spite of our constant rebellion. He has shown us His kindness through daily sustenance and continual provision (Acts 14:17). As the climactic act of His faithfulness, God fulfilled His promise to humankind by sending His only Son. However, we may still doubt His care and control over everything. When left to our own merits, we find ourselves naked before God and His impending judgment.

Doubting the sufficiency of God's Word puts us in danger of His judgment. This comes from replacing God's truth with something else. Our lack of trust in God could be followed by a trust in ourselves.

Read Mark 9:17–27 and consider how Jesus responded to the father's desperate request. When the father admitted the state of his faith, Jesus did not rebuke him but responded in mercy. We, too, need to confess our doubts to the Lord! And He will answer us in mercy.

Think about the questions or doubts you struggle with. Pause to take these issues before the Maker of the universe. He will hear your concerns!

LORD OF THE COSMOS

We have briefly reviewed Thomas Paine's and Roland Puccetti's arguments against the sufficiency of Christianity, which centered in the possibility of extraterrestrial life. Though no evidence testifies to the existence of life beyond Earth, the possibility exists for the discovery of extraterrestrial life. This should not raise any doubts concerning the truthfulness of the Christian faith.

The apostle Paul encountered attacks on the Christian faith similar to those leveled by Paine and Puccetti. Members of a young congregation in Colossae were expressing doubts about the sufficiency of Christ for the redemption of humanity. Paul responded by defending the full deity of Christ and His sufficiency to reconcile people to God.

Paul repeatedly argues for the universal effects of the reconciliation wrought by Christ (Colossians 1:15–20). In the space of six verses, Paul mentions the universal consequences of the person and work of Christ eight times. "All" is used two times, "all things" five times, and "everything" once. This supremacy or universality of Christ's person and work is asserted in all six verses. In verses 15–16, Christ's authority over creation is declared. Christ created "all things" for Himself. Verse 17 affirms Christ's authority in divine providence. In Christ "all things hold together."

In the incarnation, the man Jesus is also fully God (v. 19). (Theologians refer to this as the two natures of Christ.) The universal sufficiency of Christ's reconciling work for "all things . . . on earth or in heaven" is declared in verse 20. Verse 18 affirms both the sufficiency of Christ for eternal life for all believers through His resurrection and Christ's superiority and headship in the Church.

Thus, this brief passage pictures Christ not as the Reconciler of humanity alone but as the Reconciler of all creation—things visible and invisible, earthly and extraterrestrial.

This portion of Paul's letter defends Christ's sufficiency for the reconciliation of all creation as *universal* or, we might say, *cosmic*. Paul stresses the authority and superiority of Christ throughout space, time, and human existence.

The climax of the work of Christ took place at His crucifixion on Calvary. This unjust act against the Son of God brought about God's reconciliation of "all things, whether on earth or in heaven, making peace by the blood of his cross" (v. 20). Paul here presents Christ as the One who not only brought the cosmos into being and continually sustains it but also brings it into harmony with God. Jesus is truly the Lord of the cosmos.

Recall the arguments against Christianity offered by Thomas Paine and Roland Puccetti. Since it is obvious on the basis of Colossians that the work

of Christ has cosmic implications, Paine's and Puccetti's arguments are .
They fail to take into consideration what Paul asserts here in Colossians
that the central Christian teaching (the reconciling work of Christ) includ.
the entire universe. Should extraterrestrial life be discovered, Christian theology would stand firm.

Even in the scope of His cosmic work, the death of Christ has personal
benefits for each of us. Christ's reconciliation of the cosmos becomes personal when we trust in this act. Faith grasps the peace with God brought
about by Jesus' work. Hence, it is faith that connects us to the oneness with
God won for us by Christ.

This faith that connects us to Christ's merits on our behalf is a gift to us
from God as well. In 2 Thessalonians 2:13, Paul states, "God chose you as
the firstfruits to be saved, through sanctification by the Spirit and belief in
the truth." On account of God's grace revealed in Christ, we are considered
righteous (and are therefore saved) through faith in the person and work of
Christ.

Colossians 1:15–20 reveals a crucial part of the classical Christian worldview: Christ is the center of the cosmos, over which He is also Lord. Not only
is He Creator and Sustainer of the universe and the life within it; He is also
Reconciler of an alienated creation. Christ's death on the cross and subsequent resurrection mark the center of human history. It is also the center of
the cosmos *beyond* the scope of human existence.

Thus, Christianity presents a Christocentric worldview. Christ existed
before the creation of the cosmos. He has always existed with God the Father
and God the Holy Spirit. Also, He came into time to carry out God's redemptive work in the midst of human history. Christ is the center of all Christian
theology.

Points to Ponder

People work very hard to justify the possibility of extraterrestrial life;
they often work just as hard to argue against the existence of God, who took
steps to redeem His creation. What kind of spiritual hunger drives this view,
and how does the work of Christ more than meet our need?

Words to Remember

And you, who once were alienated and hostile in mind, doing evil deeds, He has now reconciled in His body of flesh
by His death, in order to present you holy and blameless
and above reproach before Him. (Colossians 1:21–22)

5

CONTACT?

n 1938, panic struck America when Martians landed on Earth! As Orson
᱐es's *War of the Worlds* sounded over the radio waves, strange as it may
 m today, some listeners thought that Martians truly had invaded Earth.
 e continually see this theme perpetuated in movies, such as *The Avengers*,
᱐acific Rim, Independence Day, Signs*, and many more.

In a positive light, many books and movies look at the possibility of
human-alien contact. In the 1960s, Robert Heinlein's *Strangers in a Strange
Land* depicted a half-human/half-Martian who taught earthlings "true religion." In 1982, *E.T.* portrayed a kind yet misunderstood extraterrestrial
endowed with superhuman gifts and powers. In either case—terrifying or
peaceful—the prospect of contact with extraterrestrial life fascinates the contemporary mind.

Most people would classify movies and books about alien-human contact
as science fiction. You might even know someone who takes such accounts
seriously. Most of us have probably been exposed to some media or possibly "scientific" discussions concerning alien-human contact. Or we know
someone who either takes them seriously or expresses a serious ambivalence
with a phrase like "you never know—maybe there is something to it." Many
people, including some Christians, believe in the existence of extraterrestrial
life and may even believe in contact with aliens.

Though the radio program, movies, and literature referred to at the beginning of this section are typically classified in the genre of science fiction,
researchers and extraterrestrial enthusiasts strive to discover and make contact with extraterrestrial intelligence.

Combining scientific research with science fiction, Carl Sagan's book-
turned-movie *Contact* tells the story of a young woman engaged in the search
for radio signals from advanced alien extraterrestrial civilizations. This story
parallels the real-life research begun by American astronomer Frank Drake.

In 1960, using an 85-foot radio telescope, Drake started his search for
signals from extraterrestrials. This later gave birth to the organization SETI
(Search for ExtraTerrestrial Intelligence), which dedicated itself to making
contact with alien extraterrestrial civilizations.

When congressional funding for SETI ceased in 1993, Jill Cornell
Tarter continued the search for extraterrestrial, intelligent civilizations.
Privately funded by the founders of such organizations as Hewlett-Packard,

Intel, Microsoft, and others, Dr. Tarter headed up Project Phoenix (a 1995 continuation of NASA's SETI).

Reports of flying saucers and human contact with extraterrestrial creatures from unidentified flying objects (UFOs) have grown in number, and these reports occur worldwide. Dr. Allen Hynek has developed a classification system for UFO/alien contact, or close encounters (CE):

CE-1—encounter with UFO at a distance
CE-2—UFO with physical impact on the environment
CE-3—contact between humans and UFO occupants

Alleged cases of alien abductions and encounters number in the thousands. Conspiracy theorists circulate stories of government cover-ups of advanced technological information received from extraterrestrial intelligent beings. Even cults have developed around such phenomena—for example, the Raelians, the Church of Scientology, Heaven's Gate, the Urantian Group, the Solar Cross Foundation, and the Aetherius Society.

Beauty-pageant contestants used to be the ones who gave advice for establishing world peace. Now, many believers in accounts of alien-human contact maintain that aliens are able to provide answers to humanity's problems—and even to promote world peace. What could be some scientific explanations and nonscientific explanations for increased "contact" with UFOs?

Tarter's essay "SETI and the Religions of the Universe" (published in 2000 in *Many Worlds: The New Universe, Extraterrestrial Life and the Theological Implications*) explains the possible religious significance and consequences of contacting extraterrestrial civilizations. It also helps explain the irrational actions and beliefs of UFO religious groups. Tarter draws up two possible consequences of contact with extraterrestrial civilizations: (1) If God exists, then a single, universal, scientific religion informed by extraterrestrial civilizations will replace the crude, superstitious religions of the world. (2) If there is no God, advanced extraterrestrial civilizations are in a better scientific position to inform us of this, and religion and belief in God will cease.

Both the scientific and nonscientific placement of authority in extraterrestrial life, should contact be made, revolves around the idea that extraterrestrials live outside the human situation. They would, by virtue of their location outside the planet Earth and all its problems, be able to give a more objective account of how things are in the universe. They might even be able to explain the existence of the universe. If they were an ancient alien civilization, they could offer advice for sustaining peaceful life on Earth for thousands of years to come. Should they make contact with us, this act would show their advanced communication and technological skills—skills greater than ours. Hence, they would be able to offer us technological advice.

However, the quest for contact with beings outside our planet tells us more about the human desire for knowledge and understanding of our world than it does about advanced extraterrestrial civilizations. A key truth is that both religious and nonreligious persons desire to hear a voice from beyond.

Think of a submarine crew. Nuclear subs are so advanced that they could run for decades. Though the crew needs to restock food supplies, the subs are essentially self-sufficient. Once a submarine crew gets underway, it could go for three months without any contact with the outside world. Essentially, submarines are their own little world. However, when the potential exists for the reception of news via the radio, the submarine crew gets excited, even about sports scores. News from home, though rare and minimal, offers hope to the crew members and makes the deployment easier to endure.

The same is often true with us. Though our science and technology are well advanced, the potential of hearing an outside perspective offers hope and excitement. The possibility of new technology and new ideas intrigues us. It gives us hope and optimism for the future.

WISHFUL THINKING

Scientifically speaking, the human quest to make contact with something or someone beyond our planet has ended in failure. Looking through a telescope in 1877, Giovanni Schiaparelli observed what appeared to be channels (or *canali*) on Mars. American astronomers then formed a theory that life exists or did exist on Mars. In 1907, Percival Lowell took pictures of Mars from a telescope in Flagstaff, Arizona. He opined that Schiaparelli's channels were artificial creations (probably water canals) made by intelligent Martian life. This life, concluded Lowell, must be more advanced than life on Earth since its engineering projects (canals) surpassed human engineering capabilities.

This Martian theory came to a halt in the middle of the twentieth century. When more powerful telescopes were used to look at Mars, astronomers did not observe these supposed canals. They did observe seasonal darkness on the surface. From this they concluded that Mars must contain some sort of vegetation. The *Mariner 4* probe took over twenty pictures of Mars's surface in 1965. They all showed Mars to be a wasteland covered with craters. Hopes were crushed until 1976, when the *Viking* orbiter took a photo of Mars's surface that displayed a facelike feature. Some scientists speculated that ancient Martians had probably formed it. Yet *Viking* discovered no signs of life on Mars. In fact, it found no trace of organic molecules at all.

Then on August 7, 1996, NASA spokespersons in Washington DC announced the findings of Martian meteorite ALH84001. Discovered in Antarctica, this potato-sized rock appeared to contain Martian fossils. However, most scientists found the evidence inconclusive, and many concluded that the meteorite contained no fossils at all.

The January 2002 issue of *National Geographic* devoted an entire
to the prospect of extraterrestrial life. Besides positing the possibility of
tian life, the article reported that one of Jupiter's moons—Europa—co
contain water, which could harbor life. In an insert, the *National Geograph*
article raised questions about what extraterrestrial life might look like.

In 2004, NASA landed two remotely controlled exploratory robots,
named *Spirit* and *Opportunity*, on the surface of Mars. Even though images
sent back from their work have occasionally sparked intense speculation
about life on Mars and government conspiracy theories that aim to hide the
discovery of life on Mars, no definitive evidence has turned up to prove that
life exists or ever existed on the red planet. It is fascinating to see how many
times people's hopes for evidence of life on Mars have been raised, only to
have them dashed when more or better data become available. Yet the cycle
of raised and dashed hopes keeps repeating itself, suggesting that it is driven
more by human desires than by scientific thinking.

Concerning claims of close encounters, Dr. Allen Hynek's research demonstrates just how greatly human psychology can dupe groups of people. The
hundred or so alleged nightly sightings and contacts made with UFOnauts,
which gave rise to the three close-encounter categories (CE-1, CE-2, CE-3),
share common, unscientific characteristics. For all the alleged UFO sightings
and contacts, not one shred of empirical evidence survives. Careful investigation conducted by respectable UFO experts has produced neither credible
photographs nor material evidence. In the absence of empirical evidence,
investigators are left solely with eyewitness testimony. After a "cross-exam-
ination," the majority of witnesses prove unreliable. Collaboration becomes
apparent in many cases. Drug and alcohol abuse during reported incidents
comes out frequently during the examination of witnesses. Eyewitnesses often comment on the great speed at which UFOs travel. Yet when the alleged
times at which the encounters occurred have been compared with environmental factors, such as evidence of landing or a sonic boom made from great
speeds, no concrete evidence has been produced.

Despite the lack of evidence for alien-human contacts, untold numbers
of people still believe the stories. The majority of those who claim to have experienced contact with extraterrestrial beings typically believe in the abundance of life throughout the universe—even prior to their personal "close
encounter." If life exists throughout the universe, for them there is no real
problem with believing in contact between humans and aliens. Yet, as seen
in the previous discussions, the possibility of such contact is so low that most
scientists consider it nil.

Nevertheless, an interesting fact arises in light of the eyewitness testimony about these alleged encounters. Studies show that a large majority of

who "experience" close encounters have prior involvement with the ⌐lt. John Keel—an investigator, author of books dealing with strange phe-¬mena, and self-proclaimed agnostic—sees a clear parallel between alleged ⌐ien encounters and ancient and modern occult practices. Dr. Hugh Ross, astronomer and UFO expert, shows that many alleged participants in close encounters have had actual experience in the occult—for example, with Oui-ja boards, crystal balls, or necromancy.

Italian-born physicist Enrico Fermi (1901–54) asked where the so-called intelligent-alien civilizations were if the galaxy is around ten billion years old. Fermi had argued that a civilization with interstellar-propulsion capa-bilities would have colonized the universe by now. For example, astronomers predict that it would take only five million years to colonize the entire Milky Way. Hence, if the assumptions of astronomers are true concerning the age of the universe and the rate of colonization, alien life forms would have made themselves known on Earth by now. Yet they have not. Why? In the 1970s, four prominent astrophysicists (Frank Tipler, David Viewing, Ronald Brace-well, and Michael Hart) reexamined *Fermi's Paradox* and concluded that it was difficult to get around. The logic is still solid, and the lack of evidence is still real.

An even greater argument against the existence of intelligent life beyond Earth arises from the condition of Earth itself. In an earlier section, we ex-amined the *Rare-Earth Equation:* Earth's unique ability to sustain life. Those people who believe that there must be a host of alien civilizations scattered throughout the universe also assume that earthlike conditions exist through-out the universe. However, upon scientific investigation of the conditions that make life on Earth possible, the probability of such conditions existing elsewhere in the universe appears very low if not zero. Yet in spite of these odds, as we have seen, the desire for contact with extraterrestrials seems deeply rooted in human nature.

Think about the famous painting by Michelangelo on the ceiling of the Sistine Chapel, with Adam's hand reaching out for the hand of God. What human desire do you think Michelangelo tried to express? Humans desire a "voice" from outside their own situation. A critical look at what humans do to one another and themselves demonstrates their frequently pessimistic dis-position. However, if people could make contact with something or someone outside the human situation, they might be more hopeful.

Having searched throughout his life for hope and certainty, the early Christian theologian St. Augustine wrote, "Our hearts are restless, till they find their rest in Thee [God]." These words help explain Michelangelo's paint-ing. Created in the image of God, even though now fallen into sin, we remain restless apart from a relationship with God. Many people try to find hope in science and the potentials of technological and moral advancement. However, this is simply a mask for the uneasiness we feel in living differently from how God intended us to live.

Spurred on by media attention and bold "scientific" claims, many people believe in the possibility and likelihood of contact with aliens. *The X-Files* was a popular mystery/science fiction television series that aired from 1993 to 2002 with the slogan "The truth is out there." Government conspiracies to hide the truth were a recurring part of the story line, but the protagonists never gave up on their search for the truth. After a century filled with atrocities committed against human beings on our own planet, we know that we have to look outside ourselves for hope. Rather than turning to God, many persons look elsewhere. They don't want a hope that might cramp their lifestyle or demand accountability.

CONTACT: A CASE STUDY

The pagan religions of the Greco-Roman Empire pictured their deities much differently than did the monotheistic religions of Christianity, Judaism, and Islam. Pagan gods were thought to dwell on mountains or in the sea. They acted like humans and had bad tempers and other vices. One wonders why people even considered them gods.

Early Greek philosophers such as Xenophanes and Socrates got in trouble when they pointed out that the gods were imaginary. Xenophanes wrote that just as human gods are similar to humans, the "gods" of cows are probably similar to cows.

Around AD 46, the people of a town named Lystra thought they had received a visit from two extraterrestrial beings. They had heard of previous visitations to an earlier generation (recorded by the Latin poet Ovid) and were perhaps eager to witness the next visit. One of the two visitors healed a man who had been crippled since birth. Seeing this, the people of Lystra thought that two gods had come to their town in the form of men: Zeus and Hermes. They cried out, "The gods have come down to us in the likeness of men!"

As was appropriate in pagan religions, the priest at Lystra brought bulls wrapped with garlands to the city gates in order to offer sacrifices to these two visitors. This was done in order to win the favor of the gods. Otherwise, as happened so often in pagan mythology, the two visitors might have turned their wrath on the town.

The people of Lystra interpreted the visitors' identity according to their pagan worldview, and this is consistent with the way people make assumptions and develop interpretations of facts or events. Often our worldview determines the meaning of facts. If some people's worldview holds that aliens exist, it is not a great leap for them to think that aliens make contact with human beings. The people of Lystra are a prime example. They believed in ods who came and went. When they saw a supernatural event take place, they interpreted that event in light of their worldview.

Recall previous discussions of the methods of science and the religion of science. Assuming a worldview to be true is a form of religion, whether it is a naturalistic, biblical, or polytheistic religion. The questions remain: What assumptions are true? How do we know if they are accurate? Assuming that there is no God, that life came about by evolution, and that contact can be made with life on other planets is in many ways a greater step of faith than the step of Christian faith. Such grandiose assumptions must be challenged.

No wonder some people today believe that aliens from outer space make contact with us. Numerous books and movies, though they may be classified as science fiction, presuppose a universe inhabited with uncountable extraterrestrial beings. Numerous cartoons teach children to expect life from other planets. This viewpoint is strengthened by the belief that the universe came about through a random, natural process that after billions of years yielded a diversity of life. For if life popped up on Earth as a result of natural processes, why shouldn't it pop up in the far reaches of the universe?

Acts 14:8–20 shows us that the apostles Paul and Barnabas were the visitors at Lystra. By the power of God, they healed a crippled man. The miracle caused an uproar, and they could hardly keep the people from sacrificing to them. In the end, an angry crowd stoned Paul. Perhaps extraterrestrials haven't visited us because they've witnessed the fickleness of human behavior!

The issue of contact with extraterrestrials remains unresolved, though, because the data have serious shortcomings. If the evidence were adequate, researchers would prove or at least refine their theories.

John Keel, author of *UFOs: Operation Trojan Horse* (published in 1970 and reprinted in 2013), claims that the inhabitants of UFOs are demons. Keel does not write as a Christian; as noted earlier, he is a self-proclaimed agnostic. He stresses that the messages given to those who have allegedly made contact with "UFOnauts" are in line with occult and demonic activity throughout history.

An early-twentieth-century philosopher, Ludwig Wittgenstein, once wrote that to have any certainty we must have a voice or information from outside our world. In his opinion, our quest for certainty regarding the knowledge of our universe and God is bound to fail. Humans cannot escape the limits of space and time. Only something or someone *outside* time and space is in the position of telling humankind about its existence and about the world of space and time. Most scholars think that Wittgenstein believed this knowledge from outside the human situation to be unachievable.

In a sense, though, Wittgenstein was right! Our scientific progress can tell us only so much about the world. We have an innate knowledge that something exists beyond us. But in our audacity, we define it as whether we search for extraterrestrial beings in hopes of furthering s̶ knowledge or whether we seek God on our own terms. Though we grop something that offers an explanation for our universe and our relations. with its Creator, by ourselves we are left unknowing and uncertain.

The universe testifies to a Creator, but is there any way science or our own mind could ever describe this Creator by means of rationalization? More personally, could we ever know, on our own, what the Creator's attitude is toward us?

A strong case could be built, on the basis of natural evidence, to establish the possibility and perhaps high probability for God's existence. To understand or describe what He is like would be less attainable. We might be able to determine that since we have the idea that certain things are wrong and others right, there must be a moral lawgiver. It would not be a grandiose assumption to call God all-powerful (omnipotent) and ubiquitous (omnipresent). A few other descriptions could be added.

However, notice that these attributes are (1) beyond our experience and (2) quite frightening in light of our shortcomings. Therefore, how could we say much at all about God's attitude toward us? At best, in light of all our shortcomings, it would be reasonable to assume that God is not pleased with His human creations. And this is exactly what the Scriptures state.

Contact: Case Closed

There are numerous stories of Christians who experienced doubts about their relationship with God. Jesus' own disciple Thomas responded in disbelief after hearing news of Jesus' resurrection. His famous words, "Unless I see in His hands the mark of the nails, and place my finger into the mark of the nails, and place my hand into His side, I will never believe" (John 20:25), display the attitude of a scientist. Thomas wanted hard evidence of Jesus' resurrection. No stories of supernatural phenomena would convince him. Then Jesus appeared. After He presented Himself to Thomas, Thomas responded in faith, "My Lord and my God!" (John 20:28).

What was Thomas responding to? He had been with Jesus during His earthly ministry. Surely the clear testimony of Jesus rang in Thomas's ears: "For God so loved the world, that He gave His only Son, that whoever believes in Him should not perish but have eternal life. For God did not send His Son into the world to condemn the world, but in order that the world might be saved through Him" (John 3:16–17). And the climactic act of the resurrection *verified* that Jesus was truly the Son of God and his Savior. Paul added this testimony: "For in Him all the fullness of God was pleased to dwell, and through Him to reconcile to Himself all things, whether on earth en, making peace by the blood of His cross" (Colossians 1:19–20). ...aith contact is made with Jesus, forgiveness and certainty follow.

...an people who live nearly two thousand years after Thomas made his ...fession still be certain of their forgiveness and thus their right standing ...efore God? Consider the idea that there can be no certainty without contact with something outside the human situation. The only possible way to be certain of our forgiveness before God is to trust that the words of the Bible are reliable and inspired. God Himself in the person of Christ treated both the Old Testament and the forthcoming (at His time) New Testament as totally reliable and inspired.

We cannot be certain of our forgiveness by *hoping* that God forgives us. Certainty can only be had if God *assures* us of forgiveness. God's Word assures us of our forgiveness and right standing before Him through the person and work of Christ.

God "did not leave Himself without witness" (Acts 14:17) in creation or in the Church. We still have contact with our Lord through means established by Christ, which we refer to as "the ministry of Word and Sacraments."

Consider the ministry of the Word. Jesus, God in flesh, regarded the Old Testament as the very Word of God (Mark 7:13). Throughout His earthly ministry, Jesus quoted the Old Testament to verify His teaching authority. Before His crucifixion, Jesus assured His disciples that the Spirit of God would come to them. This Spirit taught the disciples all things and reminded them of what Jesus Himself had taught (John 14:26). It was Jesus' apostles who wrote most of the New Testament. In the case of Luke and Mark, the apostles approved of the truthfulness of their writing even if they did not personally take pen in hand. Hence, we trust both the Old and New Testaments. God Himself, in Christ, certifies His Word.

The ministry of the Word is more than transmitting the letters on the pages of the Scriptures. It is the ministry of Christ Himself. Through the words of the Bible, we encounter and hear from Jesus Himself. Christ's death and resurrection stand as the ultimate act of God, an act that redeemed all people.

Christ also promised contact with Him in the Sacraments. Through the concrete, visible elements (water, wine, and bread), we receive forgiveness of sins and eternal life because of the promises of Christ. Before His crucifixion, Jesus instituted the Holy Supper; after His resurrection, He instituted the Sacrament of Baptism.

Matthew 26:26–28 and 1 Corinthians 10:16 speak about Holy Communion and the benefits it offers. Holy Communion is the eating and drinking of Christ's body and blood along with bread and wine. Some theologians describe the presence of Christ as being "in, with, and under" the bread and wine. They use these terms because we are limited in our knowledge of how

Christ becomes present. However, we know that He is present. When we ta
Holy Communion, we are in fact communing with God Himself.

In Holy Communion, not only do we proclaim the Lord's death until
He comes, but we receive forgiveness of sins and eternal life as well. We are
united with the Lord Himself in newness of life. Because the Savior instituted
Holy Communion, we can be certain of our forgiveness and eternal life when
we make intimate contact with Him in His Supper.

Matthew 3:11; 28:19; John 3:5; and Colossians 2:11–15 speak of Baptism and the benefits it offers. John baptized as part of God's Old Testament
teaching about purity and holiness. John also proclaimed a different Baptism,
which Jesus would bring. This Baptism would be a Baptism in the Holy Spirit.

Christ speaks of Baptism early in His ministry. He states, "Unless one is
born of water and the Spirit, he cannot enter the kingdom of God" (John 3:5).
Baptism is the application of water (sprinkled, poured, or through immer-
sion) in connection with the words of Christ.

Paul explains the benefits of Baptism with an analogy from Old Testament circumcision. Circumcision was an act of entering into a covenant with
God. Paul alludes to the fact that Jesus' death and resurrection finalized the
covenant God had established with His people. Baptism applies all the benefits of Christ's death and resurrection to us. It is God's act of the new covenant. Baptism puts to death our sinful nature and raises us to newness of
life in Christ.

Plagued with doubt and uncertainty, the sixteenth-century church reformer Martin Luther spent most of his young-adult life seeking God's
forgiveness and the certainty of His divine favor. The problem was that he
sought to escape the wrath of God on his own terms. Luther physically beat
himself, fasted to the point of exhaustion, performed many good works, and
went to church often. However, it wasn't until he came to realize the full sufficiency of Christ's death for his forgiveness that his conscience was eased. All
his subsequent teaching placed the person and work of Christ at the foundation and center.

Through God's Word, Luther saw that Christ came to save us from
ourselves. Luther wrote: "This is the reason why our theology is certain:
it snatches us away from ourselves and places us *outside* ourselves, so that
we do not depend on our own strength, conscience, experience, person, or
works" (AE 26:387; emphasis added). Jesus came from eternity into time. He
made contact with us. He continues to reach us through His Word and Sacraments. Close encounters with Jesus bring forgiveness.

POINTS TO PONDER

People hoping for contact with extraterrestrial beings often seem to expect that they would come to Earth from advanced civilizations and that they would bring peace and wisdom that our world sorely lacks. It is almost as though they hope for an external intervention that would improve the lot of humanity. However, God already intervened in human history by sending Jesus to die for our sins and, when the time comes, raise us to eternal life. How can we joyously share this Good News to slake the spiritual thirst of those who sense a need for intervention?

WORDS TO REMEMBER

And you, who once were alienated and hostile in mind, doing evil deeds, He has now reconciled in His body of flesh by His death, in order to present you holy and blameless and above reproach before Him. (Colossians 1:21–22)

Photo: © Shutterstock, Inc.

THE QUEST
FOR SPIRITUALITY

INTRODUCTION

Four days in August 1967 made Eastern spirituality a permanent part of Western subculture. The Maharishi Mahash Yogi—leader, teacher, and advocate of the Transcendental Meditation movement—announced that he would give a final lecture before he took a vow of silence. One of the most popular rock groups of that generation, The Beatles, rushed to catch the lecture. The next day, they followed the Maharishi on retreat in Wales to learn his technique for meditation. While they were on retreat, The Beatles' friend and manager, Brian Epstein, suddenly died, and the icons of British rock and roll publicly committed themselves to the quest for enlightenment.

Since the cultural ferment of the late 1960s, new types of spirituality have spiced Western religious life like saffron-topped burgers or curry-filled hot dogs. The quest for spirituality in the years since then has become more and more sophisticated, combining science-based methods and ancient traditions to offer ever more credible approaches.

This section will introduce you to several of the most popular quests for spirituality. It will critique their claims and consider them in view of the teachings of the Bible. "There is nothing new under the sun," according to Ecclesiastes 1:9, and you can find parallels between these quests and the many similar quests that spring up like dandelions on the lawn. And our discussion will reveal to you God's quest: how in loving kindness He seeks you, through His Son, Jesus Christ.

Oh, and incidentally, the Maharishi never took that vow of silence in the summer of 1967.

SPIRITUAL ENCOUNTERS

In the Book of Acts, Luke records early Christian encounters with unbelief. In one instance, the apostle Paul visited Athens, the center of Greek culture. While Paul waited for his traveling companions, he noticed the Athenians' fervent spirituality (17:16–34). In response, Paul "reasoned in the synagogue with the Jews and the devout persons, and in the marketplace every day with those who happened to be there" (v. 17).

When faced with objections from Jewish people, Paul argued from the Old Testament to demonstrate that Jesus was in fact the promised Messiah. When faced with other brands of spirituality, Paul took a different approach. But before the people and philosophers of Athens, Paul used man's natural knowledge of God to teach the Athenians about their spiritual needs. He quoted pagan philosophers and poets to connect with his audience. Only then did he point to Jesus Christ as the answer for full and certain knowledge of God.

The spiritual fervor of today is not unlike the religious fervor of ancient Athens. New or renewed religious beliefs appear each day. False religions and superstition threaten the unwary. Contemporary spirituality offers answers to spiritual questions and often even claims scientific backing.

However, spirituality not established by the Creator lacks a firm foundation. True spirituality is grounded in and shaped by Christ. How do Christians testify to this spirituality? The apostle Peter writes, "In your hearts honor Christ the Lord as holy, always being prepared to make a defense to anyone who asks you for a reason for the hope that is in you" (1 Peter 3:15). Peter exhorts Christians to always be ready to defend Christian hope. Martin Luther wrote, "Therefore it follows from this that every Christian should account for his faith and be able to give a reason and an answer when necessary" (AE 30:105).

READY TO SPEAK

In an age of increasing spirituality, the Christian faith stands ready to give solid answers about God and His relationship to humanity. God's appearing in the flesh through Jesus Christ takes away the need for spiritual speculation. Jesus assures us of our standing before God and the genuine spirituality that follows. When circumstances call upon us to testify to this truth, we must be ready.

Readiness takes training. Luther wrote that when you "have to engage in controversy . . . you must use all your cleverness and effort and be as profound and subtle a controversialist as possible" (AE 26:30–31). As you journey into the world of contemporary spirituality, you will encounter many spiritual claims. Familiarity with spiritual trends and the ability to critique them are necessary skills. Perhaps the most basic skill you will need is the ability to apply God's Law and God's solution in the Gospel.

Apart from Jesus, the human quest for spirituality is doomed to failure. However, a prepared Christian can act as a guide for someone lost on the journey.

6

ENLIGHTENED

They hold hands. Incense billows about the room. Sitting silently in a circle, the three radio hosts prepare for the Saturday night broadcast of *ShadoWorlds: Chronicles of the Paranormal*.

Once the hosts reach a state of enlightenment, they are ready to begin their three-hour discussion on spirituality. Occasionally, Wiccan priestesses, tarot card readers, numerologists, dream interpreters, and other guests join the show. Listeners phone in and participate. The goal: to attain spiritual enlightenment through paranormal experiences.

Ideas expressed on *ShadoWorlds* illustrate a steadily growing, though not always well publicized, spiritual worldview. In matters where traditional religion remains silent, enlightened spirituality whispers answers. It offers explanations about the unknown.

The mysteries of the paranormal are said to expand our spiritual horizons. For example, Extrasensory Perception (ESP) enables a person to contact spirit guides in order to map past lives. Mediums contact deceased loved ones to ease the grieving process. Mental telepathy and telekinesis result from parapsychological abilities. Astrologers, tarot card readers, numerologists, dream interpreters, and others provide insight into future events. Aura readers and psychic surgeons heal the body, and hypnotism heals the mind.

This form of spirituality may be popular in your social and professional circle, or perhaps not. Yet it is easy to find such paranormal "spiritual guides" online or in small business establishments in towns and cities across the country.

Cult researchers and apologists have noted at least two major reasons for this type of spirituality. First, anthropological studies in human history show that when traditional and historic religions decline in a culture, superstitious and individualistic spirituality arises. Walter Martin, founder of the Christian Research Institute, notes that what was once considered New Age spirituality is now considered enlightened spirituality. By assigning scientific names to spiritual practices and drawing connections to scientific research, enlightened New Age spirituality appeals to younger generations. If a spiritual movement or practice can make scientific claims, it appeals to the noncritical mind.

How do those seeking this type of enlightened spirituality think about life? In other words, how do they view life and the world around them? One of the difficulties with studying spiritual trends, such as enlightened spirituality, is that people who practice these trends hold views of reality that differ from classic Western thought. Even though the trends appear scientific at times, they are grounded in Eastern spiritual thought. To understand the logic of a religion or philosophy, you must define how it sees the world (worldview). In fact, in many cases you have to develop working definitions of key words, since they may mean different things in Western versus Eastern vocabularies.

At a basic level, enlightened spirituality has a *monistic* worldview. Monism affirms a oneness to reality. That is, all things share the same essence. Everything that exists, according to monism, exists eternally.

Monists believe humans can connect to all things past, present, and future. Drawing from universal psychic energy, modern spiritualists claim that they can contact eternally existing spirit beings. For example, the claim a person's fate can be known by reading tarot cards and that dreams can offer insight into past and future events. If people are enlightened enough, they believe they are able to connect to sources of knowledge that lie hidden somewhere within the whole of reality.

A *U.S. News and World Report* article stated that religion and spirituality in America are "as important as ever, no matter what you believe." You may run into this view in a slightly different form: "It does not matter what you believe, as long as you are good and sincere."

What are the implications of "no matter what you believe" for this study and for classic Christian spirituality? In his book *The Closing of the American Mind*, Allen Bloom states that by the time a young person enters college, he or she has learned that there is no absolute truth. American culture teaches this pluralism through and through.

The belief that nothing is really true directly challenges Jesus' statement: "I am the way, and the truth, and the life" (John 14:6). Warning against false teaching, Jude wrote, "Beloved, although I was very eager to write to you about our common salvation, I found it necessary to write appealing to you to contend for the faith that was once for all delivered to the saints" (v. 3). In the face of unbelief and false teaching, God calls Christians to proclaim and defend the universal truth of the Gospel. Many attitudes expressed in the *U.S. News and World Report's* April 28, 2002, article "Faith in America: It's as important as ever, no matter what you believe" are intellectually sloppy and spiritually destructive. If you hold the truth of the Gospel of Jesus Christ, you must face the claim made by others that nothing is absolutely true.

The article includes charts and graphs from the *Britannica Book of the Year 2001* that show how Americans think about religious and spiritual matters. Individuals are asked questions about the truth of one's particular religion, how often one feels God's presence or a spiritual force, and so on. One person interviewed in the article states that disbelief does not characterize

Americans. He says that Americans will believe anything. A chart tracking the growth of non-Christian religions proudly notes, "The more the merrier."

A LIGHT ON THE HIDDEN AND UNCERTAIN

Today's enlightened spirituality recognizes and endorses the ability of people to experience the paranormal. According to this view, profound spiritual insight lies in the realm of the unknown. People emerge from these encounters awakened to their true self and the true nature of reality.

Beginning in the nineteenth century, scientists and psychologists have studied unexplainable, extraordinary events. Early on, psychologist and philosopher William James amassed evidence about the reality of paranormal experience. In the late 1920s, Clark University in Massachusetts held a symposium on paranormal events. Included in the panel of presenters, and an avid supporter of paranormal research, was Sir Arthur Conan Doyle, author of the Sherlock Holmes stories. With the exception of two presenters, all the experts were convinced of at least the possibility, if not the certainty, of genuine paranormal experiences.

The 1960s saw tremendous growth in paranormal research. Universities such as Stanford and Duke led the way and continue to engage in rigorous scientific tests of paranormal experiences. Many so-called scientific studies on the paranormal lend credibility to its acceptance. However, careful analysis raises important questions about these studies.

Though scientific research has attempted to establish credibility for paranormal events, psychologists raise doubts about their regularity. *The Journal of Research for Psi Phenomena* published an essay in 1979 that revealed difficulties in distinguishing these experiences. The author, M. A. Persinger, noted that paranormal experiences are usually accompanied by excessive emotional reactions. Persinger suggested that these traumatic and emotion-laden experiences weaken critical thinking skills. This causes people to offer a paranormal interpretation for an otherwise normal event. In other words, the event was "normal," but the person's thought about the event was "paranormal."

Lawyer and theologian John W. Montgomery brings to light certain philosophical and historical problems with paranormal experiences. In his book *Principalities and Powers* he argues that the term *paranormal* is now used to describe events that were once attributed to supernatural forces (angels, demons, or God). He attributes this to an anti-supernatural bias.

Though some unexplained events are best attributed to paranormal phenomena, Montgomery raises the question: how do we know that paranormal experiences are not encounters with demonic supernatural forces? Establishing a supernatural cause for events is outside the sphere of scientific proof. Montgomery's analysis shows the difficulty of establishing differences between paranormal and supernatural events.

Paranormal events are, by definition, unexplainable. Causes and explanations for the paranormal remain concealed. The Latin word that means concealed, *occultus*, gives us our word *occult*. Enlightened spirituality parallels and comingles with the world of the occult. Like the Ouija boards found in children's toy stores, paranormal experiences may appear harmless and even scientific. However, you never know what spiritual force lurks in the unknown.

To be sure, the Holy Scriptures and the Christian faith affirm an invisible reality. For example, the ancient Nicene Creed confessed that within God's creation there exists things visible and invisible, seen and unseen. The Scriptures record angelic appearances and angelic discussions with humans. Christians do not deny an invisible element to creation. Yet the unseen typically remains "unseen" in Christian thought.

Compare the *ShadoWorlds* perception of the unseen with the Christian perspective. Groups such as *ShadoWorlds* claim that humans have the power to perceive the invisible aspects of creation. Modern spirituality's thought about creation, visible and invisible, differs from the Christian view. A so-called enlightened spirituality sees no distinction between creation and the Creator. Everything, seen and unseen, is connected by some sort of psychic energy. This energy, if tapped into by an enlightened mind, increases one's awareness of past, present, and future.

Christianity paints a different picture. Christians maintain that God exists apart from creation. That is, God is eternal. Creation depends on God for its existence. Humans depend on God as well. Reliable knowledge of unseen realities and spiritual truths comes from God. That is, God discloses what He desires humans to know concerning spiritual realities. *ShadoWorlds* and contemporary spirituality work the other way. Humans, by their own psychic abilities, perceive and define their own spirituality.

Arriving at spirituality on our own accord remains uncertain. By its very nature, modern spirituality can never be sure it has drawn the right conclusions from spiritual experiences. However, in Christianity God gives us conclusions that can be trusted because they come from God Himself. Biblical Christian spirituality is the only sure spirituality because the Creator supplies the information.

When criticized, those who claim knowledge of paranormal events insist that a person must achieve enlightenment in order to experience and correctly perceive and interpret the paranormal. In other words, you've got to try it to know it is real.

However, trying spiritual options in order to prove they are true is not without danger. Spiritual experiences do not validate a religion. They could result from hallucinations, self-deception, or demonic deception. You can never be sure what lies behind spiritual experiences.

There remains only one sure way of validating spirituality. It must come from the Author of experience and spirituality Himself. By taking on human flesh, the Author of Life unequivocally demonstrated true spirituality—a spirituality of mercy. Christ's incarnation, death, and resurrection validate this spirituality.

Christianity does not ask a person to try it out and see if your experience validates its truthfulness. Rather, Christianity stands as the truth. The Spirit of God reveals this truth to us. Apart from the Spirit of God, the life, death, and resurrection of Jesus are mere historical facts. The Holy Spirit enlightens our minds in order that we may know that Christ's death was for us (for help see *The Holy Spirit* by Korey Maas in the Lutheran Difference series [St. Louis: Concordia, 2001]).

THE DARKNESS OF UNCERTAINTY

Modern paranormal spirituality appeals to many people. It proposes answers where traditional religion and science are silent. Such spirituality appeals to many Christians as well, since almost all of us have unanswered questions at one time or another. Contemporary spiritualists use Christian terminology, pray, and read Scripture. Yet the worldview of contemporary spirituality, even though it uses Christian terms, opposes the worldview of classic Christian spirituality.

Contemporary enlightened spirituality finds God's revelation insufficient. Unsatisfied with a humble trust in God, modern spiritualists turn away from faith in the Creator and trust answers they arrive at through their spiritual quest.

Consider the following story. A starved man is placed in a pitch-black room. He is told that there is food and a black cat in the room. He feels something rub against his leg. He concludes that this must be the black cat. He reaches down to pet the cat and learns that the cat is much larger than he expected. In fact, the cat is a panther, and the man is the food!

Modern spirituality encourages people to enter the room of the paranormal to find spiritual sustenance. But the paranormal remains unexplained and uncertain. It keeps people in the dark and in spiritual danger. Their trust turns from God's certain Word to hidden and uncertain realities.

Read Jesus' parable of the wise and foolish builders found in Matthew 7:24–27.

Contemporary enlightened spirituality foolishly builds on uncertainty. Mystical experiences, however delightful or spectacular, do not offer a reliable basis for a spiritual belief system. Like sand, spirituality backed by human experience and opinions does not offer a firm foundation.

However, Christian spirituality builds on something different and strong. For example, Jesus testified to the authority of the Old and New Testaments. Throughout Jesus' ministry, He quoted the Old Testament Scripture in support of His claims. A key feature of Jesus' ministry was the fulfillment of Old Testament prophecies. Through such testimony and fulfillment, Jesus demonstrated His credibility. Prior to His death, Jesus promised to send the Spirit of truth to His disciples. The Holy Spirit would teach the disciples and remind them of everything Jesus said to them (John 14:26), and He would guide them into all truth (16:13). In this way Jesus shared His authority with the apostles—the writers of the New Testament. God's Word in Christ and His Word in Scripture are reliable. From them, Christians receive a firm foundation for faith.

Spirituality built without a foundation results in uncertainty and insecurity, with both short-term results and eternal consequences. Doubt follows uncertainty. "One who doubts is like a wave of the sea that is driven and tossed by the wind" (James 1:6). Without a firm foundation, we cannot stand firmly in God's promises. Foundationless spirituality leads to doubt, despair, and deception.

Faith built on uncertain and wavering spiritual experiences and the endeavors of humans is doomed to destruction. Without certainty, there is no light. Without light, there is no hope.

Sometimes you might find examples of enlightened spirituality that claim to be compatible with the Christian faith. For example, "enlightened" writers or leaders might speak of a cosmic Christ or angelic messengers. Some will even quote Scripture. Because attempts at showing compatibility are often taken out of context, be on guard about how Scripture and the person of Christ are distorted in popular spirituality.

God's revelation is final in Christ and the Scriptures. True spirituality can only be informed and shaped by God's revelation. From God's revelation we are informed of the sure Means of Grace. True spirituality encounters God in His Word and Sacraments. These are the only sure means of spiritual renewal.

Spiritual realities remain hidden from our eyes, so how can we be sure they exist, and who alone can be the ultimate authority on spirituality? We are assured of spiritual realities because of God's revelation. Because God is the Creator, He is the only authority on the subject. Check all claims of knowledge about spiritual realities (e.g., angels, human fate) with Scripture. If these claims are not drawn from a proper interpretation of Scripture or if they contradict Scripture, they must be rejected or corrected.

The Book of Proverbs says, "The beginning of wisdom is this: Get wisdom, and whatever you get, get insight" (4:7). How and where do we get spiritual wisdom and insight? Solomon writes, "The fear of the LORD is the beginning of knowledge" (Proverbs 1:7). All truthful spiritual wisdom and insight comes from God in His Word. We fear the Lord and humbly approach Him, allowing Him to have the final say.

Shedding Light on the Darkness

Claims of extraordinary events grab our attention. New scientific discoveries or paranormal events challenge our views of nature and reality. However, much remains in the dark.

The darkness of the human situation prods us to seek God (Acts 17:27). Questions about human identity and future events motivate our quest for spirituality. Throughout the history of humankind, God has graciously delayed His rightful judgment of our ignorance and disobedience. Finally, in one decisive event, He called all people from spiritual darkness into "His marvelous light" (1 Peter 2:9).

In Jesus Christ, God Himself is manifested. Jesus illuminates the hiddenness of God. All that we need to know concerning humanity and spirituality comes to light in Jesus. "And this is the judgment: the light has come into the world. . . . Whoever does what is true comes to the light, so that it may be clearly seen that his works have been carried out in God" (John 3:19, 21). The focal point of this light shines on the cross at Calvary.

On the cross we see God as He identifies with the human situation. He came to us as a man. He suffered as man suffers. He faced death as man faces imminent death. He died as man dies. And He returned to the dust as man returns to the dust. If this were the end of the story, our situation would remain the same. The search for authentic and enlightened spirituality would continue in the darkness of doubt and uncertainty. However, something extraordinary and unexplainable happened. The disciples saw Jesus three days after His death on the cross. He rose from the dead!

This changed everything. Jesus' claim to be equivalent with God the Father had new meaning. His claim to *be* the only true spirituality meant something new and different (John 14:6). The Scriptures had new meaning. Our situation had new meaning.

The consequences of sin, namely death, were overturned. Jesus' death and resurrection assure us of a right standing before God for all eternity. True spirituality radiates from His cross. Our spirituality has a visible starting and ending point in Christ on the cross.

Christian spirituality is certified in Jesus' resurrection. John records that the resurrection assured the disciples of Christ's and the Scripture's authority. "When therefore He was raised from the dead, His disciples remembered that He had said this, and they believed the Scripture and the word that Jesus had spoken" (John 2:22). The resurrection assured the most doubtful that

Jesus is "Lord" and "God" (John 20:28). The resurrection of Christ separates the Christian faith from all other religious faiths.

The truth of the Christian faith depends on Christ's resurrection from the dead (1 Corinthians 15:14, 17). The Christian faith is, in principle, verifiable. What does this mean? You can check the truthfulness of the Gospel with actual historic events. Instead of guessing what God is like and what He is capable of doing, Christians can speak positively of God because of the things He has done in history.

Other religions make claims about God and human spirituality, but they remain empty assertions because there are no witnesses. For example, Muhammad claimed to have received revelations from God, which he recorded in the Qur'an. The Mormon Joseph Smith claimed to have found golden tablets, which portrayed a visit by Jesus to early America. Gautama, the Buddha, claimed that nirvana is achieved through Dharma. A host of other spiritual and religious claims exist, but they all lack one thing in comparison to Christianity. They are not verifiable. That is, their truthfulness does not depend on any verifiable facts.

The incarnation of Christ marks a difference between Christianity and all other religions. God came into time and space. He verified this by miracles and by rising from the dead. All other religions make spiritual claims. Their human founders claim they have the way, yet their claims remain only claims. Jesus didn't claim to be the Son of God and to have the power to forgive sins without offering supporting evidence in the face of unbelief. John records these words of Jesus: "I told you, and you do not believe. The works that I do in My Father's name bear witness about Me" (John 10:25); "Even though you do not believe Me, believe the works, that you may know and understand that the Father is in Me and I am in the Father" (John 10:38). On one occasion Jesus claimed to forgive the sins of a paralytic (Mark 2:5). When the religious elite questioned His authority to do so, Jesus responded by restoring the boy's ability to walk. He performed this miracle in order to testify to His divine authority. The miracles of Jesus and, in particular, His resurrection, separate Christianity from all other religions.

After His resurrection, Jesus enlightened His disciples about the Scriptures. "And beginning with Moses and all the Prophets, He interpreted to them in all the Scriptures the things concerning Himself" (Luke 24:27). God incarnate showed His disciples that the Old Testament Scriptures pointed to Christ. In the Old Testament, the story of human redemption unfolded before the time of Christ. Jesus is the key to unlock the Scriptures. Scripture should be read through the lens of Christ's person and work. That is, the fulfillment of the Law in the Gospel sets the theme of all of Scripture.

Jesus' resurrection from the dead proves the Christian revelation (Acts 17:31). Nevertheless, mere acceptance of historical facts excludes a personal rust in the death and resurrection of Jesus for us. How then do we become certain that these events took place for us? How do we become enlightened in this spirituality?

The death and resurrection of Jesus give us certainty of God's love for human beings. God graciously continues to assure us of His love for us as the Holy Spirit works in our hearts and minds through the Scripture and the Sacraments. Repentance results from the working of the Spirit. That is, we are faced with our sin and rebellion against God (contrition), and our minds are changed from trusting ourselves to faith in Christ. The Means of Grace enlighten our minds to the knowledge of forgiveness of sins and the spirituality shaped by it. God does the work; therefore, it most certainly is true!

Points to Ponder

What makes paranormal activities and mysteries so interesting to people, and why do so many people keep traveling those avenues for answers to spiritual questions? Jesus is the way, the truth, and the life; we need to joyously and lovingly proclaim this to our friends and neighbors!

Words to Remember

I do not cease to give thanks for you, remembering you in my prayers, that the God of our Lord Jesus Christ, the Father of glory, may give you the Spirit of wisdom and of revelation in the knowledge of Him, having the eyes of your hearts enlightened, that you may know what is the hope to which He has called you, what are the riches of His glorious inheritance in the saints. (Ephesians 1:16–18)

7

VOICE FROM BEYOND

A man shakes and sobs. His sister's eyes well up with tears. The family just received wonderful news. Their mother is okay after all.

Four months earlier, while the surgeons operated on their mother, they had waited anxiously in the hospital emergency room. When news of her death came, it crushed them. Uncertain of what comes after death, they visited a psychic for help. The message the psychic shared with them was just what they wanted to hear: their mother was in a better place.

Psychic mediums have received a lot of media attention. This story and similar ones are prevalent on televised psychic readings. John Edward, a contemporary psychic following in the tradition of Uri Geller, Shirley MacLaine, and James Van Praagh, recently wrote a *New York Times* best seller, appeared on *Larry King Live* and *Dateline,* and had his own weekly television show on the SyFy Network from 1999 to 2004. Edward claims that his work as a medium is a gift from God. According to him, God is a force whose energy allows him (and other psychics) to create their own psychic energy, whereby they are able to communicate with those who have "crossed over." He claims to use this gift in order to heal people grieving the deaths of loved ones. By speaking with relatives and friends who have "crossed over" to a different reality, he assures the grievers that life and death are part of a continuous cycle.

Reflect on the rising popularity of spiritual advisers such as psychic mediums. Psychic mediums are common, and many people seek them out. Often people will go to a psychic because they desperately want spiritual advice. Many people seek out mediums when faced with questions concerning life after death. However, such spiritual advisers have a rather small view of God and cannot speak truth to the full breadth and depth of our spiritual needs.

Psychics such as John Edward see God as an impersonal force. Oftentimes in psychic circles there is no distinction between man and God. Man is typically viewed as either a part of God or even as a god. God is often referred to as energy. Psychics claim to tap into psychic energy, which allows them to contact others who share in the same psychic divinity.

Many psychic mediums believe in reincarnation or a variation of this teaching. When a person dies, psychics believe the deceased can be contacted. The deceased is typically seen as a bodiless spirit who remains present but is no longer visible. There is no heaven or hell in psychic thought. Man goes on existing eternally as a spirit being who may or may not come back as another person. In contrast, Christianity sees death as final. When a person

..ies, he or she enters either eternal blessedness (heaven) or eternal damnation (hell).

The Christian God has revealed Himself as a personal being as opposed to an impersonal force or energy. The God revealed in Scripture desires a relationship with humanity and creation. Though He is everywhere in creation, He is not part of creation. In classic Christian spirituality, a sharp distinction remains between God and humans. Humans are subject to God in Christian thought, whereas psychic thought places humans and God as equals.

Christians often seek advice from their pastor. However, a Christian worldview cannot fit with seeking and trusting spiritual advice from a psychic. This is because Christian spirituality cannot be synthesized with psychic spirituality. A psychic worldview not only contradicts Christian teachings about God and humans, but it also contradicts the redemption of man won by the death and resurrection of Christ.

Voices from Beyond?

Psychologists have analyzed respected and famous psychics. Their research demonstrates the deception that lies behind the psychic industry. Research shows that psychic mediums masterfully take advantage of the human psychology of belief.

Generally speaking, clients of psychic mediums find psychic readings edifying and applicable because they already believe in the medium's ability to contact the dead. Research indicates that clients tend to fit the broadest psychic reading into anticipated results. James E. Alcock, a psychologist from York University, noted that mediums might offer completely generalized readings. Nonetheless, someone who already trusts in a psychic will accept the readings as personal and genuine. Astonishment and vulnerability increase for someone who has suffered the loss of a loved one. Psychics know that a grieving family member will welcome any supposed positive news from a deceased loved one.

Beginning with supposed premonitions from the dead, mediums rattle off a list of names, colors, diseases, and so forth until they receive a "hit." Once an audience member or a client acknowledges that something from the list is familiar, such as a name or disease, the reading begins.

Some televised psychics appear convincing. However, it should be remembered that what you see on television is the edited version. After years of analysis, researchers have classified psychic readings into three categories. More often than not, the following reading techniques are utilized and are fairly easy to spot.

Hot readings obtain information on subjects ahead of time. For public readings, some mediums plant their own people in the audience in order to gather information from their conversations either before or during the session. Private readings use information from prior conversations with the client. For example, when someone sets up an appointment with a personal psychic, the psychic will often ask what the appointment involves. By the time the appointment takes place, the psychic has a good idea about the cares and concerns of the client. Clients typically forget what they told the psychic when they made the appointment.

Warm readings either feed off of hot readings or use psychological principles that apply to most people. For example, many people who have experienced the death of a spouse keep the wedding ring as a token of remembrance from that person. Psychics take advantage of these situations. They may say, "That ring on your necklace; it belonged to a loved one, didn't it?" Psychics learn through other subtle hints such as body language, which they use to pry information out of a person.

Cold readings are perhaps the most convincing of all psychic readings. They are made without any prior knowledge or acquaintance with a person/client. These usually take place in an audience with many members. The psychic will usually begin by "reading" the entire group, making fast statements such as "I'm getting an 'S-name'; it could be a man or woman, a spouse or sibling." After getting head nods from the audience, the psychic stops and probes a little further, "Is it a Steve, Scott, or Sarah?" You can imagine how many people in a large group know a Steve, Scott, or Sarah. From there, the psychic continues to probe for more hits.

Most psychics are uncomfortable with cold reads because they involve the most guesswork. For example, one researcher from *Skeptic Magazine* reviewed tapes of John Edward's cold readings. He concluded that Edward's accuracy was about 10 percent, even after editing.

Time magazine also investigated episodes of John Edward's psychic television show, *Crossing Over*. A review compared an actual public reading to the edited version for television, showing that through editing, Edward manipulated reads to boost his accuracy rate. Producers used small portions of the original reading to patch together a credible thirty-minute show, complete with commercials to break up inconsistencies. Imagine if you could take a live two-hour football game and edit it down to less than thirty minutes. You could tailor the results to reflect well on your favorite team. This is what John Edward did. He took the highlights of his tapings and edited them into a clean, believable program.

Historians report that the famed magician Harry Houdini sought out reliable psychic mediums for years. His experience in magic and illusions enabled him to detect the most sophisticated of frauds. He went to the most reliable psychics he could find, but he always uncovered the psychics' tricks. Hence, Houdini was never able to find a reliable psychic.

Though some psychics might provide a disclaimer, saying their spiritual advice is for entertainment purposes, others claim that they are, in fact, connecting with spirits of the dead. Some appear very accurate on television.

By applying our knowledge of how hot, warm, and cold readings work, a psychic's spiritual hoax is fairly easy to detect. However, some psychics still appear very convincing, and the psychic may stumble onto the truth by mere coincidence. Scriptures inform us of other possibilities: the psychic could receive information from the devil or demonic spirits.

Psychics often, if not always, speak of the dead as those who have "passed on" or "crossed over." These terms can indicate, though not always, a psychical worldview that may not fit with what we know as revealed truth. The only certain explanation for our reality is found in the Author of our reality. When God created, He brought reality as we know it into existence. A scriptural worldview is informed by the One who created time and space. Scripture offers us a voice from outside the human situation that informs us of reality.

A psychic's god is a false god. The true God who reveals Himself in Scripture commands His people to reject mediums. Hence, a psychic's notion of god cannot be the true God. Following a psychic and his god is idolatry.

When a psychic claims to be gifted by God, he misleads those who trust him. He leads to false knowledge about God and also to false hope for the future. In the end, he leads to damnation. Trust is placed in man and his false promises rather than in the reliable promises of God in Christ.

Logically speaking, a medium's claim to speak with the dead is either true or false. The psychic really divines the dead or he does not. If not, he is a charlatan. Though debunking popular mediums does not prove difficult, the possibility remains that some mediums make contact with spirits. On the other hand, mediums may not only speak with unidentifiable spirits, as mentioned above, but they also offer a false hope in life after death apart from Christ.

Psychics often offer personal advice with tragic consequences. In his 1997 book *Psychic Mafia,* former psychic M. Lamar Keene testifies about the dependence of clients on their psychics. As a psychic, he offered all sorts of advice, from marriage to professional, and his clients almost always followed it—many times, he sadly recounts, to their detriment. Marriages dissolved, jobs were lost, and so forth, and still his clients came back. He also tells of how most of the prominent psychics he knew died tragic deaths from alcoholism, mental illness, depression, and the like.

WORDS THAT CONDEMN

Psychics typically view death as a crossing over from one reality to the next. Hence, there is no heaven or hell. Regardless of one's faith or lack thereof, psychics such as John Edward assure relatives of their deceased loved one's security. There is no need for a Savior in this line of spiritual thought. A person simply transfers from one reality to the next. However, classic Christian spirituality tells a different story.

Jesus' death and resurrection put to death our old sinful nature and raised us to new life in Christ. His actions also give a picture of our bodily death. Like Jesus, when we die we will be physically raised from the dead unto eternal life. This bodily resurrection will come at the Last Day, when Jesus judges all the living and the dead. Those with faith in Christ will rise to eternal life. Those trusting anyone other than God in Christ will descend to eternal damnation.

Consulting spirits of the dead (necromancy) is expressly forbidden in the Old Testament. Necromancers and those who consulted necromancers were, under the old covenant, subject to the death penalty. Why such harsh consequences? The Old Testament recounts tale after tale of Israel's rejection of the true and living God. Israel continually adapted spiritual trends from their neighbors and consequently turned from worship of the one true God to the spurious and false gods of their neighbors.

The author of 1 Samuel records the account of King Saul consulting a medium (28:1–20). Learning of God's plan to give David the throne of Israel, Saul's jealous anger caused David to flee Israel. Though David had ample opportunity to take Saul's throne, he waited patiently for the Lord to fulfill His promise (16:1, 13). Aware of his impending doom, Saul turned to a medium for advice.

Read the story of Saul and the medium of En-dor in 1 Samuel 28:1–20. Saul asked Samuel how to defeat the Philistines (v. 15), but Samuel responded that the Lord's condemnation on Saul's kingship would remain. Prior to Samuel's death, he delivered these words to Saul: "Has the LORD as great delight in burnt offerings and sacrifices, as in obeying the voice of the LORD? Behold, to obey is better than sacrifice, and to listen than the fat of rams. For rebellion is as the sin of divination, and presumption is as iniquity and idolatry. Because you have rejected the word of the LORD, He has also rejected you from being king" (15:22–23).

Why would Saul seek out a medium even after he expelled mediums from Israel years earlier (1 Samuel 28:3), and what lessons regarding revelation apart from God's Word can be drawn from Samuel's response? Through Samuel, God delivered His word of judgment on Saul. Yet Saul continued to disobey God. Threatened by the Philistine army, Saul made a final attempt to escape God's judgment. After his prayers went unanswered, Saul sought out a medium. God's original judgment (15:22–23) compared Saul's rebellion to divination. Faced with imminent judgment, Saul committed the sin of divination itself.

When God speaks, His Word does not change. God's Law does not change. Likewise, His promises do not change. Seeking out mediums treats God's Word as insufficient. The response that the spirit of Samuel gave to Saul demonstrates the sufficiency of God's Word. When God says He will do something, He will prove faithful to His Word. Psychic council undermines God's Word and blatantly doubts God's Word.

Consulting psychics turns our reliance from the certainty of God's mercy to the uncertainty of man's spiritual whims. However, we may turn our allegiance away from God in numerous ways. We doubt and turn our back on God when we seek answers from spiritual or earthly philosophy contrary to God's Word. Whether it favors a psychic medium or our own abilities, the sinful heart continually doubts God and His Word.

Think back to the account of Adam and Eve in the Garden of Eden. When the devil appeared to Eve in the form of a serpent, what was the first thing he asked Eve? "Did God actually say . . . ?" As the story continues, Eve doubted God's command about fruit from the tree in the middle of the garden. Adam followed suit. Here lies the origin of sin and death—doubting God's warning and care.

Paul explains the consequences of Adam and Eve's disobedience: "Sin came into the world through one man, and death through sin, and so death spread to all men" (Romans 5:12). Doubting God's Word leads to sin and death.

Though many psychic mediums prove false, Scripture informs us that necromancy is sometimes real. The National Spiritualist Association of Churches claims that the Bible endorses spiritism (necromancy). So how can we discern between competing claims of spiritual truth? When faced with such competing claims, theologians from the apostle Paul to Martin Luther to C. S. Lewis have asked: "How do these views interact with what Jesus said about Himself and His work?" This question helps sort out the spiritual implications of a belief or practice.

Modern spiritism denies the person and work of Christ. Many psychics view Jesus as equivalent to any other man. Some may claim that He was more enlightened spiritually than normal man. However, psychics believe that the same power that Jesus was able to tap into remains available to all people because all people share in the same psychic divine energy. Concerning Christ's work, many psychics reject Christ's atoning death on the cross. There is no sin and eternal damnation in psychic thought—and, hence, no need for a Savior.

Surprisingly, despite the contradictions between spiritism and Christianity, some Christians try to appeal to both belief systems. For example, Jean Dixon (1904–97), a noted twentieth-century psychic, was also a practicing Roman Catholic. A common feature of modern spirituality is the mixing of different belief systems (syncretism). However, this is like mixing oil and water, and in the end it won't work.

THE ONE FROM THE DEAD

Perhaps our greatest fear is our fear of death. Despite our advances in science and medicine, death appears undefeatable. Most people who seek psychic mediums do so in order to be assured of their loved one's fate.

Christianity's answers to life after death are the only certain answers. We can tell those who fear death the message that Jesus' death and resurrection paid the ransom price for sin and defeated death. This is the essential truth. On the basis of the death and resurrection, God declares man righteous before Him. Death is no longer frightening. The penalty for our sin was paid. God is no longer our Judge but rather our Redeemer.

Throughout the history of His people, God has revealed Himself and His will to man. Immediately after the fall, God promised to crush the work of Satan (Genesis 3:15). God restated this promise throughout the history of Israel. Speaking through the Old Testament prophets, God foretold the way in which He was going to redeem creation from death.

As Old Testament history unfolded, specific details of God's agent of redemption were revealed. Finally, a baby was born in the town of Bethlehem, as foretold by the prophet Micah. This baby was the one appointed by God who would bring about His promised redemption.

Indeed, this was no ordinary baby. In the flesh of this boy was God Himself. Three decades into Jesus' life, God fulfilled the ancient promise given from the beginning. Jesus—the God-man—went to the cross. By substituting His righteousness for man's unrighteousness, Jesus crushed the work of Satan.

Jesus' resurrection from the dead finalized the redemption of humankind. The consequence of sin, which He took upon Himself, had no power over Him. Christ defeated death.

This isn't just a story or spiritual wishful thinking. Nor is it a mysterious event that occurred in another realm of reality. Seeing, hearing, and touching Jesus after His resurrection convinced the disciples of His divinity (1 John 1:1–4). The reality of the resurrected Christ overwhelmed the disciples. Many of them wound up paying the ultimate price as martyrs for testifying to this truth. The events of Jesus' death and resurrection shaped the spirituality of Christ's early disciples. It was these events that fulfilled God's promise of redemption, whereby humans truly have fellowship with God Almighty.

Speaking of the witness of Christ's early disciples, the author Paul Maier states, "Myths don't make martyrs." In response to those who deny Jesus' resurrection from the dead, the martyrdom of the early disciples testifies to the truth of Jesus' resurrection. Men who were hiding in fear after the crucifixion became bold, outspoken witnesses after seeing the resurrected Christ—risking all, to the point of death, for the joy of proclaiming the Gospel.

In the face of unbelief, Christian apologists have used this argument ("myths don't make martyrs") to establish the historicity of the resurrection. The word *martyr* comes from the Greek word that means "to witness or testify." The early Christians were killed because they testified to the resurrection of Jesus Christ. All the apostles, with the exception of John, were killed because of their testimony to Christ's resurrection.

When faced with the choice either to withdraw their claim that Jesus rose from the dead or to die, the apostles chose to die. Why? They *saw* Jesus after His death. To withdraw their testimony was to deny the truth they saw with their very eyes.

The apostles must have seen Jesus alive after He died. For them to willingly die for a lie they knowingly concocted would have been nonsense. When faced with choosing death for something they claimed to be witnesses to or freedom for denying what they saw, the apostles chose death. Surely myths don't make martyrs.

Paul argued that if Christ did not rise bodily from the dead, Christianity is useless and a false faith (1 Corinthians 15:14). Furthermore, Paul stated, "If in Christ we have hope in this life only, we are of all people most to be pitied" (v. 19). However, Christ rose from the dead. Therefore, we can be certain of our resurrection to eternal life.

During His lifetime Jesus raised people from the dead. However, these people eventually returned to death. Jesus is different. Forty days after His resurrection, He ascended into heaven. Jesus is the only authority on life after death. He is the only one who can speak of it with firsthand experience. Mediums may speak as if they are able to contact the dead. However, only Jesus can give conclusive answers regarding life after death. From eternity, He stepped into human time and space. Within the sphere of time and space, He died and came back from the dead. He then ascended back into heaven to take His place at the right hand of God the Father. He alone is able to offer authoritative answers to our greatest fear. He alone is "the way, and the truth, and the life" (John 14:6).

Read 1 Corinthians 15:12–23, where Paul states that death came through one man. Through Adam, we are born into sin. Because we are sinners, we ignore and rebel against God's promises. Spiritual beliefs shaped by humans are limited to humans. Humans are bound to their experiences, and our experiences often deceive us. In our rebellion, we find ourselves choosing our own path, which leads to spiritual uncertainty. The only thing for certain is death.

Jesus, born from Adam's seed yet from divine origin, walked the same path that humans walk. He did not rebel against God. Yet He still died. After

His death, Jesus returned from the grave. Jesus paved the way to life afte death. He made the way from humans to God. Trusting in His work for us, we are led to new life.

Paul's argument in 1 Corinthians has important implications for shaping our personal spirituality. According to Paul, Christian spirituality is founded in and shaped by Christ. In order to stand firmly in the truth, our spirituality must begin and end in Jesus. Apart from Him, His person and work, our faith is in vain. This is spirituality as God reveals it. See *The Spirituality of the Cross* by Gene Veith (St. Louis: Concordia, 2010).

The spirituality of the cross shapes our congregational spirituality as well. Our corporate worship and fellowship focus on Jesus' person and work. The Means of Grace not only remind us of Christ's death and resurrection, but they also apply forgiveness of sins to us. The Means of Grace certify our forgiveness and right standing before God and one another.

Points to Ponder

Curiosity, confusion, fear, or desperation can drive people to seek answers from psychics and the occult, but these false sources of truth can string people along and eventually lead to a dead end. You might know people who are searching for spiritual answers but may not realize what they really need. How can you point them to Jesus Christ as the true source of answers to their need?

Words to Remember

Jesus said to her, "I am the resurrection and the life. Whoever believes in Me, though he die, yet shall he live, and everyone who lives and believes in Me shall never die. Do you believe this?" (John 11:25–26)

8

YOUR DESTINY

Donald Regan's 1990 book *For the Record* shocked Americans. The former chief of staff to Ronald Reagan reported that most of the president's appearances and actions were approved in advance by Mrs. Reagan's astrologer.

The roots of astrology reach back to the second millennium BC. Astrologers from the early civilizations of Babylonia developed horoscopes based on the position of stars and planets. These horoscopes predicted what would most likely happen from month to month. Babylonian astrologers also developed the signs of the zodiac—astrological categories based on twelve divisions in the sky. Each division was assigned a name drawn from the planets and constellations found within each sphere. The twelve signs of the zodiac correspond to twelve periods over the course of a year. Zodiacal signs (e.g., Scorpio, Libra, Virgo, Leo) were thought to determine personality traits and relational compatibility.

Once astrology made its way into Roman culture (a few centuries prior to the birth of Christ), astrologers fashioned horoscopes for individuals, much like today's horoscopes.

Astrology remains popular today. According to professional astrological organizations, there are more than ten thousand professional astrologers who serve twenty million clients. Horoscopes can be found today in every form of media. Newspapers have daily readings. Television and telephone services offer astrological readings. Internet astrologers offer daily readings on the web or through email. Because of its popularity in the media, astrology has a definite place in American society. Horoscopes are a part of many people's lives. People seek out astrologers for personal and professional advice.

Despite its apparent popularity in some circles, astrology poses logical, scientific, and moral difficulties for Christian. Why would a Christian turn to stars and planets for guidance when the Creator of those stars and planets offers us a personal relationship with Him?

SCIENCE AND THE STARS

Horoscopes based on astrological readings pose a variety of difficulties. As discussed earlier, historians have observed an increase in superstition when historic, traditional religions decline. Some contemporary astrologers argue that mathematical and scientific formulations confirm astrological predictions; however, scientific and logical analysis reveals problems with astrology.

According to the Committee for Scientific Investigation of the C.
the Paranormal, rigorous scientific tests have discounted the claims of .
ogers. For example, when a test was conducted on more than three thous
astrological predictions, only 10 percent proved to be reasonably accurate.

In an attempt to rescue the reputation of astrology, supporters claim tha.
among the many frauds there still remain a few authentic astrologers. This
raises the question "How do you know which astrologer to trust?" The astrologer typically answers, "The one whose readings come true."

Another scientific investigation showed the difficulty of resting astrology's legitimacy on experimental proof. A researcher took out an advertise-
ment in a French newspaper promising a detailed, ten-page horoscope for
free. Approximately 150 people sent in their zodiacal information. The researcher responded to all the inquiries by sending them the horoscope of a
serial murderer. He enclosed a questionnaire with the horoscope asking for
the accuracy of the astrological reading. Ninety-four percent of the inquirers
claimed the readings were accurate for them! Ninety percent shared the positive results with friends and family.

Where science sheds light on astrology's inconsistencies, logical analysis
points out a fallacy in reason. Astrologers who devise horoscopes do so on
the basis of the twelve zodiac signs. Horoscopes given in the newspaper, on
television, or through personal readings do so on the basis of twelve zodiacal
divisions in the sky. This begs the question "What are the reasons or grounds
for dividing the sky in such a way?" Some contemporary astrologers argue
for anywhere between eight and twenty-four zodiac divisions in the sky. How
could we know which zodiacal scheme is the correct one? What guarantees
that the stars or a person's zodiacal sign really contains information about
one's life? These and other questions remain unanswered.

The historical roots of astrology reveal another major problem with the
system. Astronomical research shows that when the signs of the zodiac were
established, the constellations in each division were different than today. Science has shown that in the last two thousand years, constellations have shift-
ed thirty degrees. The constellations that determined the zodiacal divisions
moved over to the next division. Where Virgo was found two thousand years
ago, Leo is now located.

Ten percent of astrological predictions were not discredited by the Committee for Scientific Investigation of the Claims of the Paranormal. Chance
could account for some of the accuracy of astrological readings. After all,
wildcat drillers find oil about 10 percent of the time!

A former astrologer's client (we'll call him Ken) described his last weeks
before turning from relying on his astrologer to embracing Christianity.
Ken's astrologer told him that he was going to be safe and healthy for at least
the next few weeks. A few days later, Ken broke his arm. When Ken asked his

ser how this could happen in light of his previous astrological read-
ie astrologer answered, "Think of everything else that could have gone
ng. Be happy that you only broke your arm."

Supporters of astrology claim that despite the charlatans, genuine astrologers still remain. Every astrologer will claim to offer authentic readings.
However, scientific and logical analysis exposes the weaknesses of astrology.
There is no evidence supporting claims that celestial bodies dictate human
behavior and foretell future events. Though a horoscope or an astrologer may
appear accurate, chance and faulty inferences can account for some accuracy.

Walter Truett Anderson, author of *Reality Isn't What It Used to Be*, comments that astrology and horoscopes might appear to be the national religion
of Americans. He made this observation on the basis of the large number
of media appearances by astrologers and their services. Polls and question-
naires show that horoscopes are read and are often considered reliable by
people from all religious and cultural backgrounds.

All religious and philosophical systems of thought follow some sort of
authority. For example, Muslims follow the authority of the Qur'an, and a
rationalist follows the authority of reason and experience. The authority one
follows typically prescribes one's view of reality and truth (worldview). However, what is astrology's ultimate authority, and what is the worldview of an
astrologer?

Astrologers base their readings on planetary and astral alignments.
Hence, an astrologer's authority is the planets and stars. The worldview of
astrology connects human behavior and circumstances with the planets and
stars. Because celestial bodies dictate human behavior, free will is foreign to
the thought of astrologers. With no free will, people have no choice in their
behavior or future. The stars dictate human destiny.

There is no room for God in an astrologer's worldview. If the stars rule
everything, what place could God have? Though astrologers may speak of
God, it is empty talk.

As noted above, historians have observed a culture's movement toward
superstition when traditional and historic religious thought declines. The
early-twentieth-century Christian writer G. K. Chesterton argued that superstitious and arbitrary spirituality is dull. Meanwhile, a Christian spirituality that wrestles with the tension between faith and reason is difficult yet
exciting and the only guarantee of sanity. In contrast, superstition is rooted
in fear and does not seek understanding.

Stars and Scarecrows

The prophet Jeremiah warned God's people against associating with foreign religious practices such as astrology (10:2–5). Jeremiah compared the
practice of astrology to the absurdity of worshiping a wooden idol carved

from a tree. He also compared trust and fear of astrological signs to reverse a scarecrow in a melon patch.

Both the stars in the sky and wood from a tree are created objects. Both stars and trees owe their existence to the Creator. Without God creating them, the stars and trees would not exist. Worship and trust of created objects bewilders Jeremiah. What would cause someone to trust in a temporal object? Only the living, eternal God, proclaims Jeremiah, deserves worship. He is the only true God (10:10).

Jeremiah compares stars and wood to demonstrate the absurdity of worshiping anything other than the God of Israel. Jeremiah compares fear about "signs of the heavens" to an idol carved from a tree. To highlight the foolishness of worshiping man-made idols, Jeremiah compares the impotence of the wooden idol to a scarecrow. "Their idols are like scarecrows in a cucumber field, and they cannot speak; they have to be carried, for they cannot walk" (10:5). Like a scarecrow, idols carved from trees are powerless. The thought of worshiping them is foolish. So, too, the stars in the sky are powerless. As created objects they have no power over humans.

We could push the argument further to illustrate the logic of reserving worship and reverence for God alone. A scarecrow owes its existence and place in a melon patch to the farmer who puts it there. Therefore, just as a scarecrow owes its existence to the farmer who formed him, we owe our existence to God the Creator. He alone controls and rules our lives. He alone is worthy of worship.

Why do you think the prophets warned ancient Israel about falling into the religious practices of other cultures? To begin with, Israel's neighbors practiced idolatry, which was forbidden in the Second Commandment. The Israelites were to worship the God of Israel alone. Turning away from God's commandments invited God's wrath on Israel. The prophets continually warned against this.

In addition to idol worship, many of Israel's neighbors practiced child sacrifice. Practicing the idolatry of their neighbors could entice Israel from idolatry into even more detestable practices. These practices invited God's consuming anger.

Astrology presented serious moral difficulties for ancient Israel. Just as Christians today are surrounded by a variety of religious opinions, the Israelites were surrounded by cultures that practiced astrology, among other pagan rites. Moses warned the Israelites not to place their trust in created things on earth or in the heavens (Deuteronomy 4:15–19). To do so would provoke God's wrath (vv. 23–24).

In the New Testament, Paul repeated the command not to trust in created things. He argued that those who follow the authority of created things such as stars and planets are in spiritual bondage (Galatians 4:3).

Following the authority of astrological signs and astrologers breaks the first Commandment. Although astrologers and their clients break the First Commandment, all of humanity violates this law. Our human nature entices us to trust and worship gods other than the one true God. Astrology and horoscopes are symptoms of an idolatrous heart, and all people share this same condition.

It is our nature to turn from God toward ourselves and other created things for temporal blessings and eternal salvation (Romans 1:25). Our actual and visible sin is not the fundamental problem; it's who we are as children of Adam—children born cursed under the Law.

The First Commandment teaches us to have God first in our lives: to fear, love, and trust in God above all things. How does fearing God differ from fearing an astrologer's forecast? In his Large Catechism, Luther explained what it means to fear God. He cites Exodus 20:5–6: "I the LORD your God am a jealous God, visiting the iniquity of the fathers on the children to the third and the fourth generation of those who hate Me, but showing steadfast love to thousands of those who love Me and keep My commandments." Luther notes that God wants to be feared, not despised. However, Luther notes, God does not let wickedness go unpunished. His anger does not cease until the wicked are exterminated. God's Law judges completely. There is no escape from His punishment. On account of this, we are to fear God. For unlike the mute stars and planets, our Maker speaks His judgment against sin. Our destiny is in His almighty hands.

When astrology made its way into Roman culture, the planets and constellations within the zodiacal divisions were worshiped as individual gods. Luther noted that the Romans worshiped these "gods" because they desired the attributes associated with them. For example, Mercury was worshiped and trusted for wealth and prosperity. To have this god on your side guaranteed your success.

However, trusting in God does not imply that Christians can "take it easy" in their careers, schoolwork, or family life. Some may say that Christians are destined for success, but this can become a form of idolatry in its own right. What does it mean to trust solely in God for daily provisions and blessings while maintaining a strong work ethic and Christian lifestyle? Trust, fear, and love of God push us to work harder. God blesses us with careers, education, family, and so forth. He entrusts these things to our care. The attitude "I don't need to work hard; God will take care of me" is quite the opposite of what it means to trust God.

We trust God for every good gift. We work hard as stewards of God's gifts. By fearing God, we strive to keep His Commandments. In loving and trusting God, we gladly act according to His Commandments.

Christian spirituality fears, loves, and trusts in God for all ⸌
eternal blessings. Seeking astrological advice violates God's Comma⸌
It finds comfort and hope in created objects. Simply put, astrology ent⸌
created objects as gods and dethrones God, the Creator of these very ob⸜

Christian spirituality places its fear and trust in God alone. God's pror⸌
ise of temporal and eternal blessings assures us of our future. Mature Christian spirituality seeks to fear, love, and trust in God above all things in every
part of life.

"Sign" of Salvation

A philosopher said that if you accept astrology, you have to accept that
you are a born loser or a born winner. Astrology maintains a deterministic
worldview. That is, human fate is already predetermined. The choices that
humans make have already been made for them. A person's zodiacal sign
determines his or her fate.

In contrast, Christ's death on the cross and God's universal mission to all
people inform us of God's perspective on fate and predestination. Over the
centuries, philosophers and theologians have debated issues about free will
and predestination. More often than not, these debates end in a stalemate.
However, the Gospel gives us God's answer.

From the beginning, God promised humanity a Savior (Genesis 3:15),
and God promised this Savior to all. At the appointed time, this promise
was fulfilled in Jesus. His saving work effected the forgiveness of sins for all
people (1 John 2:2). In Christ, our fate is sealed, our sins forgiven, and our
salvation certain. Apart from Christ, we remain accountable for our sin and
subject to God's punishment. Reading Scripture through the lens of Christ
gives us this answer: salvation is God's work, and damnation is man's.

The Gospel of Matthew records the visit of the Magi from the East to
Jerusalem (2:1–12). Though little is known about the Magi, they were most
likely wealthy astronomers/astrologers or magicians from the area of Per-
sia. Something extraordinary drew them to Jerusalem. Some sort of unusual
sign in the sky appeared, which aroused their curiosity. So they followed this
"star" (the Greek word for star can refer to any celestial body apart from the
sun).

Upon their arrival in Jerusalem, the Magi asked, "Where is He who has
been born king of the Jews? For we saw His star when it rose and have come
to worship Him" (v. 2). After King Herod heard of the Magi's request, he
asked the Jewish scholars and priests where this king was to be born. From
the book of the prophet Micah, written about seven hundred years prior to
this event, the scribes were able to point to Bethlehem, the city where the
"king of the Jews"—the promised Messiah—was to be born.

the Magi finally made it to the place where Jesus was born, they ... and worshiped Him" (v. 11). What prompted rich, Gentile Wise ... om the East to bow down and worship this infant? The promise given after the fall of Adam and Eve (Genesis 3:15) and repeated throughout ...ael's history was to be fulfilled in this child. The shepherd of God's people (Matthew 2:6; Micah 5:2)—all people—had come.

When the Magi asked where the "king of the Jews" was to be born, the Jewish scholars turned to Scripture for their answer. They knew that the only sure information concerning the Messiah had to come from God. The Scriptures record God's Word throughout history, and this is where we find certainty about God, our life, and eternal life.

In the example of the Magi, is Christianity viewed as a religion bound by cultural walls, or does it transcend such boundaries? Rather than being a local or regional religion, Christianity is designated as *the* world religion. The Magi's visit to Jesus demonstrated this. Some scholars think the Magi may have been Zoroastrians. To be sure, they were not Jews, though they may have had some contact with Jews in their lifetime. In spite of their culture and religion, God led them to their Savior. By using the stars to guide them to Jesus, God met the Magi where they were in their religious understanding. He also fulfilled the prophecy of Numbers 24:15–19.

Three decades after the Magi visited Jesus, He was put to death on a cross and then rose from His grave. His death paid the debt for sin, and His resurrection certified the destruction of the work of Satan and the consequences of sin—death.

Christ's death shows the consequence of our sinful nature. It took more than a cursory show of spirituality and good deeds by humans to reverse the effects of sin. No amount of religious piety or godly living could change our natural inclination toward sin and outright rebellion against God. (Good works and piety for the purpose of meriting God's favor are, in fact, a form of self-idolatry.) The effects of our sinful nature were not reversible by human efforts. Only the death of God's Son could reverse the judgment for a sinful humanity. The resurrection of Christ validates the victory won in the death of Christ. It certifies the destruction of sin, death, and Satan's stronghold over us.

Following the sign of a bright star, receiving the certain location from the Scripture, the Magi were led to an infant child. In a manger lay the Savior of humankind. God's mission in the world extends to all people. The star the Magi followed led to the Scriptures, and the Scriptures told of the Savior's birth. In the Scriptures we find Christ. In Christ all people find salvation.

POINTS TO PONDER

The easy availability of horoscopes, astrological readings, and sin. "spiritual advice" reflects a widespread hunger for guidance that is almc fatalistic in its search for meaning. These people search for something that they don't have and cannot find, yet keep coming back for more as if admitting that the search is endless. God answers this darkness and futility with light and freedom—light and freedom found only in Jesus!

WORDS TO REMEMBER

But now the righteousness of God has been manifested apart from the law, although the Law and the Prophets bear witness to it—the righteousness of God through faith in Jesus Christ for all who believe. (Romans 3:21–22)

9

CONTEMPLATE

What do Electroencephalography (EEG), Computerized Axial Tomography (CAT), Magnetic Resonance Imaging (MRI), Single Photon Emission Computed Tomography (SPECT), and Positron Emission Tomography (PET) have to do with spirituality? As of late, quite a bit.

Work begun by the late Dr. Eugene d'Aquili of the University of Pennsylvania's medical school opened up fascinating avenues for scientific research into how the brain functions during religious experiences. Dr. d'Aquili and his colleague Dr. Andrew Newberg have observed neurological changes in the brain during meditative states.

Their research has developed into a new science called *neurotheology*. This science explores links between spirituality and the human brain. During a 2001 interview with *Reader's Digest*, Newberg remarked that man's idea of a higher reality might actually be real. The interviewer asked Newberg what he meant by "real." He responded that the existence of a higher reality might be as real as a table. Such a thing, Newberg continued, is definitely not inconsistent with science. The interviewer asked Newberg if such a thing is observable in a scientific way. Newberg responded that it is. According to neurotheology, observations and pictures of the brains of Buddhist monks and Franciscan nuns during meditative states demonstrate the human ability to connect to a higher reality.

Though Westerners often view meditation and contemplation as an Eastern religious practice, Christian mystics from the early Middle Ages engaged in contemplation/meditation as well. In fact, medieval clergy were distinguished as either "contemplative" or "secular." The goal of Christian mysticism was to achieve a unity with God, a mystical union. The world's great religions share a common tradition of meditation or contemplation.

Do you know anyone who practices meditation? Read and reflect on Psalm 1:2 to see a biblical perspective on meditation and its goals and consider how this compares with meditation practiced in the context of non-Christian worldviews. The discussion below will touch on how neurotheology attempts to invoke science to finesse or perhaps sidestep these distinctions.

Science is a gift from God, but science gets in trouble when it speaks outside the realm of its inquiry. Scientific investigations of meditation and attempts to investigate spiritual matters can look into physical things such as brain activity, pulse rate, or other phenomena, but cannot really measure mental processes such as ideas, feelings, or consciousness.

Meditation can relieve stress involved with work, school, or
ships. Used as a relaxation technique, it can be a great blessing. He
professional meditation facilitators oftentimes have Eastern religious
ences. Meditation associated with Eastern ideas of monism and divine s
awareness contradicts the Christian faith. Christians who practice medita
tion should be wary of this.

SCIENCE AND GOD

Using sophisticated scientific tools, Newberg's research found that during meditative states the human brain is deprived of neural information
necessary to distinguish between the self and the external world. Thus, he
concludes, while a person is meditating, he or she experiences a union with
God and/or a "higher reality." However, a "higher reality" may not be God
and may not even be "higher."

The research pursued in neurotheology falls within the realm of science. The research tools used and the experimental method all fall within the
realm of science as well. However, conclusions drawn from neurotheological research reach past the limits of practical science. In effect, the research
makes a leap from observation of certain neurological activity to statements
about humans and their connection to God, something that lies outside the
scope of scientific observation.

The faults of neurotheological research lie not in experiments and observations, but rather in its theological conclusions. Here's why. Science typically reasons inductively. Observations from various experiments provide
hard scientific data. Upon establishing all the evidence, scientists interpret
what the evidence means. That is, from the evidence a scientist reaches a
conclusion.

Newberg's tests observed monks during meditation and nuns at prayer.
Using SPECT (Single Photon Emission Computed Tomography) measurements, scientists took pictures of the blood flow in each subject's brain. After
studying the pictures, scientists noticed that the left parietal lobe of the brain
showed a steady decrease in blood flow as the subject reached a spiritual
peak. The left parietal lobe is responsible for distinguishing between the self
and external reality. In these experiments, science discovered a neural-phys-
iological explanation for interconnectedness that Buddhist monks feel and
the mystical union that Christian mystics feel. However, Newberg attempts
to go further. Using the same evidence, he infers that these religious experiences are more than a feeling. He claims this is evidence of a higher reality,
even though there was no way that the investigation could detect that reality.

Although scientists are able to observe changes in neural activity during
a meditative state, they are unable to observe God or a higher reality. When
neurotheologians claim that meditation or any other religious experience

.onnects one with God or a higher reality, they step outside the
of scientific observation. True, certain neurological activities occur
. someone meditates; this is observable. It does not follow that someone
 ɔ meditates or engages in contemplative prayer is actually connecting
.ɪth a higher reality or even God.

From a scientific perspective, the idea that religious experience makes a
man aware that he is connected with the divine is shown to be nothing more
than neurological processes in the brain. Thus, when the statement is made
that man is able to connect with a higher reality through meditation and
prayer, science shows that it is only the decrease in neurological activity that
causes man to *feel* he is so connected.

The claim that meditation or prayer connects one to God has certain
theological problems as well; namely, how would one know he or she is in
fact connecting with God? Can feelings identify the God we pray to? The
world's religions have different views about God. The variety of contradictory definitions and ideas about God show how difficult it is to pin down the
true God on the basis of religious experience. Which religious experience
is really connecting with the true God? What about other religious experiences? Could they be hallucinations? Theologians have been pondering these
questions for centuries. Because of the limits to human knowledge regarding
God, the only knowledge of God that we can achieve is that which God gives
or reveals to us. All other knowledge is speculative at best.

Neurotheology assumes that observing human religious experience can
lead to knowledge of the human relationship to God. It goes on to assume
that the evidence found within a human gives us data about God. Analysis of these assumptions brings to light a few problems. First, there are no
scientific grounds for concluding that evidence found in nature can tell us
about the supernatural. Second, the different subjects studied hold to different spiritual beliefs. A person's religious presuppositions affect the way he or
she interprets religious experience. For example, some subjects claimed to
feel a mystical union with God. Others felt a sense of awareness of a higher
reality. Still others talked about an awareness of interconnectedness with all
of reality. A Franciscan nun's idea of God is much different from a Buddhist
monk's. Which experience proves to be authentic, and how could science
ever measure that authenticity?

A theologian's method of obtaining information about God differs from
a neurotheologian's approach. Theologians begin with what God has revealed
to man. From there they speak of God within the framework of accepted language and vocabulary. Neurotheologians extract knowledge of God through
scientific observation of human brains. There is no way to measure whether
these experiences come from God.

Over the centuries, philosophers and theologians have devis
rate proofs for God's existence. Though he does not claim to offer fo
evidence for God's existence, Newberg claims that neurotheology may
evidence of God's existence. At the very least, Newberg's theory and the ot.
natural theological arguments show that it is not irrational or absurd to be
lieve in God. Even so, we remain a long distance from discovering God by
scientific means.

Natural proofs for God's existence divide into two approaches. The first
are the empirical or evidential approaches. For example, the world exists;
therefore, someone or something must have caused it to exist (cosmological).
Another example: the apparent design of the universe requires the work of a
designer (teleological).

The second kind of approach is rationalistic. For example, all people have
a sense of moral law or right and wrong; therefore, a moral lawgiver (God)
must have placed this knowledge in humankind (moral argument). Another
example: a higher power must exist because it is absurd to think that there is
no higher power among the powers in the universe (ontological argument).

Arguments for God's existence fall in the realm of what is called natural theology, but what can natural theology tell us about God? (See The
Lutheran Church—Missouri Synod's Commission on Theology and Church
Relations publication *The Natural Knowledge of God in Christian Confession
and Christian Witness* for an in-depth perspective.) As noted above, natural
theology at the very least shows that it is not absurd to believe in God. Scientists, philosophers, and theologians have developed extensive proofs that
they claim make it absurd to not believe in God. However, these proofs from
time to time meet challenges. The church reformer John Calvin claimed that
natural theology is at its best when it renders man without an excuse for
disbelief.

Natural theology, though, is limited to knowledge of God. The Gospel
cannot be found in natural theology. Though theologies drawn from nature
offer some insight into the nature of God as Creator and Judge, the Gospel
is found only in revealed theology—theology drawn from Christ and the
Scriptures.

DIFFERENT GOSPELS BE DAMNED

Meditation and contemplative prayer often invoke deeply religious experiences. These experiences can excite or calm us. Feeling personally connected to God or a higher reality charges our spiritual fervor. Spiritual experiences offer an exciting substitute to life's mundane activities. Some find such
religious experience a thrilling alternative to traditional religious practices.
Nevertheless, we should examine where religious experiences lead us.

ɪg religious experiences, our feelings lead us to believe that we have ᴛed to a higher reality. Newberg's research informs us that this is the ᴄ of neurological processes in the brain (or are the neurological pro- ᴄes a consequence of the religious experience?), yet the experience feels ᴏ real. Perhaps it is.

Scientific evidence is unable to prove or disprove authentic spiritual encounters with God or a higher reality. However, the experience itself may give some indication of the value of religious experience. Practices such as deep meditation and contemplative prayer begin on human initiative. As these experiences intensify, feelings of spiritual awareness arise. People feel a connection or a communion with something bigger than themselves. This mystical union or interconnectedness cannot be described. They "just know" that they experienced something deeply religious.

Some call the thing or essence encountered in religious experiences "God." Others call it a "higher reality." Mystics of all stripes offer a variety of descriptive and nondescriptive names. But here lies the problem with religious experience.

Terms like "higher reality" and "God" suggest a sort of anonymity found in religious experiences. A connection or union to something bigger than us may be perceived. But what is it? Does this higher reality or God have a name? Is it the God of the Bible? Because religious experience is so personal, it is difficult and perhaps impossible to arrive at universal descriptive terms. By its very nature, religious experience can only lead to an unknown God.

An unknown God is a safe God if it is the true God who has revealed Himself in history in no uncertain terms. However, religious experiences can lead us to the God *we want to find*, which can be a risky proposition.

Read Exodus 19:3–25, where Moses had an intense religious experience. How did the rest of the Israelites know that Moses was in fact receiving revelations from God? God told Moses that He would come to him in a dense cloud. The Israelites would hear God speaking to Moses. God did this, providing validating evidence, so that the Israelites would know to trust Moses and the words he delivered from God.

This experience must have been awesome in the fullest sense of the word. Moses did not talk about subjective and private feelings of interconnectedness. This was a public display of God's glorious presence.

On Mount Sinai, God provided a revelation about Himself and His relationship with His people. God began His dialogue with Moses by identifying Himself as the One who delivered the Israelites from the Egyptians. Then God made a promise: "You shall be My treasured possession among all peoples, for all the earth is Mine; and you shall be to Me a kingdom of priests and a holy nation" (Exodus 19:5–6). God's promise was part of a covenant.

Shortly thereafter, God gave the Ten Commandments to the Isra... were to obey them, and God would bless them as a nation.

God's covenant showed that He desired to be in relationship w... people. The chapters that follow in Exodus lay out how God's people we... approach Him. These regulations would identify the Israelites as God's ch... sen and blessed people. This relationship was not based on religious feelings but on a specific set of rules and promises given by God.

Throughout the history of Israel, God revealed Himself in terms of rules and promises (Law and Gospel). Every time Israel disobeyed God's Commandments, God disciplined them. However, God's grace was quick to follow. God constantly reminded the Israelites that they were "a kingdom of priests and a holy nation" (Exodus 19:6). Through the nation of Israel, the Messiah was to come. This Messiah, God promised, would be a blessing to all nations. The Messiah publicly displayed the Good News of forgiveness of sins. The Law of God was fulfilled in the Gospel of Jesus.

The unknown God of religious experiences is often foreign to the God who revealed Himself in history. Genuine religious experience encounters God as He reveals Himself in Law and Gospel. Where the Law reveals the gap between humans and God, the Gospel builds a bridge across the gap. God's revelation of the Gospel came in the person of Jesus Christ. According to the apostles who lived with Jesus and witnessed His resurrection, the forgiveness of sins in the Gospel of Jesus offers the only genuine religious experience.

Reports of spiritual experiences during meditative states and contemplative prayer are often quite distant from the Gospel. In Galatians 1:8–9, Paul offers a specific way to distinguish between misleading and genuine religious experiences: "But even if we or an angel from heaven should preach to you a gospel contrary to the one we preached to you, let him be accursed. As we have said before, so now I say again: If anyone is preaching to you a gospel contrary to the one you received, let him be accursed."

Let's apply this to the religious experiences covered above. God's revelation to man is identified in the Law and Gospel. An experience of God's Law condemns humans. The Gospel brings humans into union with God. The Gospel is found in the person of Jesus. The unity with God found in religious experience must identify with Jesus Christ. Apart from Christ, it is a different gospel, which is really no gospel at all. Different gospels be damned!

To what could religious experiences apart from an experience of the biblical Christ be attributed? Knowing that Satan is the great deceiver, we should remain cautious of religious experiential claims that contradict the Gospel. Claims of religious experience could be explained by Newberg's research. That is, neurological processes in the brain cause certain feelings that people interpret as religious experiences.

_nt churches offer a variety of worship styles. In an attempt to ap-
_fferent people, many churches advertise new and fresh worship "ex-
_es." Regardless of whether a historic liturgy is used or a contemporary
_ of worship, Christian worship should always line up with the Scriptures,
_e Law and the Gospel. Our worship should always present the biblical mes-
sage of the Gospel. God established means by which we can be certain our
worship is biblical. When the Gospel is preached and the Sacraments are dis-
tributed rightly, we can be sure that our worship is genuinely Christian and,
hence, our worship experiences are authentically Christian.

FREE TO EXPERIENCE THE GOSPEL

Martin Luther spent his youthful days in meditation and prayer. He
chose a contemplative life. But his attempt to find union with God resulted
in self-inflicted injuries. Luther refrained from food for long periods of time,
whipped his body, and slept on a cold stone floor. Despite his efforts, Luther's
conscience could not be eased. No amount of meditation and prayer, acts of
penance, or good deeds satisfied Luther. He was sure of his separation from
God because he could not do what was right.

Luther's anxiety resulted from the self-awareness of his unrighteousness.
He experienced the demands of the Law. Luther knew full well that he could
not stand before his righteous Creator. The demands of the Law and God's
justice kept man from union with God.

But in Scripture, Luther learned the Gospel of the forgiveness of sins
and righteousness before God. He saw that man's sin and alienation before
God were placed on Jesus at the cross. God reconciled the world to Himself
through the death of His Son.

As Luther continued to contemplate the cross, he asked how this reconciliation could become his own. He found the answer once again in Scripture: "The righteous shall live by faith" (Romans 1:17). Righteousness before
God comes through faith. A simple trust in the merits of Christ unites people
to the righteousness of Christ—a righteousness that assures them of their
right standing before God.

The wonder of the Gospel is not that we can reach God through meditation or some other form of religious experience. Instead, God has reached
out to us through His Son, Jesus. Religion is not spiritual hide-and-seek, with
us groping after God. As John 1:18 tells us, we can know Him because He
made Himself known in Christ!

We often associate meditation or contemplative prayer with Eastern
religions, which emphasize emptying the mind. However, as we see in the
example of Luther, Christian meditation and/or contemplation is not a non-
cognitive, mind-emptying practice. Christian meditation is full of content

(Psalm 1:2). Luther wrote that true knowledge of God comes from "prayer, meditation, and fear of God." The Scriptures and the person of Christ are the proper objects and source of Christian meditation and contemplation. God reveals Himself here. Here we truly encounter God.

During Christian worship, God comes to us in the gifts of grace—the Word and the Sacraments. In the reading and preaching of God's Word, we experience God as He reveals Himself. When the pastor announces the Absolution, we experience the forgiveness of sins as if spoken by Christ Himself. During Holy Communion we feed on the very body and blood of Christ. God invites us to an intimate, personal union with Him in the eating and drinking of Christ's body and blood. The Word and Sacraments assure us of an authentic religious experience. We can be sure that in this we are united with the one true God because He Himself instituted these practices.

Like it was to Luther in the sixteenth century, the promise of authentic religious experience is available in the twenty-first century. Meditating on Christ's death and contemplating the Gospel in the Holy Scriptures, we experience the forgiveness of sins. Every Sunday, God invites us to experience forgiveness in a tangible way. With the bread and wine of Holy Communion, we partake in the body and blood of Jesus Christ. In God's Word and the Sacraments we find God as He reveals Himself—in the forgiveness of sins.

The psalmist wrote, "I rise before dawn and cry for help; I hope in Your words. My eyes are awake before the watches of the night, that I may meditate on Your promise" (Psalm 119:147–48). When faced with the turmoil of life, where can we go for hope? The promises of God in Christ offer comfort for anxiety and fear. Notice the psalmist's declaration: "I hope in Your words." The Scriptures give us authentic and reliable words from God.

Authentic religious experience begins and ends with Jesus. God meets man in the person and work of Christ. God in Christ treated our sin and inability to experience God's mercy in His death. He took upon Himself our sin and suffered our punishment on the cross. Jesus' resurrection from the grave guarantees His victory over sin and death. Now we are able to approach God with confidence.

POINTS TO PONDER

There is nothing we can do to bootstrap ourselves into spiritual riches. Left to our own devices of science, meditation, or man-made philosophies, we are nothing but the blind leading the blind. Let us thank God for the true spiritual enlightenment and the genuine spiritual riches found only in Jesus Christ!

WORDS TO REMEMBER

Let the words of my mouth and the meditation of my heart be acceptable in Your sight, O LORD, my rock and my redeemer. (Psalm 19:14)

10

MAGICKAL MYSTERY

The Harry Potter books and movies, the 1996 film *The Craft*, the 1996–2003 television program *Sabrina the Teenage Witch*, the game Magic: The Gathering. American popular culture contains hints of the ancient pagan religions of pre-Christian Europe. Modern sorcerers, witches, and warlocks claim to trace their ancestry from this era.

In 1974, various groups of witches formed the American Council of Witches. Since then, the popularity of Wiccanism continues to grow. For example, witches establish covens on college and high school campuses. In Cleveland, witches, vampires, and werewolves rent themselves out to liven up parties. Television shows and movies feature attractive witches and gallant vampires endowed with magical abilities. Seeking empowerment, feminists and environmentalists worship Mother Earth and the goddesses of Wicca.

The predominant practice of Wiccanism is some form of magick (not to be confused with the stage performance of magic). In their ceremonies and rites, Wiccans attempt to master supernatural forces. Spells, charms, and other magickal techniques alter the course of natural events. Witches use white magick to help others and black magick to do harm. Wiccanism offers power and rebellion against traditional religion and science.

Wiccanism does not seem to receive much attention in the news media, though sometimes an article will show up regarding Wiccan activity by public figures. A little research of news articles would probably show the presence of Wiccanism and its variations in your area.

Daniel Cohen, author of a 1971 book entitled *A Natural History of Unnatural Things*, observes that witchcraft has not yet been taken seriously by most of the public. Recognizing Wiccanism is difficult. Many modern witches are "normal" people. For example, Detective Constable Charles Ennis served on the Vancouver Police Department for years before identifying himself as a Wiccan priest. In 2010, U.S. Senate Candidate Christine O'Donnell mentioned that she had at one time dabbled in witchcraft, but her comments met with a mixed reception. Regardless, though some who practice witchcraft may not be involved with the occult at first, the risk of future involvement reflects an unrealized danger of Wiccan practices.

MAGICK, DRUGS, SEX, AND PSYCHOSIS

The Middles Ages saw a rise in witchcraft, but it was suppressed by the infamous witch hunts of the sixteenth and seventeenth centuries. When we think of witches, visions come to mind of ugly old women riding on broom-sticks accompanied by a black cat. However, modern-day witches and war-locks resemble the status quo of society. New converts to Wiccanism often are naive about the depths of its occultic involvement. Yet much of Wiccanism threatens the mental and physical health of those involved.

At the center of Wiccan activity lies its practice of magick. White and black magick rites deceive those involved. Research has demonstrated a high correlation between Wiccanism, occultism, and schizophrenia. Constant practice and self-persuasion of the reality of white or black magick causes a loss of the human ability to distinguish between reality and illusion. Kurt E. Koch, an expert in family counseling and author who has written books about the occult, confirms this theory. In case studies detailed in his 1978 book, *Occult ABC: Exposing Occult Practices and Ideologies*, he demon-strates the adverse effects that Wiccanism and occultism have on families.

Daniel Cohen notes that witchcraft has a definite connection to drug use and sexual deviancy. In many cases, drug use and sexual promiscuity are en-couraged during Wiccan rituals. The American Council of Witches formally states that sex is a symbol of power, the embodiment of life, and a source of energy used in magickal practices and religious worship.

Accounts of the infamous black magick champion Aleister Crowley tell of excessive drug use and ritualistic sacrifices. Police departments around America record case after case of drug-induced deaths resulting from magick rituals. More than a few murders have been traced back to black magick cults. Santoria and Satanism employ blood sacrifices. Traces of animal sacrifices of-fered to Mother Earth or Satan are common finds in areas where witchcraft is practiced. In some cases, evidence of human sacrifice has been found. How-ever, Wiccans officially distance themselves from such activities and insist they do not practice Satanism.

In 2001, the Waupan Correctional Institution in Wisconsin offered Jamyi Witch, a Wiccan priestess, a position as a prison chaplain. After this was re-ported in the media, the public protested, and the case went to trial. After all the psychiatric evidence and police reports were heard, it was deemed unsafe to have a witch as a chaplain. The scientific and legal evidence was so strong that the state could not risk having a Wiccan counsel prison inmates.

Though some witches claim that Wiccanism is innocent, the evidence shows otherwise. Certainly there are Wiccan fads that pass with little harm. However, serious involvement in Wiccanism and magick arts tells a different story.

Psychiatrists attribute psychological problems in witches to drug use and constant self-deception. The more a witch believes in her powers, the more her perceptions of reality decrease. Some psychiatrists ascribe psychologi-cal problems in witches to demonic possession since witchcraft has ties to the occult. Psychiatrists see a definite connection between occult practices and demonic possession. Since medieval times, witches have been associated with the broad diagnosis of "hysteria." The stereotype of a witch as a lonely, hostile older woman may have its root in cases of mental illness and the isolation that such women experienced.

Apart from the psychological and spiritual dangers, involvement with Wiccanism opens one up to physical danger. Magick rites vary from coven to coven. Some are physically harmless, but black magick involves sacrificial rites. Though human sacrifice is rare, scarification and other physical dangers are a real threat.

QUEST FOR POWER

Both the Old and New Testaments make repeated references to sorcery and witchcraft and condemn their practice. For example, Luke recorded Paul's run-in with a sorcerer. Acts 13:6–10 gives us interesting insight into the work of Satan. The Jewish sorcerer Elymas was the proconsul's attendant. When the proconsul desired to hear the Word of the Lord, what did the sorcerer do? He tried to interfere with Paul and the proconsul. Satan accomplishes this interference in at least two ways. False religious teachings offer alternatives to the one and only true religion. Such religions also claim to have overwhelming signs of their power. These signs seek to sway people away from God, as their power attests to some sort of spiritual authority.

Despite Elymas's attempt to curtail God's Word, Paul exposed Elymas for who he was: he accused Elymas of being a child of the devil. He identifies him as deceitful. Elymas's sorcery was used to distract the proconsul from hearing the Word of God. Paul identifies this distraction as a perversion of the right ways of the Lord.

At first, Elymas's feats of magick convinced the proconsul of his spiritual authority, but Paul took steps to convince the proconsul otherwise. Paul blinded Elymas, showing that the apostolic authority given by Christ overcomes the power of sorcery. Through this miraculous sign, God established Paul's authority as a messenger of His Word.

Like Paul's identification of Elymas's sorcery with Satan, Wiccanism and magick obtain their powers from the same source. Whatever powers a witch might display come from the devil. Satan uses these signs to deceive those who are seeking spiritual fulfillment.

At its heart, Wiccanism is a quest for power in the natural order and power over other people. Wiccanism teaches people that he or she is his or her own god. Offering earthly riches and power through magick, Wiccanism teaches human autonomy, but reliance on magick and false religious teaching offers no eternal hope.

Authorities during the Middle Ages used the Old Testament civil law to support their witch hunts. Drawing from verses such as Exodus 22:18—"You shall not permit a sorceress to live"—medieval Europeans justified their murder of accused witches. However, the elements of the Old Testament civil code do not apply today. Rather than attack witches, Christians should witness to them as they would to people of other religions. Note that Paul never called for Elymas's execution.

ETERNAL CERTAINTY

Using magic as a metaphor, British author C. S. Lewis wrote *The Lion, the Witch and the Wardrobe* to paint an image of the suffering, death, and resurrection of Jesus. (During Lewis's lifetime, laws against witchcraft were lifted in England, giving rise to the Wicca movement in the 1950s.) In order to release a boy from the spell of a witch, the lion Aslan passively submits to humiliation and eventual death. Crushed after seeing Aslan die, the main characters fear that the witch's magic had overcome the lion. However, Aslan returned to life. The lion explained to the children that the witch's magic wasn't enough to overcome a deeper magic—a magic that turned the tables on death.

In this way, C. S. Lewis creatively pictured the teachings of the Gospel throughout his Chronicles of Narnia. Just as Aslan overcame death and reversed the curse of the witch, Jesus' death on the cross and resurrection from the dead overturned the curse of sin, death, and the devil.

Wiccans and those involved with magick claim to possess extraordinary power. In a society enthralled with the pursuit of power, we should not be surprised that witchcraft finds followers. Its spectacular claims arouse interest.

Nevertheless, we need not fear. Paul sets the example for those redeemed by Christ. Through the use of magick, the sorcerer at Paphos (Elymas) managed to acquire a position as the proconsul's attendant. When this sorcerer stood in the way of God's Word, Paul defied him. Attributing his show of power to God Himself, Paul blinded the sorcerer. With the sorcerer blinded and removed from the proconsul, Paul taught him about Jesus' authority over all things. Paul received power from the risen Jesus. This same power blinded the sorcerer. When faced with this power, the proconsul believed the Gospel.

Both Christians and neopagans should remember the superstition and fear that dominated Europe in pre-Christian times. For cultures that live in fear of spirits, witches, and witch doctors, the Gospel comes like a welcome light in the darkness. The Gospel has power. All the devil's powers could not defeat the crucified Jesus. He conquered all worldly and spiritual powers in His victorious resurrection from the dead.

He continues to reign over the powers of the devil. Baptism claimed us as Christ's own. Far from an empty ritual, the act of washing connected to the promises of God assures us of our protection from the powers of the devil. This assurance never wavers. We can stand certain in God's promise at Baptism.

Each week we see God's power at work in our midst. When we confess our sins before God, our pastors pronounce powerful words of Absolution. These words—"in the stead and by the command of my Lord Jesus Christ I forgive you all your sins"—are God's words for us. We can rely on our right standing before God in Holy Absolution.

Despite the dangers that witchcraft and magick present, we need not be afraid. We can be certain that the devil has no hold over us. Jesus' resurrection sealed and certified this promise.

Spend some time reviewing the nature, blessings, power, and significance of Baptism in Ezekiel 36:24–27 and Colossians 2:9–15. Ezekiel prophesied that sprinkling "clean water" would give people a new heart and the indwelling of God's Holy Spirit. Paul compared Baptism to a new circumcision. He spoke of Baptism connecting a person to Christ's death and resurrection, by which Christ defeated the spiritual forces of this world.

Review the Office of the Keys and Confession in Luther's Small Catechism, and read Matthew 16:13–19 and John 20:19–23. Christ promised His disciples the authority to free people from their sins. He fulfilled this after His resurrection when He called the apostles to proclaim the forgiveness of sins.

Wiccanism often expresses anger toward Christianity, partly due to the witch hunts of the early modern period and the Salem witch trials, and perhaps out of a sense of rivalry. Regardless, people involved in Wiccanism need the Gospel of Jesus Christ. Using the Law to demonstrate the false assumptions that Wiccanism holds as well as the false gods it worships, Christians can throw light on the uncertainty and danger that Wiccans engage in. The Gospel brings certainty and safety to those in darkness and uncertainty.

POINTS TO PONDER

Our original sin reflects a desire for power, to be like God. Witchcraft and similar kinds of occult activities tap into this desire, but lead us away from God. Why do we want to be in control? Why would some prefer to engage with the occult rather than the living God? Let us thank Jesus that He has defeated the prince of this world and that united with Him in Baptism, we are rescued.

WORDS TO REMEMBER

Little children, you are from God and have overcome them, for He who is in you is greater than he who is in the world. (1 John 4:4)

11

Body and Mind

A woman feels tingles in her hand while holding a crystal. Having experienced foot pain for more than ten years, she decides to ask an expert on crystals how to use them. So she asks the salesman what will happen if she holds the crystal to her foot. When her foot heals, she believes that the crystal has healed it.

A television program films a Brazilian doctor performing lipoma (a lumpy, fatty deposit) removal on a patient. This doctor uses a rusty knife and no antiseptics or anesthetics, yet the patient feels no pain and receives a successful surgery. The surgeon's secret: a deceased German doctor has possessed him during the operation.

Madonna, Sharon Stone, and other celebrities swear by yoga. Although it began in India some three thousand years before the time of Christ, yoga has found its way into American culture.

Some of these health techniques may have positive aspects, but they may also carry negative aspects. The exercises taught by yoga may contribute to a healthy lifestyle. Though many yoga adherents claim spiritual benefits as well, Christians can practice yoga without fear so long as they reject the spiritual teachings of many yoga teachers. More broadly, though, New Age healers can be dangerous. For example, relying on unscientific methods for healing requires a leap of faith, and waiting for results from a psychic healer could lead to more health problems.

Health and Science

Medical surveys reveal an increasing number of health and healing alternatives. Some of these alternatives do contribute to mental and physical health. However, many threaten the physical and spiritual health of those involved.

For example, most people know of the benefits of stretching. Medical research widely documents that yoga helps decrease back pain and other sorts of bodily pain as well as relieving stress. Due to this, the general public considers yoga helpful, certainly not harmful. For the most part it is. Nevertheless, yoga practice and the philosophy behind yoga tell a different story.

The word *yoga* itself means a yoking together of mind, body, and soul. Just prior to the time of Christ, an Eastern doctor and philosopher, Pantanjali, set down a list of eight rules that lead to fulfillment in yogic practice. This list is based on Eastern religious assumptions and purposes. When followed, the yogi will find self-realization and oneness with the universe (*samadhi*). In other words, the religious aspects of yoga teach the monistic worldview described earlier.

Eastern religions such as Buddhism and Hinduism and their American New Age counterparts teach that humans share in the oneness of the universe or are actually divine by nature. Self-realization awakens us to our oneness with the universe and our divinity. With this background in mind, Christians may use the exercises associated with yoga, but need to be wary of the spiritual claims of Eastern philosophies that often accompany yoga.

Other new "medical" practices provide alternative approaches to individual health. Though positive results are documented in some cases, practices such as crystal, aura, and psychic healings lack scientific explanation. Crystals, for example, serve as energy transmitters in electronics. They are used in watches, radios, computer chips, lasers, and so forth. Consequently, New Agers assume that they must also be good transmitters of energy in the body. However, scientific research is unable to substantiate this claim.

A popular New Age magazine, *Spirit Seeker*, claims that science verifies the existence of auras around humans. Aura healing takes place when a healer senses imbalances in a person's aura. New Age defines auras as a sort of force field around a person made up of positive and negative energies. Aura healers find the imbalance and set it right. From what science can tell, human bodies do have electrical charges. Whether these electrical charges act as a force field, science does not know.

Psychic surgeons claim to perform surgeries relying on their psychic senses alone. Whether deceased doctors possess psychic surgeons or surgeons work with their eyes shut, the American Medical Association warns against such practices! They are unable to verify accounts of psychic healing.

For many, alternative healing procedures appear real. However, these alternatives lack scientific evidence and long-term tests to verify their safety or reliability, so the American Medical Association warns against relying on them at all.

Alternative medicines offer miracle cures that might be attractive to people who lose patience with conventional medical treatments or for whom conventional methods offer no relief. Further, just as some Christian groups flock to faith healers, New Agers seek out healers for similar reasons. When a person is engaged in New Age and Eastern thought, he or she may lose trust in Western medicines. An Eastern worldview caters to alternative healers and physical-spiritual exercises.

Some alternative medicines have some scientific support. For example, acupuncture can offer relief from pain where other treatments have failed. However, while science has been able to verify a cause/effect relationship between acupuncture and pain responses in the brains of animal and human patients, most alternative treatments lack such verification. Use careful scrutiny when considering alternative health options.

What could be some dangers of relying on crystals, psychics, or aura balancing for physical and mental health? To begin with, these practices may lead a person into false religious practices. Moreover, these practices have no scientific basis. Because they are connected with the occult, they pose serious spiritual dangers. While waiting for healing using alternative means, a person could grow sicker by not seeking adequate, qualified medical attention.

The Diagnosis

Former New Age believer Elliot Miller claims that powers of suggestion account for much of the alleged positive results from alternative healing. He and others do note some unexplained events that seem to vindicate positive claims, yet they are quick to point out that other powers beside psychic powers are at work.

Scripture does not inform us of psychic energy pervading the universe for use by humans. Nor does it inform us of a "divine spark" within us or some kind of oneness we share with all of reality. Scripture does, though, inform us of a deceptive power at work in the universe. Satan works through whatever means possible to deceive God's creation. When people combine alternative health options with a nonbiblical worldview and then look to these practices for healing and other desired ends, the door is opened to deception.

Scripture informs us of the first of Satan's deceptions, from which all deceptions arose (Romans 5:12–14). Yet the choice belongs to man. The foolishness of human choices has been diagnosed. The indictment is clear. On account of sin, we have fallen short of the glory of God (Romans 3:23). Rather than coming to the Great Physician with our sickness and our sin, we choose other means. The options are endless, but the result is the same. Our body and soul belong to sin.

In His great love, God created humans endowed with reason and sense. As stewards of creation, we use and develop these gifts. Medical and scientific advances are great gifts that God provides through us and to us. Nevertheless, we seek alternative means to explain the universe and care for our infirmities. Finding God's Word insufficient, we invite deception as we entertain religious positions foreign to the faith revealed through Jesus Christ.

Those who seek out New Age healers condone and trust in their religious assumptions. But our God-given reason casts serious doubts on practices such as aura and crystal healing or psychic surgery. Science does not support them. The religious assumptions of these healers contradict a Christian worldview. There really is no reason to trust these types of healers.

The Treatment

The Pharisees found Jesus sitting amidst sinners, including the former tax collector Matthew. Questioning Jesus' compliance to the Jewish laws and traditions, the Pharisees asked Matthew, "Why does your teacher eat with tax collectors and sinners?" (Matthew 9:11).

Overhearing their question, Jesus responded, "Those who are well have no need of a physician, but those who are sick. Go and learn what this means, 'I desire mercy, and not sacrifice.' For I came not to call the righteous, but sinners" (vv. 12–13).

Jesus' words offer comfort and hope for all who share the diagnosis of sin. Despite our attempts to find healing elsewhere, Jesus came to provide deeper healing. This is no ordinary health. It is eternal health.

When we experience sickness and ill health, through Christ we can approach God, the Great Physician, for healing. Poor health and sickness appear to run rampant. Cancer and other awful diseases seem to go unchecked. When doctors are unable to cure us, and our health fails, the promise of God remains.

Job experienced sickness to the point of death. Though his health failed him, Job stood firm in the sure promises of God. "I know that my Redeemer lives, and at the last He will stand upon the earth. And after my skin has been thus destroyed, yet in my flesh I shall see God" (Job 19:25–26).

We can stand firm with Job in our confession of faith and hope for the future. Christ's death and resurrection assure us of our eternal health and right standing before God.

The Pharisees asked Jesus' disciples why He ate with "tax collectors" and "sinners." Apparently, in their eyes, Jesus kept bad company, society's worst sinners. Tax collectors were at the lowest rung of the social ladder. Selling out to the Roman government, tax collectors often cheated their own people out of money. For this they were considered to be equivalent with prostitutes and other "gross" sinners.

Jesus' words in Matthew ring true. He did not spend all His time with the religious elite. Rather, He associated with the outcasts, the sick, and the unclean. Jesus' work on the cross brings eternal healing and salvation to all, regardless of social and religious status.

Think of the names of hospitals in your region or other hospitals you have visited. Most hospitals have an association with Christianity. Modern medical care has its roots in the institutional care that Christians provided for the sick as early as the fourth century (*nosokomeiä*). As the Book of Acts shows, Christians followed Christ's example by caring for the body as well as the soul (see 6:1–6).

Jesus is the only sure source of healing. Though doctors, medical technologies, and exercise are great blessings, apart from Jesus we have no certainty of body and soul.

POINTS TO PONDER

We need physical healing if we are sick or injured, and we need spiritual healing because of our sin. We cannot heal ourselves by wishful thinking or unproven techniques. For physical healing we go to a trustworthy doctor who uses proven techniques. For spiritual healing we go to Jesus, who heals us and gives us a hope of eternal life, proven by His resurrection.

WORDS TO REMEMBER

Those who are well have no need of a physician, but those who are sick. Go and learn what this means, "I desire mercy, and not sacrifice." For I came not to call the righteous, but sinners. (Matthew 9:12–13)

Photo: © Shutterstock, Inc.

THE UNEXPLAINED

Miracles, Mysteries, and More

INTRODUCTION

Teacher, we wish to see a sign from You.
—Some scribes and Pharisees
(Matthew 12:38)

This part of our discussion is not merely an encounter with strange encounters, but a tool for discerning the truth with a Christ-centered mind. The first section on miracles is not meant to be a "Ripley's Believe It or Not" that woos onlookers and creates senseless wonder. It shows that miracles have a set purpose. They focus on Christ. God's redemptive purposes are revealed through the miraculous deeds that reach their culmination in the person and work of Christ. Therefore, this Bible-based section calls you to be Christ-minded, seeing persons and events in this life in relationship to Christ.

Miracles really happen. Understanding miracles allows one to consider other metaphysical topics (metaphysics refers to one's beliefs about reality). For example, if God can intervene in history with a miraculous deed, then life is more than "natural." It is supernatural. God is present in history.

Most important, miracles are not distant or transcendent events. God does not come from behind a "heavenly curtain," perform a miracle as a magic trick to shock us, and then go "backstage" and remain there. Miracles are personal. Martin Luther liked to emphasize that God's works are *pro me*, or "for me." God is a God "for me," or as Christians say in the Nicene Creed, "for us," because He performs miraculous deeds for our salvation and brings us to faith in Him. God is close or immanent in a relational sense. This immanence is revealed chiefly in Jesus Christ. Thus, miracles and other supernatural causes are not only meant for us to "look above" to the Divine, but also to "look below" to the baby at Bethlehem and His miraculous work. In Christ, we see both the "above" and the "below" because He is God in human flesh.

THE GOSPEL PRINCIPLE

This study of unexplained phenomena will leave you with a lot of things unexplained—that seems to be a given. However, you will also find a common appeal to something I call "the Gospel principle." This principle helps Christians discern the truth about the unexplained things in life. For example, if I am wondering whether a certain miracle or teaching is from God, I *first* judge it in light of the Gospel by asking, "Does the event support or undermine the teaching of the Gospel?"

False teachings and false miracles ultimately come from the devil. If we are to defeat him, we must oppose the purpose of such falsehoods. The purpose of the devil's lies and deceptions is to keep us from salvation in Christ. The fires of the devil are extinguished by the waters of Christ in Baptism. To discern whether a teaching opposes the teaching of Christ and His salvation, one must compare it with the Gospel message. One can use this "rule of faith" as a starting point.

At the same time, the Gospel does not give us answers for *everything*. God has given us the gift of reason for discerning matters involving science, math, morality, and other daily affairs. But, when there is an event or teaching claiming to occur under the auspices of God's name within Christendom, or under a Christian name, then we should judge it appropriately.

12

MIRACLES

"Miracle Service—Every Tuesday"

—Message on a church marquee

The possibility of miracles fascinates people. A *Reader's Digest* article once told of a miracle occurring right after Christmas one year. That Christmas, Arthur Stevens received from his daughter a handy, waterproof flashlight like the kind he had always wanted. Nearly a month later, he went out to sea on the tugboat *Harkness* with a friend and the captain, Rudy Musetti.

During their trip, a violent storm erupted, and the boat began taking on water. With winds blowing up to 40 mph, the crew found itself in grave danger. Captain Musetti radioed for help as they began to sink. Three lobstermen heard the message and set out to search for them. As the lobstermen searched, they saw a beam of light. The flashlight Stevens received as a Christmas present had frozen to his friend's glove in the icy water. Its beam shone upward, leading the rescuers to the men of the *Harkness*! The flashlight saved their lives.

Has a remarkable event similar to this one ever occurred in your life? If so, do you think God directly caused it? Perhaps you have experienced such an event, or more than one, or maybe none at all. The more important point here is to consider the relationship between miracles and God's purpose behind them.

Exodus 6:1–8; 9:16; and 14:31 have something to say about the purpose of miracles and the relationship between faith and miracles. God is not a "cosmic magician." God does not do powerful and wondrous things for mere shock value. Apologist Paul Little affirmed that God's miraculous works were not done to simply astound people and mesmerize them. They had a broader purpose, namely, the salvation of souls. When a remarkable thing occurs for human benefit (such as the one that occurred for the men in the *Harkness*), it may very well be from God, and it may very well not be. If there had been no salvific goal in the act of the miracle, then it is possible that it is not from God. God wants people to receive the spiritual benefits of Christ.

In the destruction of the World Trade Center on 9/11, some people miraculously survived while others tragically died. Should we say that the survivors had God's favor upon them? If so, what should we say about those who suffered and died? The fact is, easy answers are few, and it is risky to quickly attribute things like this to God's will.

The story of Lazarus in John 11 addresses the problem of evil and how God relates to the world. Jesus allowed His friend Lazarus to remain ill and even to die. Note how Jesus said that Lazarus's illness would not lead to death (v. 4). Yet, later, Jesus stated that Lazarus had died (v. 14). Jesus speaks with *equivocation*. He uses the same word (*death*) in different senses or meanings. In verse 4, Jesus is saying that Lazarus will not die in an ultimate sense or he will not remain dead. In verse 11, Jesus refers to death in the temporal sense as one's ceasing to exist in this life (also vv. 25–26).

The story of Lazarus shows that eternal, spiritual needs take precedence over temporal, physical needs. Jesus gave faith priority over healing an illness. What happens in this life is subordinate to the promises given in Christ through faith. Christ times the whole situation in order to lead people to a greater good—faith in Him (vv. 4, 14, 41–45; 14:11).

It should also be noted that even though Christ did not prevent Lazarus's death, He did not cause it. Humanity brought death upon itself through the disobedience in the Garden of Eden (Romans 5:12–14; 1 Corinthians 15:22).

DOUBTS ABOUT MIRACLES

The eighteenth-century philosopher David Hume stated in his treatise *An Inquiry Concerning Human Understanding* that miracles violate the laws of nature. For Hume and other Enlightenment thinkers, human experience is the final criterion of truth. Experience proved the laws of nature and disproved miracles. In other words, the discovery of the laws of nature did away with the need for miracles. (See Glossary for more on naturalism.)

However, David Hume also pointed out that the traditional Christian definition of a miracle is something that occurs *outside* of the regular course of events. To understand Hume's point, we need to distinguish between something being *against* another thing and something being *outside* of another thing.

Consider the following. A fire set beneath a pan of water will heat the water even though the fire and water never touch one another. They are outside of one another. If you dumped the water onto the fire, that would heat the water too. But in that case, the items would mingle with one another. They would be against one another.

A miracle is an *extra*-ordinary event; that is, it is something outside of the regular course of nature. For example, when God parted the Red Sea, gravity did not cease to exist. He did not extinguish the laws of nature. He merely acted outside the natural laws in parting the sea.

With this point in mind, recognize that Mr. Hume's arguments against miracles do not address the same issue. He argued against miracles that violate natural law. In contrast, the Christian position asserts that miracles are outside of natural law. Hume's famous argument does not really address the miracles described by a Christian at all!

This suggests a question: can science prove or disprove miracles if miracles stand outside the normal course of natural law? Science is useful for considering any event, but cannot prove the existence of miracles. Among other reasons, this is because our experiences with our senses are very limited. We are often poorly prepared to judge the experiences of others. (You may have heard someone say, "If I can't see it, I won't believe it!")

By their very definition, miracles defy explanation. In his classic book *Know Why You Believe*, Paul Little discusses the ongoing debate about the very nature and definition of miracles. Some say that they act *against* the normal course of nature while others believe that they are *outside* of it. It may be noted that God is the Creator of the world and is therefore the Author and Sustainer of natural laws. So no matter how one defines miracles, there is a fundamental agreement that God can do what He wills with regard to the natural laws of the world—He is not subject or bound to them. Christ demonstrated His authority over nature (Mark 4:35–41; 6:45–52; John 2:5–11) in several different ways, as if to prove the point.

Many skeptics toward Christianity deny the existence of miracles because they believe that miracles go against the laws of nature explained by science. They assert that if events violate or are not explained by natural laws, these events must not have really occurred.

This is certainly a cavalier assertion. Theodore Handrich explains in his book *Everyday Science for the Christian* how natural laws do not cause things to happen. Natural laws simply describe things that ordinarily happen. Therefore, natural laws do not cause the events in the world around us but are related to them as a journalist is to news events.

Remember that natural law employed by science does not determine what *can* happen. It describes what *usually* happens in the course of nature. In other words, since natural law describes events that *regularly* occur, it leaves open the possibility that something else may occur. And, if it were something of a miraculous nature, then science would not dismiss its occurrence, but simply be left "scratching its head" because of such an event.

Referring back to our earlier discussion of the scientific method, science presents us with a set of observable facts, things that can be seen, demonstrated, and repeated. But we must remember that something's existence is not dependent on whether we have observed it or not.

Consider how Scripture describes God's relationship to the world (Genesis 1:1–27; Psalm 50:1–6; Matthew 6:25–34). These passages present God as the mighty Creator, Judge, and Sustainer of all things that exist. He maintains His care and concern for all living creatures. He is perfectly capable of doing miracles as He wishes. Jesus' words emphasize that God is our Father. But He has purpose in His actions: to care for us and call us back to Himself (Mark 10:26–27; Romans 11:33–36).

MIRACLES AND MANIPULATION

For centuries, people have sought signs or miracles. During Jesus' ministry, the Jewish religious leaders demanded that He show them His miraculous power. Christ rebuked them, stating, "An evil and adulterous generation seeks for a sign, but no sign will be given to it except the sign of the prophet Jonah" (Matthew 12:39).

Jesus, of course, was not against performing miracles. But He rebuked the religious leaders of His day because of their motives in asking for miracles. They requested miracles in order to test Him without any sincere intent to follow Him. They also disconnected miracles from the promises of God's Word. Christ rebuked them by alluding to His resurrection: "For just as Jonah was three days and three nights in the belly of the great fish, so will the Son of Man be three days and three nights in the heart of the earth" (Matthew 12:40).

People crave miracles for any number of reasons, but this can reinforce sinful motives and emphasis on self. In Deuteronomy 29:29, God tells the Israelites to rely on what is revealed to them in His Word. To go beyond the Lord's self-revelation is not only going beyond God's will but also going against it. Furthermore, it is a fruitless endeavor. Speculation is just that: speculation. How can somebody know what is not available to them for examination? God's revelation to us in His Word is sufficient for our knowledge concerning Him and our salvation.

People today test God by crying out that they will follow Him if He does something miraculous before their eyes. For example, people point to the many miracles recorded in the Book of Acts and suggest that God ought to be doing such miracles now. The Lord gives very different reasons for us to follow Him. God does not urge us to test His ability to do miracles. He invites us to test His Word and deeds. The Lord calls us to believe in Him based on whether His testimony is actually confirmed in historical reality (Deuteronomy 18:21–22; John 14:11). Thus, the Word of God is our source of truth. The ultimate action confirming its truthfulness is the resurrection of Christ (Acts 2:30–32; 3:15, 18; 17:31).

Moreover, remember that the miracles occurring in the Book of Acts were not some grand "miracle parade" that Christians must experience each day. They were done over the first twenty years of the Church's mission work. God did these miracles not only to demonstrate His presence but also to validate His work and bring people to a saving faith in Christ and His resurrection (John 14:11; Acts 2:22–24).

Many of the mighty acts of God have been open to human observation, but this does not always mean that we can understand them. Job 37:5 tells us that God does things that we cannot comprehend. We need faith as well as reason. Even though God does things that are beyond our reason, it does not mean that He does things that are *irrational.* They stand *beyond* the capacity for human reason but not *against* it. Faith is God's gift for apprehending things that we cannot grasp by our reason (Hebrews 11:1).

Understanding the miracles recorded in Scripture can be challenging, and this should caution us when we consider remarkable events not recorded in Scripture. Speculating about things God has not revealed or explained can be fruitless. If we have a minimal understanding of what is revealed, how much less will we understand what is not revealed?

Most likely you have heard of television evangelists claiming they have healed people of terminal diseases or other ailments. I remember driving by one church that advertised on its marquee "Miracle Service—Every Tuesday." A planned miracle service seems ridiculous. And any ad for a miracle service that does not give credit to God, up front, seems suspicious. Personal claims of miraculous power seem bogus.

Finally, aren't real miracles spontaneous? How can any mere person plan a miracle? God is the one who plans and initiates miracles on His own terms and to His own credit! Moreover, we must watch out for false miracles. Scripture warns that the devil has the capacity for creating miracles to delude people and direct them away from the truth. Scripture warns that God will allow such false miracles to occur as a result of His judgment (2 Thessalonians 2:9–12).

Many people reason, "The disciples of Jesus did miracles. If a religious leader can perform miracles today, he must be a disciple of Jesus." Read Matthew 24:24 and Revelation 13:11–14 to see what's wrong with this reasoning. A miracle does not validate the person who performs it. Matthew 4:1–11 shows us that even Satan can use Scripture. He may also use miracles or remarkable events for his own damnable purpose: to lead people away from Christ. The Gospel provides the surest grounds for testing deeds and claims. God came in the flesh to redeem humankind from their sins and save them through faith in Christ alone. See Galatians 1:8; 1 John 4:1–6; John 8:44; 2 Timothy 2:24–26; 1 Peter 5:8; Luke 22:31–32.

THE LORD OF MIRACLES

Miracles have a twofold purpose: (1) to manifest God's glory and name before humankind, and (2) to create faith in those observing the miracles. It may be noted that this is not an either/or. God can do miracles for the purpose of revealing His name to both believers and unbelievers (Exodus 9:16; 1 Kings 18:38–39; Isaiah 25:1–5). But, it is important to remember that miracles do, indeed, have a salvific purpose behind them. Many of the miracles of both the Old and New Testaments confirm this (Exodus 14:31; Psalm 105:26–45; John 11:38–42; 14:11).

Although we are darkened in our minds by sin and may have trusted in false miracles before, God has mercy on us in Jesus Christ. Remember, by faith in Christ, you have been brought from the kingdom of darkness to His very own kingdom of grace and forgiveness (Colossians 1:13). You have been given faith that overcomes Satan's kingdom of delusion and brings you into favor with God (Romans 5:10–11; 1 John 4:4). Indeed, God has miraculously intervened in human history in Jesus Christ, not only to grant you faith, but also to purchase salvation for you through His death and resurrection (Romans 3:23–26; 4:24–25).

Reflect on the celebration of Easter in your life and the life of your congregation. How important is the historical fact of the resurrection for your personal faith? Apologist Paul Little once said that whenever he had serious doubts with regard to his faith, he always went back to two things: (1) the objective historical facts pertaining to Christ, and (2) the subjective experience of how Christianity changed his life. Both are important. But the objective basis of our faith has more solid ground because it is not dependent on our ever-changing emotions or personal experiences.

The resurrection is the ultimate miracle of God, not only because it is the basis of salvation, but also because it verifies God's promises for us. Because Christ has defeated death, we have hope. He has opened the gates of heaven to us so that we might be glorified with Him (1 Corinthians 15:54–57; John 11:23–26). Moreover, in a world of ambiguity and fakery, we can have certainty that God has maintained His promises by fulfilling them in the risen Christ. Christ's defeat of death not only bears witness to the truthfulness of God's promises but also to the certainty of having hope that we, too, will be raised unto glory!

And your faith is not only a miracle itself but also a miracle that participates in greater miracles—the person and work of Jesus Christ (2 Peter 1:3–4). Moreover, we need not look for miracles outside the Word and Sacraments. God works miracles through the Word by leading us to repentance and renewing us in His image. He works miracles in Baptism and the Lord's Supper by forgiving our sins and causing us to be born again!

Matthew 12:38–40; Romans 6:4; and 1 Corinthians 15:1–11 speak of the importance of the resurrection with respect to our faith. The resurrection is absolutely central to our faith! The resurrection separates the Christian faith from all other religions. The ability to raise a person from the dead is a power unique to God. Scripture declares that only God has the power to resurrect people from the dead (Psalm 68:20; Revelation 1:17–18; 2 Kings 5:7). The resurrection of Christ bears witness to the fact that He is God (John 2:19–22)!

John 5:28–29; 11:25–26; and Romans 6:5–11 speak of how the miracle of the resurrection can benefit you today. The resurrection is not only central to our faith in the objective sense but also in the subjective sense. Luther wrote that the Christian undergoes a "daily Baptism," meaning that a Christian needs to repent and "drown" the old Adam daily, putting to death the sinful nature. We daily participate in Christ's death and resurrection by being raised in newness of life through the power of the Holy Spirit (Colossians 3:5–10; Galatians 5:22–26). And if the resurrection of Christ had not occurred, this subjective resurrection would have no basis. Our spiritual resurrection presupposes the victory over death won by Christ. In our "daily Baptism," we participate in a death and resurrection because of the death and resurrection of Christ (Romans 6:1–11)!

POINTS TO PONDER

If you or someone you know has experienced a miracle, why do you suppose it happened, and who should get the credit? In Christ we have new life, and we can see the world with fresh eyes. Let us bow and give Him the credit and the glory!

WORDS TO REMEMBER

We were buried therefore with Him by baptism into death, in order that, just as Christ was raised from the dead by the glory of the Father, we too might walk in newness of life. (Romans 6:4)

13

MYSTICAL EXPERIENCES

In 1999, the film *Stigmata* drew millions of people to movie theaters. It was inspired by the mystical experiences of the medieval friar St. Francis of Assisi. "Stigmata" refers to the miraculous appearance of the five wounds of Christ on a person's body. Although the film is fictional, Francis's stigmata supposedly has a historical basis. In fact, people interested in mystical experiences have recorded similar events.

Reportedly, St. Francis was the first to receive the stigmata. According to the story, after forty days of fasting and prayer, Francis proceeded up a mountain to reflect on the death and suffering of Jesus. While he was contemplating Jesus' suffering, Jesus appeared and granted Francis "copies" of His own wounds.

In contrast to the story of St. Francis, the film *Stigmata* has as its main character an agnostic, young suburban hairdresser who has been "divinely chosen" to receive the stigmata. She undergoes a series of traumatic experiences while receiving the "copies" of Christ's wounds. The miraculous wounds send her into euphoric states of shock and confusion. Although the young woman was an unbeliever, God ordained that she receive the stigmata as a powerful introduction to the spiritual realities of life. The film contrasts the corruption of organized religion with the genuineness of mystical experience, an increasingly popular theme in contemporary culture.

You have probably heard of other examples of mystical experiences. Mysticism takes on different faces. Although the term is not used very often in everyday conversation, mysticism can be found in New Age practice and belief, as well as in religions of Buddhism, Islam, and even Christianity. Additionally, practices that are clearly mystical may have quasi-scientific names, such as Transcendental Meditation.

The Greek term *mysterion* means "something that closes the mouth"— in other words, an act that makes someone speechless with amazement or causes them to keep a secret. Mysticism appears in all world religions and has a common goal: to engage the divine without the use of reason but through direct experience.

Read Acts 9:1–9, and consider how the apostle Paul's experience compared with that of St. Francis. At first glance, Paul's experience may seem very much like that of Francis. They both received direct revelations of Jesus Christ. Yet Paul's experience differs. First, Paul's experience had witnesses who observed the light that confounded and blinded Paul (22:9), while the earliest recorded statement for Francis's experience dates a century after the alleged event. Second, Francis's experience followed an extreme fast and extended meditation, two conditions known to bring on delirium. Acts does not record that Paul was fasting or meditating prior to his encounter with Christ on the Damascus road. He began a journey from Jerusalem (where the high priest was) to Damascus (about 150 miles) with the intent of arresting Christians (9:1–2). Moreover, the narrative states that Paul fasted *after* the encounter with Christ, and not *before* (v. 9). Someone may argue that Paul was in an unusual or guilt-ridden state of mind because of his murderous attitude toward Christians, but that does not necessarily mean that he suffered from hallucinations of any sort. His intense persecution of Christians was motivated by his zeal for the Law (Galatians 1:13–14).

EVALUATING EXPERIENCES

In his 1999 book *Looking for a Miracle: Weeping Icons, Relics, Stigmata, Visions and Healing Cures*, Joe Nickell mentions that medieval Christians were fascinated with the physical suffering of Christ and the wounds affected on His body at the crucifixion. They engaged in morbid curiosity regarding the Passion of our Lord. There are some reported cases of people purposefully inflicting themselves with wounds similar to those of Christ's as a way of copying His example in submitting to God's will by His death on a cross. Nickell describes such cases as examples of fraudulent stigmatics. Quite often, fake stigmatics injured themselves in a state of mental illness.

In some parts of the world, a similar fascination continues today. For example, at an Easter festival in the Philippines, penitents undergo crucifixion for several hours. But Christians are not the only people who seek greater identification with a religious figure through suffering. Many Shia Muslims whip themselves bloody at the end of the festival of Ashura in order to identify more closely with the sufferings of Imam Ali, the son-in-law of Muhammad. Other examples of self-inflicted suffering for religious purposes include the sun dance of the Sioux Indians and the piercing and suspension rituals practiced by some Hindus.

Another type of mystical experience involves people who claim that Jesus appeared to them. Have you ever encountered anyone who claimed to have received a direct revelation from the risen Christ? If so, how did that person describe the experience, and is it consistent with the truth revealed in Scripture? It is not unusual today for people to assert that Jesus appeared to them in a vision or dream. Some charismatic Christians claim to have had private revelations of Christ prior to their conversion or after their conversion.

Prior to the ascension, Christ had not undergone any outward transformation in His body (glorification as in 1 Corinthians 15:51–54; Philippians

3:21). Part of the reason for this was to establish the validity of His resurrected body and to impart clear evidence that He truly had risen bodily from the dead (Acts 1:1–3). Paul, however, encountered the glorified Christ (note Jesus' appearance with bright light in Acts 9:3–5). After the ascension, this was the only way Christ appeared to people. This distinction may be significant when considering people's claims that they have had direct encounters with Christ. Many people experiencing discouragement or suffering claim they saw Christ in an *unglorified* manner. Such experiences don't seem to fit with the appearances of Christ—post-ascension—as described in Scripture.

Read Philippians 1:27–30 and 1 Peter 4:12–16, and consider how the apostles encouraged Christians who faced suffering. Christ suffered to take away our sins, not to gain some personal spiritual experience. Genuine suffering, by nature, is something that *happens* to an individual, not something an individual seeks in order to earn a spiritual badge. Thus, suffering is passive and not active. Scripture never commands us to seek out suffering.

Further, Scripture never promises that we will live totally without suffering as Christians. Scripture offers encouragement and precepts on how to deal with suffering by pointing to Christ as our example of patient endurance. Scripture consistently describes suffering as a result of persecution and not something a person should impose upon himself or herself.

Researcher Ian Wilson has suggested that cases such as St. Francis's could simply have been a result of his extreme fasting. The friar's mental state could have led to self-inflicted wounds in light of his probable fascination with the crucifixion.

Twentieth-century Roman Catholic priest Padre Pio serves as a more modern case of reported stigmatics. Evidently, Padre Pio received the wounds of Christ for several years. It was also reported that he could remain alert for eighteen hours a day, listening to people's confessions. His experiences and his commitment to serving people by hearing their confessions of sin created an enormous following.

Oddly, when Padre Pio died, the wounds of the stigmata on his body could not be found. No scars or traces of self-inflicted wounds appeared on his hands and feet. Researchers have suggested that it may be possible for stigmata to occur through psychosomatic means. In other words, as a result of intense concentration and mental conviction, the mind could cause wounds on the body—a person might actually concentrate so hard on receiving the wounds that such wounds might appear!

If this is the case, the wounds of Padre Pio are little different from the self-inflicted wounds of other stigmatics or anyone who uses suffering as a means to gain a mystical experience.

GOD WORKS THROUGH MEANS

How do we maintain a proper understanding of Christ and the centrality of His cross? Love for Christ and keeping His Word go hand-in-hand. If we truly love Christ, we will keep His Word and see it as sufficient enough for maintaining a proper understanding of His work on the cross (John 14:23–24; 1 John 4:9–10). Both Word and Sacrament are presented in Scripture as means connecting us to Christ and His death on the cross. They connect us in both the remembrance and in the reception of His benefits—the forgiveness of our sins merited by His death (1 Corinthians 11:23–26). Therefore, one who seeks to know Christ and His cross apart from Word and Sacrament is not motivated by a love for Christ, but rather by something else—likely, spiritual pride or vain sentimentality.

Mystical experiences emphasize what theologians call *immediate* revelation, or revelation that does not come through *means*. *Means* refer to those things that God uses as instruments to reveal and present Himself to us. God's Word and the Sacraments of Baptism and the Lord's Supper are means because God uses them to reveal His will and to be present with His people.

Mystical experiences seek God in a direct or immediate way apart from the use of Word or Sacrament. Thus, one could argue that false stigmatics misuse the crucifixion of Christ. Certainly, the cross represents a central point of Christian faith. But Jesus never intended that we repeat His crucifixion in our own bodies. Rather, the cross is presented in Scripture as the basis of both our justification and our sanctification (Romans 3:24–26; 5:9; 6:6–14; 1 Peter 4:1–2).

Genesis 3:8 notes how Adam and Eve perceived God's presence. They heard the voice of the Lord in the "cool of the day." This expression uses *ruach*, the Hebrew word for "wind." In other words, God made Himself present through a physical reality—a breeze of wind. Luther notes in his commentary on Genesis how this manifestation of God occurs as a result of sin. That is, because of sin, humans can no longer be in God's presence apart from mediation. (Also read Exodus 3:1–5 and 33:9–11, 20–23 to see the different ways in which God revealed Himself to humankind.)

Mediatory forms hide the fullness of God's glory and therefore provide a way for us to approach God safely. For humans to have direct contact with God would result in death (Exodus 33:20). Prior to the fall, when Adam and Eve were without sin, humans dwelt with God in an immediate way. Likewise, St. John describes how after Christ returns, "we shall see Him as He is" (1 John 3:2), which happens at our glorification when our sinfulness will be eradicated. Also note the apparent contradiction with regard to this view in light of Exodus 33:11. If you pair it up with verse 20, you will see the distinction. Verse 11 does not deal with the *mode of God's presence* in the act of speaking with Moses, but rather portrays an image of how God will relate to His people. The same concept could be applied to the burning bush incident in Exodus 3. God conversed with Moses without any agents or messengers to communicate what God wanted to say. However, the way in which God communicated to Moses was directly person-to-person through a burning bush. Verse 20 regards the mode of God's presence. No one shall see His being as it is or in a direct, unmediated way. Such a thing is dangerous because man cannot handle the magnitude of God's presence unfiltered by physical means.

We must acknowledge that, because of our sin, God is unapproachable apart from mediation or means. God is holy; He dwells in "unapproachable light" (1 Timothy 6:16). A person cannot approach God apart from the mediating work of Jesus Christ (John 14:6; Romans 5:10). Even though there is a temptation in each one of us to make personal experience our basis for knowing God, we should resist such temptation. God provides His Word and Sacraments as ways of "experiencing" Him.

Looking for truth in experience, or from within, is dangerous. The Word tells us, "The heart is deceitful above all things" (Jeremiah 17:9). If we rely on our own hearts and opinions as a normative source for truth, we will rely on a shaky and faulty foundation. But if we look to the Word as an objective standard for truth, we will have a firm and solid foundation (John 17:17).

Even though God is physically unapproachable, John 6:63 says how God becomes present for us. The words of Christ are not mere text; they are spiritual words. The words of Scripture present God's very Spirit to us. God speaks to us, revealing His character and salvation.

Further, the Sacraments provide us with God's presence because His Spirit is present in Baptism (1 Corinthians 6:11; Colossians 2:11–12) and Christ's body and blood are present in the Lord's Supper (Mark 14:22–24).

Matthew 6:9–13 explains prayer in Jesus' words. Does prayer point us to a revelation apart from God's Word or to a revelation in keeping with God's Word? Luther's exposition on the Lord's Prayer in the Small Catechism provides a great resource for understanding the nature and purpose of prayer. Note that prayer is, indeed, relational by nature. That is, it involves man offering up petitions and supplications toward God. But, in this relational action between man and God, one is not called to ascend and lose oneself in God through mystical experience. Instead, prayer depends on the Word of God.

God's Gracious Gifts Found through Means

God comes to us in forms of mediation, presenting His gracious gifts of forgiveness and salvation. Because these means lack outward extravagance, we may find ourselves looking to things other than Word and Sacrament to find God. But ironically, what God provides for us contains dynamic and life-giving qualities.

For example, when you partake of the body and blood of Christ at the Lord's Table, you are partaking of the life-giving elements of the risen Savior. Faith, inspired by Christ, is truly a dynamic thing because it participates in Christ as its object and lays hold of "the bread" that Christ gives "for the life of the world" (John 6:51).

Moreover, when God comes to you through means, He is doing this because He loves you. By God coming to you through Word and Sacrament, He is coming to you in such a way that is "safe" and giving you an opportunity to experience His presence for your benefit rather than for your harm. For God to abide with us through forms of mediation is a witness to His unfailing love. God could have abandoned His creation and remained transcendent, and we would never come to know Him. But the heavenly Father, in His love, chose to reconcile you unto Himself by sending the one true mediator, Jesus Christ (Ephesians 1:5–7; 1 Timothy 2:5; Romans 5:10–11).

How would you describe the state of your faith relationship with Christ? Remember that it is not the degree of faith that saves, but rather it is faith alone that brings a person into salvation (John 6:29; Mark 9:24). In this life, our faith will never be totally perfect. In faith, we abide in the true Vine by continually partaking of Christ's Word and Sacrament (John 15:1–8).

Titus 3:4–7 and 1 John 4:9–10 emphatically declare God's love for us in spite of our sins. The Gospel motivates us to trust God because it declares the love of God for us! Note that what reminds us of God's love for us is the cross and the things that link us to the cross—the Word, Baptism, and the Lord's Supper.

Points to Ponder

We may sometimes hear of spiritual happenings that seem too odd or too wonderful to be easily explained. In fact, some people seem to seek out spectacular spiritual experiences and live from one emotional high to another, never wanting to come down to something as mundane-seeming as a daily walk with God. This risks ignoring something much more substantial and valuable: God's grace to us, found in Christ, and the Word and Sacraments that He provides.

Words to Remember

All this is from God, who through Christ reconciled us to Himself and gave us the ministry of reconciliation. (2 Corinthians 5:18)

14

DREAMS

New Age religious movements, such as Eckankar, and popular psychology have placed a great emphasis on dreams. This has led people to wonder if their dreams hold special meanings or foreshadow events. Some wonder whether God is speaking to them through their dreams.

The Old Testament describes numerous dreams and their interpretation. For example, Joseph told his brothers of different bizarre dreams insinuating that he would have lordship over them and all his family (Genesis 37:5–11, 18–20). Joseph was certainly bold, or perhaps naive, to share his dreams! However, Joseph's brothers took his dreams seriously and understood their implication immediately. Many people can't even remember their dreams, much less take them seriously, but that is not true for all.

Many Old Testament stories describe dreams given by God. For example, when Jacob went to sleep, he dreamed of a ladder coming from heaven. He saw angels surrounding the ladder and heard God promise land to him and his descendants. God promised Jacob and his descendants that they would inherit the very land he slept on and that He would never forsake him (Genesis 28:11–16). Many Israelis still consider this dream as evidence that God gave them the land of Israel. This dream and interpretation still affect issues of peace and conflict to this day!

DREAMS AND THEIR INTERPRETATION

Psychologists have created a significant amount of research on dreams and their meanings. Sigmund Freud, the father of modern dream analysis, believed that dreams are symbols or representations of the inner subconscious. The inner subconscious is the compartment of the mind where man's innermost desires lie. Therefore, Freud concluded that dreams represent man's deepest desires.

Some dreams come directly from God, but these are rare. More commonly, dreams come from our own thought processes. However, there is nothing we do or *can* do apart from God's omnipotence. Our very existence is grounded in His causal activity (Acts 17:24–28), and He provides for our physical and mental powers even when we use them for sinful acts. This does not mean that God works in us to commit sin or that He causes our dreams and nightmares. Theologian Thomas Aquinas made a helpful distinction between primary and secondary causes. God is the primary cause of our existence, while the secondary causes are results of human actions—those actions, in turn, affect us individually as well as the world around us. In a similar manner, God can be seen as the primary cause for some dreams, but dreams are also a result of our own secondary causes. For example, worry can cause bad dreams, and so can eating too much before going to bed. But dreams of all kinds appear to be a natural part of the REM stage of sleep and necessary for good mental health.

In a 1983 article in *The Journal of Psychology and Theology*, John Walsh described dreams as essentially symbolic. He asserted that dreams are symbolic realities that connect us with what is transcendent and otherwise unknown. He argued that dreams offer a certain Christological element by creating "incarnations" in our minds through concrete representations. In other words, spiritual things take a physical form when we dream. They communicate to us transcendent meanings through visions of physical images. Dreams connect us with the divine and transcendent.

Note that Walsh is not saying that every dream is directly related to Christ. He asserts that Christ was the incarnate Logos, or physical manifestation of God; He bridged the divine and the human by providing sensory imagery to man in communicating divine truth. In this sense, dreams act "incarnational" because they are symbolic realities of otherwise unknown meanings lying in the realm of subconsciousness. Walsh's opinion may be interesting but needs to be tested against what Scripture teaches about dreams and Christ.

Walsh also gives an interpretation for Joseph's dream in Matthew 1:18–25. Walsh states that Matthew's account of Joseph's dream seems to come from a deep conviction that God works His will through dreams. It also suggests to him that Matthew had a personal experience of God in a dream. Walsh goes on to suggest that Joseph's dream was a representation of his own desire for hero status, filtered through his current cultural context of what was considered heroic.

On one hand, Walsh has a point in recognizing how dreams have a vital role with regard to revealing God's will. Scripture gives clear examples of God revealing His will to people in dreams. However, Walsh's evaluation of Joseph is highly unwarranted. There is simply no evidence that Joseph's dream manifested psychological issues. The text merely tells us that an angel came to him and that Joseph feared for Mary's reputation because she was pregnant prior to their marriage (Matthew 1:18–20). Moreover, the text also tells us that Joseph was a just man and not someone who was struggling for the ideal image of a hero. Conclusively, Walsh's interpretation "psychologizes" the text by reading modern ideas about dreams into the story.

Notice that Walsh's interpretation becomes man-centered because he speculates on the mind of Joseph. Walsh is discounting the truthfulness of Matthew's account by not letting it speak for itself. He subordinates the text to Jungian psychological theory. In other words, he is molding the text into his presupposed psychological theories. Dreams may truly have deep roots in the inner subconscious. But we cannot assert that all dreams are symbols of our innermost struggles or desires. Some dreams have their basis in God, as other biblical narratives point out (see Genesis 28:12–15).

Walsh also emphasizes the archetypal character of dreams for spirituality. He asserts that dreams present signs or patterns about the nature of a person's spiritual life. For Walsh, dreams can indicate the state of a person's relationship to God. A person can discern how God is working in their life through their dreams. Since dreams are a pipeline from the divine life to our own, they inform us about God's will as well as the nature of our faith.

Based on Matthew 1:18–25 and Galatians 1:9–10, how may someone discern whether a dream is from God or not? Note that Joseph's dream not only involved an angel, but primarily an angel giving witness to and serving the Gospel of Christ. We should not be so apt to dismiss the reality of angels revealing themselves to us. But here is where the Gospel principle (p. 112) comes into the picture again. We should measure dreams or visions in light of their relationship to the Gospel if we want to determine whether they are revealing God's will or not. For example, does the image point to objects of worship other than Christ? Does it motivate us to violate God's commands? Is it presenting a Christ other than the one found in Scripture? Is it somehow contradicting faith in Christ alone? Such questions are pertinent to the essence of the Gospel. As mentioned previously, the devil does not do things for the mere thrill of messing with people. The devil craftily does things to thwart people's salvation and obstruct them from the Gospel.

People in ancient times regarded dreams as a form of direct communication with the supernatural. For example, Egyptians and Mesopotamians held dreams in high status because they were more than likely forms of communication from the gods.

Dreams that come from pagan gods, or gods other than the one true God of Israel, are essentially demonic. After all, such gods were set up and created by people as objects of worship (idols). They were not real. Scripture mentions that demons will use such idols as "masks" and hide behind them, in a sense, leading people astray from worshiping the true God (1 Corinthians 10:19–20; Psalm 106:35–38). Therefore, one could maintain that dreams from supposed "gods" actually come from demons.

EMPTY DREAMS

If *all* dreams are revelations of God's will, then it would be safe to say that they have an authoritative status with regard to truth. Dreams then could be put on the same par with God's Word because they directly come from God. But, as has been shown, not all dreams come directly from God. Therefore, we should be discerning about our own dreams. We should not be too quick to use them as a normative source for truth.

Read Deuteronomy 18:19–22 and Jeremiah 23:25–28, and consider what these passages have to say about false prophets. Note how the false prophets in Deuteronomy 18:19–22 speak under an appealed authority to one of two names: (1) the name of the Lord or (2) the name of their own god. God tells us that the false prophet speaks presumptuously when he claims to have received a direct revelation from God, while not receiving His revelation at all. Also, note the value God places on dreams in contrast to His Word (Jeremiah 23:28)!

People naturally look within to their ideas and feelings when they search for a standard for truth. In contrast, God urges us to look outside ourselves for truth. God's Word provides two important truths for guiding our lives: Law and Gospel. First, God proclaims His Law for our benefit. The Law shows us the true status of our sin and how we have forsaken His righteousness. The Law benefits us only if we keep it (Deuteronomy 6:3; Psalm 1; 119:1–8). The Law of God is good (1 Timothy 1:8) and an absolute standard of truth.

But the Law alone is not enough. The problem is that we naturally act against God's Law (Romans 3:10–20). Thus, we incur God's wrath (Ephesians 2:3; Isaiah 34:2; Malachi 1:10). The Lord shows us our utter failure to keep His Law and therefore shows us our need for a Savior in His Gospel (Romans 3:19; Galatians 3:19–26).

Why should we trust God's Word to be authoritative even over the dreams we have? God has created us and knows us better than we know ourselves (Psalm 119:73; Luke 12:7, 22–34). Here are two reasons to rely on God's Word above our own ideas or subjective emotions: (1) God is Creator and Sustainer of all things, and (2) God is omniscient. Since God has created all things, He knows the natural processes of our own lives as well as the world around us. Therefore, He has the authority to decide what is right and wrong. Since God is also omniscient, it is only common sense to conclude that He knows what is best for us.

Trust in these truths comes from seeing God's goodness toward us. He is not totally transcendent to the point where He is uncaring for His creation, but rather, He provides for our every need and has reconciled us to Himself through Christ (2 Corinthians 5:19). Not many people will simply trust in the authority of a tyrant or an emotionless judge. But how many people have come to trust God's Word when they have seen that He became a man who sacrificed Himself and rose from the dead so that they, too, may escape death (Acts 2:36–41; 17:24–34)!

The fact that dreams have different possible causes or sources should also tell us of the danger in relying on them for guidance. Dreams could come from God or from our own mental downloading of experiences or images.

Because of the possibility of different causes for dreams, we are already on shaky ground if we trust them.

We see an immediate difference with regard to God and His Word. God is the one ultimate cause for genuine revelation, and such revelation is found in Holy Scripture. God may have used men to write what He has revealed, but such revelation is ultimately grounded in Him (2 Peter 1:20–21). Therefore, when we rely on Scripture, we are not relying on shaky ground because we have the assurance that it comes from one source, namely God.

REAL REDEMPTION

What we dream does not create or destroy what is real. I can remember having a dream in which I was Spider-Man. But I did not wake up in a red and blue suit with the ability to fire webs at criminals or at my coffeemaker to pull in a morning cup of joe.

It may seem silly and obvious for me to state that dreams are not real. But a philosophical belief known as *solipsism* makes this necessary. Solipsism teaches that there is no reality existing outside of the mind. Under this theory the world is basically an illusion, a vast dreamland.

Although Walsh proposes that dreams may act as "incarnations" of truth, they do not offer what the Incarnate One—Jesus Christ—offers, namely real forgiveness and eternal life. In fact, the use of the word *incarnation* is a bit presumptuous, since in the entire course of human history there has been only one real incarnation!

Some modern theologians treat Christianity as an ideal. They describe Christ as a creation of the disciples to embody that ideal. But Christ is more than an ideal Savior. He is not a fictional character dreamt up by human imagination. Rather He is a historical being who really dwelt among us humans (John 1:1–14).

Why does this matter? Scripture tells us that "without the shedding of blood there is no forgiveness" (Hebrews 9:22). Since Scripture also tells us that the Law holds us condemned, we need the forgiveness of sins. We need a physical and real being to shed blood for forgiveness. As both God and man, Christ provides what is necessary for salvation: shedding His blood as a *man* and applying it with infinite forgiveness as *God.*

Read Hebrews 9:11–22; Isaiah 43:11; Mark 2:5–7 to see what these passages tell us about the necessity of a Savior being both God and man. Essentially, these verses address both natures of Christ. Hebrews 9:22 shows that it is necessary for the shedding of blood to purchase forgiveness of sins. Since God is spirit (John 4:24), He is not made up of physical flesh and blood to purchase forgiveness—this is where the necessity of becoming man comes in. And since forgiveness of sins and eternal salvation could only be granted by God, it is necessary that God grant us such benefits. The effects of Christ's death carry benefits that only God could achieve. No person can give to God a ransom for another (Psalm 49:7). Since only God has the power to forgive sins, and the blood of Christ forgives our sins, it follows that it is not the blood of a mere man, but the very blood of God Himself (1 John 1:7; Ephesians 1:5–7; Acts 20:28).

Some regard the idea of heaven and eternal peace as mere dreams, a form of escapism from suffering, a destitute life, and depression. Christ does not promise that our relationship will be void of all suffering, but He gives us joy in the midst of suffering (John 15:11). Moreover, the suffering you may experience as a Christian does not compare to the promise and glory of eternal life (Romans 8:18). You will experience the struggles of the sinful flesh and persecution for following Christ, but Christ has given you His love and the Holy Spirit to help you through the troubles of this present world (Romans 8:26–28). Furthermore, Christ has promised to bear your burdens, and He admonishes you to cast them on Him (Matthew 11:28–30).

God, in Christ, forgives you all your sins (1 John 1:9). Assurance no longer is to be found in dreams, but rather in God's promises through Jesus Christ. Rather than having assurance in the "incarnational" symbols of dreams, you have assurance in the Incarnate One, Jesus Christ. You have assurance in Christ because He is the truth. This means He not only communicates truth but also has fulfilled what He set out to do: to die as a ransom for you and to rise again for your justification (Mark 10:45; Romans 3:22–25; 1 Peter 1:21)! Our dreams do not have the creative power of Christ. He is living and active today, providing a sure and strong foundation for you through His Word.

Points to Ponder

Some of us remember many of our dreams while others might remember only one or two, if that. Once in a while, though, we might have a dream that really sticks in our mind, and we wonder what it means. None of our dreams carry value or meaning, though, compared to the value and meaning of the Word of God!

Words to Remember

We destroy arguments and every lofty opinion raised against the knowledge of God, and take every thought captive to obey Christ. (2 Corinthians 10:5)

15

DEMONS

William Peter Blatty's 1971 novel of a young girl possessed by the devil, *The Exorcist*, remains one of the most chilling and horrifying stories ever made into a film (the movie appeared in 1973). During the early stages of her possession, the girl, Regan, exhibits unusual behavior, such as superhuman strength, different personalities, and blasphemous language. The mother of the young girl takes her to a series of doctors. But after being examined by a host of doctors and psychologists, no natural explanation is found for Regan's condition. The doctors then suggest that the mother contact a witch doctor or someone with expertise in delivering spirits.

Eventually, the mother contacts Father Karras, a Jesuit priest who does not believe in the possibility of possession. (The priest was taught by modern theology and psychology that demonic possession does not occur.) After he visits the possessed girl, he seeks permission from his bishop to conduct an exorcism as a type of placebo, the idea being that a ceremony could ease the psychological pain Regan was struggling with. The bishop assigns another priest experienced in exorcism for assistance. Both priests engage in a vehement spiritual battle with the devil using the rite of exorcism as found in the *Rituale Romanum.*

Some Christians discount the possibility of demonic intervention in the world. But, if we truly take God's Word seriously, we should also take the possibility of demonic activity seriously (Ephesians 6:12). Moreover, the Lord would also have us take seriously the ministry of Christ in this specific area. For example, Mark 5:1–20 describes Jesus casting demons out of a man who was possessed.

William Peter Blatty's novel is loosely based on a 1949 case of a twelve-year-old boy from Maryland. The boy was brought to St. Louis after the spontaneous etching of "Louis" appeared on his abdominal region. Since his parents were Lutherans, they sought help from a Lutheran seminary. When the Lutheran ministers failed to help the boy, the parents took him to some local Jesuits, who performed an exorcism.

Read 2 Peter 2:4; Jude 1:6; and Mark 1:23–26; 5:1–15 to see what Scripture says about the nature and state of fallen angels, otherwise known as demons. These verses tell us that such beings are evil and act contrary to God and His will. Because of their rebellion against God, they have been reserved for judgment. That is why, in the Gospel accounts of Christ's encounter with them, they fear Christ's judgment. Christ possesses total authority over demons, and they are afraid of Him. You will note in the Mark 5 account that there are a multitude of demons possessing the man. The demons' name, "Legion," may indicate that there were thousands of them since a Roman legion at that time consisted of thousands of soldiers.

DEMONIC INFLUENCE

Many people today dismiss the existence of the devil and demons. They reason that since demons are not physical beings, no one can prove their existence. Therefore they must not exist. Of course, it is a very big step to go from cannot prove to cannot be.

It is also very common for people to dismiss the existence of demons in the same way the priest dismissed them in *The Exorcist*. That is, people often think that demonic intervention was an idea left back in the 1500s or earlier, that people of old who believed in demonic intervention were superstitious and lacked the tools of science or psychology to understand mental illness. They trust that our modern psychology explains away so-called demonic possession.

So can psychology offer a comprehensive explanation for demonic intervention? Psychology is the study of the human mind based on human behavior. Human behavior reveals what is going on in the mind. Since a psychologist learns about the mind through behavior, psychology has a basis as an empirical science.

Since demons are not physical beings, they lie outside of the range of the psychologist. But we should not disregard the use of psychology in interpreting whether someone is influenced by the demonic. Psychology helps us determine how the mind usually behaves (not everybody who acts unusual or speaks with different voices is demon-possessed). Moreover, not everyone who has been or can be demon-possessed is devoid of psychological illness. Darrell McCulley's 2002 book, *The House Swept Clean*, suggests that mental illness and possession may occur together in an individual. Ultimately, psychology may help us discern demonic influence in an individual, but not determine the demonic causes manifested in an individual.

In his book, McCulley suggests different ways in which demonic intervention can occur. He argues that demonic intervention does not necessarily mean full bodily possession, as in the 1949 exorcism case. There are other ways in which demons manifest themselves. Demonic activity is also found in the following: (1) miraculous healing, (2) "parlor tricks," and (3) direct communication. We will examine these categories one at a time.

Many people report that they have experienced miraculous healing through a spiritual medium. Such mediums may treat people with elixirs or other mysterious potions. McCulley suggests that such reports may be based on demonic activities.

One may wonder why a demon would heal someone. McCulley points out that demons can do such things to create credibility in a medium. If a medium heals someone of a disease, people may put their trust in the medium rather than in Christ. In this way, people are directed away from Christ, which was the ultimate goal of the demon working through the medium.

Read 2 Thessalonians 2:9–12 for a summary of things Satan might do in his attempt to deceive us. The work of Satan through the man of lawlessness is twofold: (1) to cause people to worship Satan, and (2) to deceive people so that they do not follow Christ. Satan wants to be higher than God and to be worshiped. Even when the devil tried to deceive Christ in the testing in the wilderness, he tried to get Christ to worship him (Matthew 4:9). He will use deception to lead souls astray from God. As long as someone does not believe in and obey Christ, they are carrying out Satan's will (John 8:41–44; Acts 26:17–18; Ephesians 2:2).

"Parlor tricks" refers to levitating objects, mysterious noises, apparitions, or objects moving without any apparent physical cause. People generally believe that such things happen because of a disembodied spirit (ghost). But Job tells us that the dead do not come back (7:9–10; see also Hebrews 9:27). This is disheartening to many because they want to contact their dead loved ones, either through an unexpected spiritual encounter or through a spiritist. Job 7:9–10 indicates that the dead do not return but demonstrates that when one dies, his soul is either (1) with God in His kingdom or (2) in hell (Philippians 1:23; 2 Corinthians 5:1–2; Luke 12:5; 16:19–31). So if ghosts do not cause "parlor tricks," what options are left for their origin?

Finally, demons also intervene through direct communication to mediums. Unlike "parlor tricks," this method goes beyond bodily manifestations to the point of relaying information. As mentioned above, the dead simply do not come back, but demons may relay false information to psychics and mediums as a way of undercutting something directly asserted in God's Word. Think about the impact such misleading information could have. If a demon relays information to a medium who thinks he or she has actually contacted a dead spirit, it could convince the medium and others that not only are the dead able to communicate from "beyond" but also that eternal bliss with Christ is unnecessary.

Read Acts 16:16–18 and 19:13–20 to see how spiritists and those who practice black magic tap into the demonic. These spirits could only be one of two things—either demons or spirits who have passed from this world into another. As shown above, souls of the dead have no contact with the living. Therefore, spirits involved in divination and the black arts are demons.

GOD WARNS US

Scripture does not explicitly tell us how demons possess an individual or why they inflict people with particular torments. However, God's Law clearly commands us to turn away from any form of divination (Deuteronomy 18:10–12). That is, we are forbidden to attempt contacting the dead through spiritists or psychic mediums.

Despite this clear warning from God's Word, popular culture encourages people to dabble in the spirit world. For example, Ouija boards are a form of divination. It is amazing how Ouija boards, things that appear so harmless that they are sold in toy stores (and made by Parker Brothers!), are actually spiritually destructive. It should be noted that the boy possessed in the true-life exorcism story mentioned above used forms of divination, including a Ouija board. (Evidently, the Ouija board was one of his direct avenues to the demonic.)

Deuteronomy 18:10–12 offers a sobering view of divination. With today's fascination for the supernatural, how should we as Christians warn others of the dangers connected with divination? This is not an easy issue to deal with directly. If you know somebody involved with spiritism or any form of divination, it is imperative to warn them of the dangers. However, recognize that they may not listen to your concerns. People who practice such things are often prideful, or they may not take such things seriously. The only way they can be delivered from such practices is through the power of God's Word and Spirit.

You may warn people directly with God's Law or point people to the love of Christ in His cross. Usually, the latter applies to people who have some degree of despair in their lives and need to hear a word of grace as opposed to Law.

I remember when I met a young man who claimed to follow Satan. He honestly believed that Satan was "on his side" and had more of a friendship role in his life. I explained to him that Satan hated him and that he only used people for his own purposes. I also explained to him that it was Satan's nature to lie. The young man seemed convinced and sat in shock and silence. Sadly, I never had the opportunity to speak with him again, but after the look on his face that evening, I would not be surprised if he gave up following Satan. The key to our discussion was helping him realize that Satan actually hated every ounce of him. Following this important point, I explained that Christ was His true friend. I communicated the Gospel to him. He appeared to give it serious consideration. Although he did not confess Christ as his Savior, the Word was sown in his heart so that it could sprout in God's time.

Another example of the effects of divination is found in an event involving two young women over twenty years ago. Gerald Brittle's 2002 book,

The Demonologist, records the account of two roommates who used a Ouija board and contacted what they thought was the spirit of a young girl named Annabelle. This spirit wanted to be brought back to this world for the purpose of finding "peace." Feeling sorry for the spirit, the women continued to contact it through the Ouija board. This led to a series of mysterious and terrifying events including the possession and movement of a doll, the appearance of written messages, and an attack on the fiancé of one of the women. The women then sought help from professional demonologists, who performed an exorcism.

Many Christians have disdain for a formal rite of exorcism. They think it is unnecessary or overly ritualistic. (One example of rites for exorcisms can be found in the traditional *Rituale Romanum of 1614*. This service book uses many elaborate and superfluous wordings for the purpose of expelling a demon.) To some extent, such criticisms are warranted. However, Christians should not throw out the practice of exorcism, which is simply calling on God to remove the influence of the demonic. We should realize its proper form and place. For example, it used to be a common practice for Lutheran ministers to conduct an exorcism prior to Baptism (see *Lutheran Cyclopedia*, pp. 287–88). Martin Luther rejected the medieval rite of exorcism because such rituals contained too many procedures and not enough emphasis on the Word of God and prayer. Luther believed that all a Christian needed to do was pray over someone who was demon-possessed to expel the demon. An exorcism liturgy could serve as a guideline for such prayer. One needs to know *what* to say in the prayer and *how* to say it. An exorcism rite would provide some of the necessary details for handling possessions. Perhaps the reason that the Lutheran minister involved with the 1949 exorcist story could not offer help was that he did not have a service for exorcism to guide him. He simply did not know what to do!

Idolatry is another avenue for demons, who can intervene in this world through just about anything one sets up as an idol. Darrell McCulley reported to me the experience of a high school friend who set up a sculpture in his room as an idol. McCulley's friend gave the sculpture a name and talked to it much like one would a pet. Then, his sculpture started appearing in different places in the room even though his friend had not moved it. Suspicious of his own memory, one night the young man made sure to set the sculpture in one distinct position. When it appeared in a completely different place, he began to worry.

Matthew 4:8–10 and Isaiah 14:12–15 describe the prideful character of the devil. The Isaiah text does not directly refer to the devil; it specifically describes the king of Babylon. However, interpreters have also viewed this passage as a comparison with the fall of Satan at the beginning of the world. (The Latin Vulgate uses "Lucifer" in v. 12, which means "bearer of light" or "son of the dawn." Note how Jesus refers to this passage in Luke 10:17–18.) Satan was once the beautiful "son of the dawn." But he wanted to usurp God's majesty and be the highest being. The devil is swollen with pride up to this day and is on a vengeful mission to overthrow God's creation.

Christ rebuked the devil and quoted the passage from Deuteronomy (6:13) about how one is to serve and worship God alone. This reminds us to shun idolatry, seeking God and His kingdom as found in Jesus Christ.

CHRIST THE VICTOR

Read about the Gerasenes demoniac in Mark 5:1–20 and Luke 8:27–39 and consider whether a Christian can become demon-possessed. Theologians have expressed different opinions on this issue. For example, Francis Pieper's *Christian Dogmatics* states that Christians can become demon-possessed (vol. 7, p. 509). The argument Pieper uses needs a serious reassessment since it robs the Christian of assurance that the Lord protects us from the evil one. He bases his statement on Mark 5:6, 18–19 and Luke 8:28, 38–39, the story of the Gerasenes demoniac. However, it is not at all clear that this man was a Christian or a Jewish believer. Other passages of Scripture emphasize the presence of the Holy Spirit in believers (e.g., Ephesians 1:13). Christians certainly struggle against Satan but remain in the possession of God's Spirit (Romans 8:9–11, 38–39; Ephesians 6:10–18).

The belief that Christians may be demon-possessed may come from experiences people have had with divination. For example, if Christians use such things as the Ouija board, then it seems that they, too, could become possessed.

It is important to distinguish between sins done *in* faith and losing one's faith. The former regards the sins committed against God's Commandments. Practicing divination is not an unforgivable sin. A doubting or confused Christian may partake in divination out of ignorance. That does not mean that person has denied his or her faith or become demon-possessed.

Read Acts 26:17–18; Colossians 1:13; Ephesians 2:1–7; and Luke 22:31–32 to see what these verses tell us about our salvation in Christ and His protection. We are transferred from one dominion to another: from the dominion of darkness and the devil to the dominion of Christ's kingdom. As Christians, we are under a new lordship, that of Christ. Satan no longer has dominion over us, nor can he have dominion over us. Christ does not share His property. The devil has no rights over the Christian anymore because the Christian has been ransomed from his kingdom. Furthermore, the examples of Peter and Job show how God protects His people from Satan (Luke 22:31–32; Job 1:9–12).

Faith grafts you into Christ. You are under His lordship. You are sons or daughters of God through faith and Holy Baptism (Galatians 3:26–27). As

Luther's Small Catechism states, Baptism "works forgiveness of sins, [and] rescues [us] from death and the devil." Likewise, the Holy Spirit is given as a deposit to you, the believer. Both your body and spirit belong to God through Christ's blood (1 Corinthians 6:19–20). Since you belong to Christ by faith, you are also a bearer of His name.

The name of Christ has tremendous power! It is the very name at which every knee should bow when He returns in glory (Philippians 2:10). As bearers of Christ's name, we have His authority, and this includes authority over the evil one.

Demons are afraid of Christ! As inheritors of His kingdom, we are given His rights and hold the power of His name. Luther mentioned in his treatise *On the Freedom of a Christian* how Christians are the Bride of Christ and are given the full benefits and blessings of their Groom. Demons are afraid of us because of the name we bear (James 4:7). Christians have been rescued from slavery to the devil and are no longer under his ownership. Christ's blood has ransomed you from the devil by bringing you safely into Christ's glorious kingdom. Now, the devil and his minions are under God's authority (1 John 4:4; 2 Peter 2:4)!

The evidence of Scripture about Christ's and the Christians' authority over the devil and demons is that they cannot threaten Christ's people. Moreover, Matthew 26:53 tells us about Christ's authority over good angels. If good and upright angels serve Christ, how could even a multitude of *fallen* angels stand up to Him! Even the devil needs Christ's permission to test one of His saints (Luke 22:31–32).

POINTS TO PONDER

Christians live in the midst of spiritual warfare. (See Robert H. Bennett's *I Am Not Afraid: Demon Possession and Spiritual Warfare* for an in-depth look at spiritual warfare found in the Malagasy Lutheran Church and a study of what Scripture has to say [St. Louis: Concordia, 2013].) God's enemies are our enemies too, even if unseen, so Ephesians 6:11–17 tells us to put on and wear the whole armor of God. Jesus has already won the victory, but the skirmishes continue, so let us stand our ground in His name!

WORDS TO REMEMBER

"In all these things we are more than conquerors through Him who loved us. (Romans 8:37)

16

ANGELS

A loud thunderclap sounds. A heavenly manifestation unfolds. Before a multitude of priests, an image suddenly appears at the altar of the church. The image brightly illuminates the altar in a supernatural spectacle. An angelic apparition appears before their very eyes! It is judged to be Michael, the angel of justice and the avenger of evil.

A group of people attending service at St. Francis Xavier Church in St. Louis described this event in 1949. They explained that this vision of an angel appeared at about the same time that the boy from the exorcist story (mentioned previously) was delivered from demonic possession. The priests who witnessed the apparition thought the angel's appearance was a sign of God's victory.

Every year Christians claim to receive visits from angels. They remain a popular topic in our culture and, recently, in television and movies. Angels may be depicted as fat little babies on greeting cards or guardians/companions in TV shows and movies. These depictions of angels do not agree with biblical teaching, so do not be surprised if you find that you need to change your attitudes and ideas about angels.

SCIENCE AND ANGELS

Angels are definitely not something you see every day. Since science primarily investigates material causes or tangible realities, it does not seem possible for scientists to investigate angelic beings. Angels cannot be placed under a microscope. They are spiritual "heavenly beings." It is important to remember, however, that there are many examples in Scripture where angels were observable.

Angels, though often described as "incorporeal" (having no physical body), appear to have taken physical form as described in Genesis 19:1–13. They not only appear in dreams (as one did for Joseph in Matthew 1:20) but also in history. Isaiah describes the angels that surround God's throne (6:1–7). Multiwinged seraphs, they fly about serving the Almighty and praising Him with powerful voices.

Subjects for scientific investigation are usually observed repeatedly (such as the sun rising or snow falling). But angels don't appear in a regular way, so repeated observations are out of the question. However, the quality of an observance, rather than quantity, can help validate our knowledge of something's existence. For example, astronauts who observed the round shape of the

Earth from outer space for the first time made such a quality observance of the planet. The Earth stood before them in its mass and shape so convincingly that they did not need a series of tests to validate whether it was really round or not.

We often doubt things that are not readily available to the senses, so how can we have any certainty for the existence of angels? Accounts of angelic appearances are often personal. For example, Isaiah seemed to be the sole witness of the angels who appeared to him. Joseph and Mary were also each visited individually by angels (Matthew 1:20; Luke 1:30–35).

The account of the angel appearing at the church in St. Louis has some credibility. After all, a number of people testified about what they saw. It is hard to dismiss the event as a hallucination or mere "dreaming" because more than one person claimed to have observed the angel. At the same time, one should not make belief in such an event a basis for the Christian faith or a point of obsession. The Lord's angels serve the Lord and want us to focus on Him.

Since most people do not see angels, they rely on the testimony of those who have. The surest testimony on this topic comes from God's Word and not accounts from popular culture.

THE LORD'S MESSENGERS

People today seek hope, but often from sources other than the Lord. Even angels can become inappropriate objects of hope. Two worldviews influence our sense of hope: naturalism (belief in only the material or physical) and supernaturalism (focus on the heavenly and immaterial). We live in an age of paradox. Some people are apt to dismiss the reality of things unseen, while others focus almost completely on the supernatural.

Matthew 4:1–11 and Luke 1:30–38 describe the primary role of angels as messengers and servants. Hence, they are subordinate to God not only in their *being* but also in their *role*. Angels are not equal to God, for they are created beings. They do not deserve worship. Although God sends angels to our service, their service to us is ultimately founded on His direction. Hence, their service to us is their service to God. Psalm 91:11 tells us that it is God who gives His angels the charge of our protection.

The First Commandment expressly forbids us to set up anything as an object of worship in place of God (Exodus 20:3). If we look for salvation from something other than the Savior, Jesus Christ, we are also guilty of idolatry and unbelief. Angels are not our saviors; they are servants of God. They do not do anything apart from God's command on our behalf. God is the ultimate cause for their protection over us; thus we can thank God for angelic protection.

Read Psalm 91:9–13 and Hebrews 1 for more perspective on the interaction between God, angels, and humans. The emphasis here is to show how it is God who sends angels. He is the one giving His angels "charge" over the psalmist. This represents the reality of how angels receive their "orders" from

God. They do not act in an autonomous way or choose to do as they please. Angels will not act apart from God's will or usurp their own desires above God's; otherwise they would fall into the same judgment as the fallen angels or demons (2 Peter 2:4, 11; Jude 1:6). Moreover, Hebrews 1 deals with the issue directly. We read in Hebrews 1:14: "Are they not all ministering spirits sent out to serve for the sake of those who are to inherit salvation?" The entire chapter of Hebrews 1 presents angels in a servant role both to Christ and the saints. Christ is clearly stated as having a superior office to the angels as they answer *to Him*.

Psalm 8:5 declares that God made humankind "a little lower than the heavenly beings." Because of our natural propensity toward idolatry, we will even make an object of worship out of something that is at a lower status than God. Although angels are truly magnificently created beings and possess far greater power than ourselves, they are still less in power and authority than God.

Psalm 8 tells about God's majesty and authority over the world. While there is not a direct reference to God's status with regard to angels, we may infer that since God's glory exceeds all else in His creation, angels, being created by God, are subordinate to His power and glory.

If an angel appears to us in a dream or in any other manner, we should not be too quick to assume that it is directly from God. We are called to test the spirits and to see whether they are from God (1 John 4:1). In case of such an event, one should "catechize the spirit." This does not mean you play Bible trivia. Even false spirits may come across as well-instructed in the faith. Instead, request that the spirit confess Christ as its Lord. Only by the Holy Spirit can a person confess that Christ is Lord (1 Corinthians 12:3), so simply ask the spirit who is its Master or Lord. If the spirit can confess Christ as Lord, then it is sent from God. But if the spirit is unwilling or evades the question, then it is a false spirit and a messenger of Satan. You must always remember that even the devil can disguise himself as an angel of light (2 Corinthians 11:14).

What do you think of testing the spirits? Is the question of lordship a valid criterion for establishing the truthfulness of a spirit? We should not go out on a witch hunt or actively engage in seeking the supernatural for the purpose of examination. Rather, if a spirit or their doctrines confront us, we are to test them to see if they are from God. In an audio lecture, the late apologist Walter Martin described an event in which a certain gentleman had a direct conversation with a spirit masquerading as his dead wife. The man thought that since his wife had died in Christ, she must have seen Jesus. Before the man knew it was a false spirit, he asked it about Jesus. The spirit continued to evade the question. Perturbed, the man questioned the true identity of the spirit and pressed the question as to whether it could call Jesus "Lord" or not. The spirit wasted no time in retreating, being unwilling to answer the question.

ANGELS ARE SERVANTS OF THE GOOD NEWS

We may regard the protection God provides through angels as one of the blessings of the Gospel. Although they did not purchase eternal life for us, as did Christ, nonetheless, they are sent to care for us (Acts 27:23; Psalm 34:7; 91:9–13; Hebrews 1:14). The concept of a personal guardian angel is alluded to in Scripture but is not emphasized (Matthew 18:10; Acts 12:15). Scripture emphasizes a general protection of angels over the saints, instead of a "Clarence" (the guardian angel for Jimmy Stewart's character in the film *It's a Wonderful Life*). Additionally, Scripture does not teach that either adults or children become angels when they die.

The concept of a personal guardian angel may provide us comfort, but how might too much emphasis on such an idea confuse people? Out of His love for us in Christ, God truly sends angels to help His saints. Whether this help is in the form of a general blanket of assistance or a personal angel assigned to us, we cannot say. In either case, angels are not our spiritual "pets." They are mighty servants of our almighty Lord. One may certainly pray to God for the protection of His angels, but one should not pray to or worship angels.

There is much superstition regarding the person and work of angels. During medieval times, people generally held to such high supernaturalistic views that they tended to perceive a spirit "behind every bush." Today, we may often find people believing that angels come to comfort people in a random manner. Angels tend to be viewed as divine "pillow-fluffers" that help us in every little discomfort we experience.

Isaiah 37:36 and Joshua 5:13–15 explain that angels are not the soft and cuddly comforters that our culture so often depicts them to be. Scripture gives us a varied perspective of angels and their actions. God will use them to smite entire armies. In fact, you will note that in both passages there was only one angel involved in inflicting violence on the enemies of God's people. If only one angel can do this, imagine what several of them can do!

Scripture does not tell us that angelic protection is random. There seems to be a definite and set purpose as to the nature of their protection. Since angels work according to God's purpose and at His command, we can only conclude that there is a definite and organized principle behind it. Although how angels work may be mysterious to us, we can be assured that their purpose is for the glory of God. God does not do things chaotically or randomly but carries out His plan to His glory while working all things in conformity with His will (Ephesians 1:11).

Angels serve God by serving His plan of salvation in the Gospel. For example, the angel Gabriel announced to Mary that she was going to bear the Son of God (Luke 1:26–31). Likewise, we also see a similar event in the case of Samson's birth (Judges 13:1–5). Angels are servants to Christ and act on Christ's command (Matthew 26:53). Since they have a subordinate role to Christ and His will, we can have confidence that angels will be there for our good.

Read Colossians 2:18–19, where Paul warns us against false humility and the worship of angels. Christ is our Lord, but because of the old Adam within, we often diminish the lordship of Christ in our own life. It should be noted that it is not what we do with our life that makes Christ our Lord, but rather He is our Lord by faith through the power of the Holy Spirit (Romans 8:9–11; 1 Corinthians 6:19–20; 12:3). When we hold to Christ as the substance and center of our faith and life, we can place everything else subordinate to Him and His lordship. We are free to serve Him and refrain from the captivity of idolatry, which can occur even toward heavenly things such as angels.

The devil is so good at deceiving people that he would not mind for an instant if Christians were to worship the *good* angels. As long as people are worshiping something other than Christ, they are doing the devil's will.

In spite of our idolatry or trust in things other than God, Christ forgives our sin. Angels point you to the Savior who removes your guilt. They are God's messengers who serve the most important message—salvation wrought through the death and resurrection of Christ. Angels are always there for you because you belong to Christ.

We should remember that our one true security is offered us in the blood of Christ. We contact this source of true security in the Word and the Sacraments. Tangible things give certainty, and such tangible realities can be found in the preached Word of Christ's forgiveness, the certainty of your bond with God through Baptism, and participation in the body and blood of Christ at the Lord's Table. If you feel the need to find security in angels, recall that even angels worship the Son of God. Moreover, angels would not exist if Christ had not created them in the first place. Therefore, Christ alone is your hope and trust who bought you with His own blood (Hebrews 1:3–6; 9:11–22; 10:10, 19).

POINTS TO PONDER

Just about every time God sent an angel to speak with someone in the Bible, the angel would have to start out by saying, "Don't be afraid." Angels must not be the cute little figurines seen in stores and curio cabinets! Fortunately, they must obey Christ. Are you on a first-name basis with the One who is in charge?

WORDS TO REMEMBER

He will command His angels concerning you to guard you in all your ways. On their hands they will bear you up, lest you strike your foot against a stone. (Psalm 91:11–12)

HEAVEN AND HELL

The Edge of Eternity

INTRODUCTION

Attaboy, Clarence!

—*George Bailey*, It's a Wonderful Life

Popular misconceptions about the afterlife run the gamut from abject denial (atheism, nihilism, annihilationism) to the fanciful: clockmakers like Clarence become angels after death, earning their heavenly wings through earthly deeds (hyperspiritualism).

Some people ask quite glibly, "How can a loving God send good people to hell?" as if the reality of evil logically justified the denial of God's existence. Perhaps those asking such a question err not by going too far but by not going far enough. We must also ponder, "How can a just God allow sinners into heaven?"

That question can be answered only in Jesus Christ, true God and true man. By His bloody cross and empty tomb, we are fully forgiven. Baptized into Him, our bodies will be raised to perfection and life on the Last Day. Through the deposit of His Spirit we now yearn for the new heaven and the new earth.

Jesus Christ is God in flesh and blood. The two natures of the one Christ remind us of the dangers of pitting one aspect of our faith against another. By maintaining the tension between what only appears to be a contradiction, the Clarence of film can become the Clarence of faith. The erstwhile clockmaker enjoys heaven because of God's grace in Christ and will be resurrected in his perfect, human body. No wings are necessary.

Little Zuzu's bell still rings. But this time its cheerful sound reminds us not of rewards outside the body, but of God's grace in Jesus Christ experienced in the body—here and now and in the life of the world to come.

17

Scientific Eschatology

Before considering our individual fate, let us set some context by reviewing some popular views about the end of the world, or even the end of the universe. Think about book titles such as these: *The End of the World*, *The End of the Age*, *The Last Three Minutes*, and *The Ultimate Fate of the Universe*. In what section of your local bookstore might you find these books?

All of these books (and many more) were found in the science section of a chain bookstore. For interest, you might want to stop at a local bookstore and look over the available popular literature dealing with the fate of the universe—you might be surprised at how many different titles and viewpoints are on the market! The topic of eschatology usually excites people, especially in view of all the discussion generated in some Christian circles.

Eschatology. A study of the last things, such as death, resurrection, life after death, the second coming of Christ, Judgment Day, and heaven.

At a conference at New York University in 1978, physicist Freeman Dyson optimistically expressed his hope that discussion of eschatology would continue in the sciences. Our first reaction as Christians might be uneasiness about including a traditionally theological topic in the field of science. However, in view of the gloom-and-doom outlook current in most scientific eschatology, the factual events of Jesus' death, resurrection, and return provide the contrast of eternal hope.

On August 10, 1972, an asteroid 42 feet in diameter passed through Earth's upper atmosphere, just 30 miles above southern Montana. Looking back in geologic time, the Canadian province of Quebec contains a meteorite crater over 2 miles in diameter and 400 feet deep—the Ungava-Quebec crater. And on February 15, 2013, an asteroid up to 60 feet in diameter exploded in the atmosphere about 14.5 miles above Chelyabinsk, Russia, shattering windows and injuring fifteen hundred people seriously enough to require medical attention.

Observers with the Lincoln Near Earth Asteroid Research Project (a program funded by the United States Air Force and NASA) once detected a 1.2-mile-wide asteroid, which they named 2002 NT7. Some catastrophe theorists predicted that this asteroid could collide with Earth on February 1,

2019, and throw it out of orbit. Those persons who survived the initial impact would eventually starve or freeze to death as Earth spun away from the Sun. Better measurements and calculations of orbits have since debunked the prediction, but there are many other potentially hazardous asteroids out there, and astronomers keep finding more.

The possibility of extraterrestrial debris colliding with the Earth usually invokes fear. A sizable meteorite or asteroid striking a populated area could cause serious damage. If one landed in the ocean, tidal waves could destroy various coastal cities. Movies such as *Armageddon* and *Deep Impact* (both popular in 1998) develop this theme.

Isaac Asimov's 1979 book *A Choice of Catastrophes* categorized and described potential disasters that threaten us. Asimov described the most disastrous catastrophes as those that would affect the entire universe, destroying the potential for the continuation of life, or as those that would merely bring about the destruction of humanity.

Asimov's book also correctly identified problems with various millennial groups (e.g., the Seventh-day Adventists and Jehovah's Witnesses). But the author made the mistake of describing biblical pictures of the end times as mythical and treats potential natural catastrophes as purely scientific phenomena. His conclusions, of course, derived from several assumptions.

Asimov, and in fact all other naturalists, hold certain assumptions. To begin with, God and a purposeful creation are mere fiction to those with a naturalist worldview. So a naturalist can logically call the Christian conception of the end times and final judgment mythical.

Because it rejects a Creator, naturalism also fails to recognize God as the sustainer of life. Therefore, it admits no supernatural intervention in connection with potential disasters. Scientific naturalism can ultimately be reduced to an extreme form of determinism—that is, all things happen by necessity. A natural catastrophe cannot really be called a catastrophe in a naturalist worldview. The very term *catastrophe* implies some sort of "bad" event. However, in naturalism there can be no objective "good" or "bad." Things simply happen. They carry no meaning or meaningful implications.

In light of the scientific method studied in the first part of this book and in view of other things you have learned, what difficulties does the very nature of scientific eschatology present? The end of all life is by its very nature an unobservable event. Who's going to record the scientific data? (An observable event implies that those who observe it will remain to report the facts of the event.)

Also, scientific eschatology is limited in its knowledge of the existing universe. The fact that eschatology deals with the end of time implies prediction of future events. Of course, science can speculate about the fate of the universe. But since we cannot actually observe the end of the universe, prediction of the future falls outside the realm of science.

The only way scientists could be certain in events of the future, both near and distant, is for them to receive data from outside of time—that is, from a timeless vantage point.

INEVITABLE DECAY

In addition to positing theories about flying objects colliding with the Earth, physicists have also considered the implications of the laws of physics for the future of the universe. Since the nineteenth century, physicists and astronomers have studied the potential for the destruction of the universe. What is known as *thermodynamics* pointed toward the probability of energy "burning itself out." Physicists called this the "heat death" of the universe, although at first glance the phrase is a bit misleading.

What does all this mean? The first law of thermodynamics states that the heat or energy content of the universe is constant. The second law of thermodynamics states that the heat or energy in the universe evens out over the course of time. This equalizing process—called *entropy*—will bring about the end of change and motion. The universe will be "frozen" in time like a wound clock slowing down as the spring unwinds (only much slower—millions of years slower).

Imagine pouring water into a bottle until it is three-fourths full and then pouring water into another bottle until it is one-fourth full. If you connected the two bottles by a hose and then turned them upside down, water from the three-fourths-full bottle would flow into the one-fourth-full bottle. Eventually, the water level in both bottles would equalize and all movement (energy) would cease. This analogy paints a picture of entropy, or what would happen to bring about the heat death of the universe. All available energy would reach a state of equalization. Hence, there would be no change or motion—the planetary revolutions would cease, life would end, and the universe would "freeze" in time. These ideas for how the universe might end have been superseded by other theories, but not before they sparked their own derivative theories.

Freeman Dyson, a physicist at the Institute for Advanced Study in Princeton, New Jersey, pioneered the idea of *cosmic optimism*—that life could overcome the fate of an open universe doomed to entropy. Through a series of sophisticated calculations and hypotheses concerning the deterioration of the universe, Dyson concluded that life could continue to exist. However, it would not continue as we think of it. Rather, flesh-and-blood humans would have to embody themselves in a cloudlike assemblage of dust grains. Dyson further concluded that if humans learned to develop skills for hibernation in order to conserve energy, life could continue forever.

Another optimistic view of scientific eschatology was presented in 1986 and developed further in 1994. John D. Barrow and Frank J. Tipler (in *The Anthropic Cosmological Principle* and *The Physics of Immortality: Modern Cosmology, God and the Resurrection of the Dead*) expand on ideas concerning human survival after the thermodynamic death of the universe. Barrow and Tipler describe a situation in which life begins to leave Earth in order to colonize outer space. They envision life ultimately spreading throughout the universe. As life spreads, they theorize that it will be able to obtain and process information at an enormous speed. Barrow and Tipler suggest the possibility of life at some point obtaining and storing a tremendous amount of information. This information would enable life to gain control of all matter. At this point in time, which Barrow and Tipler call the "Omega Point," life would achieve the godlike attribute of knowing everything, including how to live forever. They conclude that this point in time would be the end of life as we know it, but also the beginning of eternal life.

Even though the foregoing optimistic proposals seem as if they were pulled out of a science fiction novel, some scientists have taken them seriously. However, when closely examined, Dyson's theory fails on two levels. To begin with, his work assumes that a variety of constants in physical laws will continue to the very distant future. If any one of his assumptions does not hold true, then his entire theory is shot. Furthermore, according to the laws of thermodynamics, Dyson's theoretical, hibernating life forms will also expire in the heat death of the universe.

William Press (b. 1948), who taught at Harvard's Center for Astrophysics, exposed the scientific weaknesses of Barrow and Tipler's work. He showed that their work is based on faulty mathematical calculations and even accused them of misleading their nonmathematical readers. Besides, he argued, their broad conclusions are based on a minimal amount of empirical data.

Another critique, offered by Fred W. Hallberg, showed in 1988 that Barrow and Tipler's optimistic eschatological theory rests on nine assumptions. Hallberg pointed out that not one of their assumptions is known to be true. If even one were not true, he concludes, the Barrow-Tipler theory would prove faulty.

The decay of the universe seems inevitable. But why would scientists expend time and energy studying possible happenings that may be millions of years in the future? They apparently feel that the question is worth study but don't want it to become too personal. A far-distant heat death of the universe is easy to talk about with no emotional qualms about the fate of humans. An end that lies a million or more years in the future does not give rise to fear.

Placing the end millions of years away helps us feel safe. But what if the end comes sooner? What about biological death and what follows? What if Jesus does return quickly, as He promised He would? All these questions and more could be asked to spark conversation with those persons who treat eschatology as a merely scientific discipline.

Think about what the possibility of the thermodynamic death of the universe or the fear of natural catastrophic events fail to take into consideration. Read Colossians 1:17 and Hebrews 1:3 for perspective. God sustains the universe through Christ. He remains intimately involved with His creation. So how good are answers about the fate of the world if they don't include God?

DEATH: ARE YOU READY?

In theory, science has pretty well established that millions of years from now the universe will cease to support life. This, of course, begs the deeply intellectual question: so what?

But what if the universe and life come to an end sooner? That's a different matter. It would be interesting to compare the scientifically calculated time scales for (1) the life of the Sun, (2) the interruption of Earth's orbit, and (3) the time when the expanding universe will collapse onto itself. A gambling pessimist would probably bet that a major asteroid would get us first. News of meteorites bound for Earth and nuclear threats from terrorists arouse immediate fear. Yet many people do not ask themselves if they are ready for life to be over. Death is a very personal thing.

Think back to the material discussed above. What does Barrow and Tipler's or Freeman Dyson's apparently sterile explanation for the potential of life's surviving the "heat death" of the universe tell you about humanity's preparedness for death? Dyson, Barrow, and Tipler manifest the human desire to continue living. Though death gets masked in a variety of ways, most humans ultimately fear it. Twentieth-century atheistic philosopher Bertrand Russell was asked what would happen to him when he died. He calmly responded that he would rot. He may be the exception to the rule: death usually frightens the average person.

What happens to us when we die? This question has occupied the minds of thinkers throughout human history, and hosts of opinions have been offered. Some persons see death as a new beginning in a cycle of life. Hence, they favor the idea of reincarnation. Others see death as the transition from a physical presence to a bodiless, spiritual presence. Even the position of Russell offers an answer, fatalistic though it may be, to the question concerning what happens after death. The problem is that we cannot know through philosophy, science, or religious speculation what happens to humans after they die. In spite of all our proposals, all we can know on our own accord is that the end is the end.

Scientific theories and contemporary developments such as cryogenics focus on the possibility of cheating death. But what if time as we know it came to an end? Would we simply cease to exist?

The Bible addresses these questions for us. We know that we will go on living for an eternity. God created humans as eternal creatures. His original intent was for human beings to live eternally within His creation. But Adam and Eve disobeyed God and brought the curse of sin upon all creation.

Strange as it may seem, death is actually not natural, but came with the curse of sin (see 1 Corinthians 15:21, 26). We were originally intended to live forever. At the outset of creation, God breathed His Spirit into the body of Adam (Genesis 2:7). God wanted to live in constant communion with His human creatures forever. However, all of creation is cursed on account of Adam and Eve's sin (Genesis 3:17–19). This cursing includes the curse of death. Like Adam, we are accountable for our transgressions against God's Law. Our lives are lived in painful toil and constant turmoil.

In addition to imminent death, we face the threat of the final judgment. This is not the distant heat death of the universe. This threat lies closer at hand. A day awaits us, hidden from scientific discovery and theological insight, when the Creator will bring His judgment upon all people.

In light of current events, many people think that the last days have arrived. Rather than asking themselves whether they are ready, some people use fancy calculations in order to estimate the time of the Last Day. Others dig up long-standing prophecies from nonbiblical figures such as Nostradamus. Yet they all miss or avoid the all-important question: how can we prepare for the Last Day?

The final day for human beings and Earth does not lie in the comfortable and distant future. Rather, it lies in the (unexpected) near future. In Matthew 24:42–44, Jesus compares the Last Day to the coming of a thief in the night. Nobody can predict when a thief will come. If one could predict, there would probably be no thieves. We hope that we will never have to deal with an intruder in our home. However, such hope alone is worthless. So we turn our thoughts to what we can do. We lock our windows and doors at night. We keep our valuables locked up and make other preparations for safety. Still, cunning thieves are able to evade the most sophisticated preparations.

There will be a Last Day, either when you die or when Jesus returns. Either way, you need to ask whether you are ready to face your impending judgment.

Ready through Christ

The uneasiness people feel when faced with their impending fate is widespread. We have seen how some scientists try to look optimistically toward the future in light of thermodynamic eschatology. But not only do their attempts fail in light of their own assumption, but these scientists also fail to take into account the present threat of death and the promise of a soon-returning Messiah.

St. Paul describes all of creation as waiting in eager expectation for the end (Romans 8:19–21). For those people who place their hope in Christ, waiting is not fearful. We know that in Christ we are redeemed and have already become a new creation. So we eagerly await the visible return of Christ, when we will physically obtain the prize Christ has won for us. We can stand confident in the face of death and the Last Day. We already know the future through the promises of the Gospel.

We live now in the certainty of our redemption. However, our eternal home in the glorious kingdom of God has not yet come. In spite of all appearances, we hold the status of adopted sons and daughters of God (Romans 8:16–19). This was brought about through Christ's death and merit. Hence, theologians speak of our redemption and consequent eternal life as realized *now*. However, we still have the old Adam in us. This is the *not yet* part of redemption. The two cannot be separated. Our redemption now is sure because of Jesus. His resurrection and ascension into heaven assure us of our future resurrection to eternal life, which has yet to come.

Jesus will return to bring His followers to their heavenly home. Hence, those who belong to Christ are ready. All who trust in the death of Christ for the forgiveness of their sins are ready for the end, whether it comes through death or Christ's return.

There is no need for us to fear the threats of science or the thought of death. We can be certain that our eternal life is already secured for us. By Christ's death on the cross, He atoned for the sins of the whole world (1 John 2:2). As the final act of His redemptive work, Christ came back from the grave to prove His conquering of death. Hence, the resurrection of Christ assures us that He conquered death for us and that we, too, will rise to unending life.

Concerning questions about signs of the times or predictions of dates, Paul responds: "For you yourselves are fully aware that the day of the Lord will come like a thief in the night" (1 Thessalonians 5:2). Paul goes on to reassure believers that they are already prepared for Christ's return. Because they trust Christ for their salvation, they are ready and should live in keeping with this readiness.

A life characterized by eager expectation of Christ's return is one that is centered in Christ. All preparation and expectation is rooted in the decisive act of Christ's death and resurrection.

At the appointed time, the Lord Himself will descend from heaven. At that moment all deceased believers in Christ will physically rise from their graves. Meanwhile, those believers who are still living will rise to meet those who rose first. Just as Christ ascended into heaven forty days after His resurrection, we will ascend into heaven to live eternally with God, our Father. (See 1 Thessalonians 4:13–18.)

The Scriptures do not speak of a resurrection of believers before a seven-year "great tribulation." The final judgment will take place as one decisive event. The believers will receive the crown of life Christ won for them. Those people who chose to go their own way will receive their just punishment of eternal condemnation.

The punishment for our sin and guilt was borne by Jesus. Therefore, we, who trust in Him, stand righteous in the sight of God. Our names are written in the Book of Life. When God looks at us, He sees the righteousness of Christ. Hence, His final verdict on us will be *innocent*.

POINTS TO PONDER

No matter how hard scientists try, they cannot investigate anything past the end of time. On a more personal level, we cannot really investigate what happens to a person after the body dies. Yet the world will someday come to an end. And meanwhile, nobody gets out of here alive; we all die sooner or later. Science is left speechless, but even though we can't see it from here, we can look forward to eternal life because of Jesus.

WORDS TO REMEMBER

I know that my Redeemer lives, and at the last He will stand upon the earth. And after my skin has been thus destroyed, yet in my flesh I shall see God. (Job 19:25–26)

18

THERE IS A HEAVEN—REALLY!

A young Christian mother lay in pain, dying of cancer in a hospital. Her unbelieving husband listened as the pastor ministered to her. The husband's only comment was "Nobody ought to suffer like that!" Indirectly, he was saying, "Where is your God now?" The pastor could only respond, "This is why she loves her Savior. She knows that when mysteries and disappointments confront us in our earthly life, they cannot rob her of eternal life in heaven."

The wife's and the husband's views of suffering sharply contrasted because one believed in heaven and the other did not. This underscores the importance of our study on heaven. It points us to our need for the sure and clear promises God makes in His Word, which free us from all doubts and fears about the afterlife.

Some people have said that all we know about our future life in heaven is that everything is good. It is true that our knowledge about heaven is limited by (1) what God has chosen to reveal to us and (2) our limited understanding of spiritual things. Yet there's much that we can learn.

Stop to take stock of what you do know—and do not know—about heaven. As you go through the following discussion, you may be surprised at the large number of scriptural references about eternal life in heaven. Surely, God has reasons for revealing these things to us before we get there.

The promise of heaven offers comfort in time of bereavement (see John 14:1–2) and a challenge to live a godly life on earth (see Colossians 3:1–2). Curious beings that we are, we may wish for more details about our future life in heaven. However, the writers of Scripture did not attempt to answer every question about life or the afterlife (John 20:30–31). When some of our questions remain unanswered, we do well to focus on the chief purpose for which the Scriptures were given to us: to help us know Jesus for eternal life. For other matters, we can trust that God has revealed all we need to know now in His Word.

EXPLORING LIFE AFTER DEATH

Is there a renewed interest in heaven in our times? Yes and no. Yes, because many people are beginning to realize that there must be life beyond what we see now. Some in the scientific community accept the possibility of some kind of spirit world beyond the physical. However, we must also say no because society in general seems less and less interested in what the

Bible says about the matter. Belief in some kind of afterlife is not necessarily the same as accepting the Christian teaching of heaven that is based on the authoritative Scriptures.

Romans 8:38–39 is often read at Christian funerals. This passage states that God's love is stronger than death. Death is not the end and cannot separate us from a glorious life in heaven. God's love for us in Christ Jesus transcends every natural and supernatural experience.

More and more we hear claims of near-death or after-death experiences indicating that human life is not limited to the body. Some claim to have hovered over their own body on an operating table. But do these claims in any way relate to your belief in heaven?

Such experiences may be genuine. Scientists have difficulty confirming or denying them. The fact that so many people have such experiences could indicate that there is life beyond the physical things we experience, but it may not tell us much about that life.

Charles Darwin's theory of evolution has convinced many people that humans are nothing more than a higher form of animal life. They have concluded that humans have no immortal soul and that there can be no resurrection of the body with eternal life in heaven. The Christian heaven is, therefore, often the object of ridicule by some intellectuals and skeptics. Even if not an object of ridicule, this assumption still finds its way into how many people look at life. It finds its way into their worldview.

The secular world may ridicule Christian belief in heaven, as well as nurture gross distortions and misconceptions of that belief. However, Jesus and the apostles emphasize that heaven is not merely something added to our Christian faith but also an essential part of it. If there is no afterlife, the unbelieving world is better off than we are.

Matthew 6:19–21 and 1 Corinthians 15:12–20 speak to the importance of heaven in our faith. Life in heaven should be our ultimate goal. Its promise affects how we live on the earth. The surety of Christ's resurrection gives us hope and courage even in this life. Because of Him, we look forward to our own resurrection.

Even though God has included so much about heaven in our Scriptures (the New Testament uses the term "eternal life" over forty times!), Christian beliefs in heaven have suffered some erosion in modern times. Surveys show that even some church members have doubts and are woefully ignorant of what the Bible teaches about heaven.

Bumper stickers often display Christian words and symbols as well as more mundane thoughts like "I'd rather be fishing." If we truly believe in heaven, why don't we display bumper stickers proclaiming "I'd rather be in heaven"?

In most situations even those who look forward to heaven are not anxious to leave behind their life on earth. Life on earth seems too precious. Relationships here are treasured. For most, heaven seems nebulous and far away. (Exceptions may be those who are terminally ill.)

The apostle Paul gives us a good perspective for life here and now versus life in the hereafter (Philippians 1:22–26). Wanting to go to heaven or stay on earth can be rooted in selfishness, or it could reflect a genuine ambivalence that gives way to accepting God's choices for us. Like Paul, we may continue to serve others through a longer life, but we always serve our brothers and sisters at our Lord's pleasure.

Atheism dogmatically denies the existence of any supreme being apart from and outside of the physical universe. That denial precludes the assertion of divine revelation and any future life with God in heaven. Agnosticism does not explicitly deny the existence of deity, but rather asserts that any certain knowledge about the divine or an afterlife has not been and cannot be reached. On the basis of ancient religious texts and traditions, those believing in reincarnation assert that after death a person's life force or soul transmigrates into other bodies—including plant or animal life.

These beliefs conflict with the Bible's teachings. Atheists, agnostics, and those believing in reincarnation reject the clear, authoritative teachings of the Bible that humans are created in God's image, that we are fallen by nature, and that Jesus came to rescue us from eternal death and give to us eternal life.

The Book of Revelation has much to say about heaven. Revealed to His servant John, these promises are God's truth (1:1–3). As surely as God lives and speaks, there is a life in heaven for all who believe in His Son, Jesus (ch. 22). This truth is a tremendous source of comfort and joy.

If doubts come to you regarding heaven, learn from Paul in 2 Timothy 1:12. We should and can be convinced of heaven and freed of doubts by continuing in God's Word and Sacraments. Through the Word, written and proclaimed, and the promises of Baptism and Absolution, the Lord uplifts and encourages us (see John 8:31–32). In the Lord's Supper, we literally taste the very joys and comforts of heaven itself, given to us in Christ's true body and true blood.

Heaven is real. God's Word is clear on this point. Life in Christ is eternal life. Don't be influenced by the unbelieving world that doesn't know Christ or His Word. Any doubts and fears you may have about the afterlife can be dispelled as you focus on God's sure promises.

Put your confidence in Jesus Christ. He promised that His truth will set you free. Remember that when your sins condemned you to hell, He put you on the road to heaven by His suffering, death, and resurrection. Prayerfully reflect on the "pictures of heaven" in this study and pray that your family, friends, and neighbors will be convinced, with you, of the glories awaiting all who trust in the Lord Jesus.

POINTS TO PONDER

No matter what you read or hear about medical advances, the mortality rate in this country is 100 percent. We all die sooner or later! Yet it is just our body that dies, and this only until we are raised for Judgment Day. And because of Jesus, we are raised for eternal life with Him!

WORDS TO REMEMBER

I consider that the sufferings of this present time are not worth comparing with the glory that is to be revealed to us. (Romans 8:18)

19

NEAR-DEATH EXPERIENCES

When Holly went to the hospital for carpal tunnel surgery, she couldn't have anticipated the surprising events of that day. During surgery, Holly experienced a violent seizure in reaction to a medication. Despite the efforts of doctors and nurses, Holly died. Suddenly, she heard a beatific voice. She saw no one but heard the voice telling her that she could come away now with the person speaking to her or she could come later. She did not know exactly what was happening. She felt blissful. She responded to the voice, saying that she had to go back because she wanted to continue taking care of her family and her responsibilities as a mother and wife. At that point, the doctors resuscitated Holly. She remains alive today and remembers her experience, believing it was God Himself who spoke to her. She attributes the peace she experienced in that event to the promise of salvation God has provided in Jesus Christ.

Not every near-death experience is so peaceful. For example, a young man involved in a horrible auto accident was brought to an emergency room. In a state of incoherence, he suddenly felt himself rising up. He looked around and saw the hospital room. He looked down and saw a body that had lost two of its limbs. He felt sorry for the person who had been disfigured, but it soon occurred to him that he was looking at his very own body. He believed that he had passed out of his body and had been separated from it.

Have you ever talked with someone who has had a near-death experience? People may be reluctant to share personal near-death experience because of self-consciousness, doubts and unspoken questions, or other factors. The section will discuss the claims that are out there and the research being done on them.

MODERN RESEARCH

Many people discount any possibility of near-death experiences because they believe in only naturalism rather than supernatural causes. Some regard these experiences as the result of psychological illnesses, side effects from medications, or mere dreams.

Yet another reason for denying near-death experiences comes from nihilistic assumptions. Nihilism is the philosophical belief that life has no meaning. For the nihilist, nothing happens when a person dies; that person merely ceases to exist. The nihilist believes that when a person dies, he or she does not experience an afterlife, nor have any conscious awareness of anything, because there is nothing existing outside of this life. Unfortunately, both nihilism and naturalism contain unwarranted philosophical claims and do not sufficiently explain away near-death experiences.

A Gallup study estimated in 1982 that nearly eight million people in the United States have had a near-death experience. The poll was subdivided into the different types of near-death experiences people had. The most common experiences reported were visitations to another dimension, life reviews, feelings of bliss, out-of-body experiences, and encounters with other beings.

However, do the numbers of near-death experiences prove the validity of such experiences? Fundamentally, it is difficult to answer this question absolutely because the nature of such events lies outside the realm of science. Near-death experiences are extremely subjective. They can only be observed by the individual involved. In a sense, this phenomenon is one of those "I won't know until I see it for myself" things. However, we should assess the evidence available to us and examine it in light of Scripture.

Near-death experiences are often argued to be the result of three major types of mental illnesses: schizophrenia, delirium, and autoscopic hallucinations. On the other hand, researcher Raymond Moody (b. 1944) has carefully researched near-death experiences and argued that they are not the result of psychological or mental illnesses. Moody offers substantial explanations to refute each of these claims.

Moody notes that near-death experiences contradict many traits of schizophrenia. For example, schizophrenics usually cannot function in society and lead a life of isolation, while most people who have had near-death experiences cope with society better after their experience than they did before it. They are characterized by love and peace and function better in the world around them. Fundamentally, the effects of the near-death experience are positive, while the effects of schizophrenia are negative.

Near-death experiences are also not caused by delirium. Delirium results from a significant chemical imbalance in the brain, which causes disjointed thought patterns or even random hallucinations. In contrast, a near-death experience is characterized by lucid and coherent perception. Moody describes how people suffering from delirium observe images in an impersonal or detached manner, as if they were watching them on a movie screen. A near-death experience, however, is usually described in a highly detailed and personal manner.

Finally, there is the claim that near-death experiences are actually autoscopic hallucinations. Autoscopic hallucinations are when a person sees himself or herself in a third-person manner (i.e., their double) but is aware that this other "them," their double, is a separate distinct person. Moody notes that these hallucinations are only from the perspective of one's own physical body and are therefore limited. In contrast, people with out-of-body experiences have a solid perception of their own body and are able to float or roam around to observe places their body could not occupy. During that entire time the person recognizes their body as theirs and not that of another person or "double." The essential difference is that a person undergoing an out-of-body experience holds a totally different center of perception than the one with a hallucination.

Moody's explanations are fairly well thought out, yet uncertainty remains. Human experience and scientific proposals offer insufficient help for evaluating such experiences. We need the certain testimony of God's Word.

Death as a Result of the Fall

A discussion about near-death experiences, of course, presupposes the reality of death. God's Word does not specifically explain much about near-death experiences. But since the discussion involves death, we must consider the fundamental cause of death: sin.

Scripture tells us, "God made man upright, but they have sought out many schemes" (Ecclesiastes 7:29). When God created Adam and Eve, they lived in a state of perfect righteousness, enjoying peaceful fellowship with God in a life where there was no death. The command God gave Adam and Eve was to abstain from eating from the tree of the knowledge of good and evil in the middle of the garden. If they ate from that tree, death would result (Genesis 2:17). By disobeying God's command, Adam and Eve brought spiritual and physical death to themselves and their posterity (Romans 5:12). Moreover, disorder resulted from their sin.

Medieval theologian Thomas Aquinas noted how the fall resulted in the disorder of human reason and will. People no longer live with unified purpose, thinking and willing what is right. They often place what is wrong ahead of what they know to be right. The disorder resulting from the fall has resulted in an unnatural separation between body and soul, which we call "death."

Martin Luther made special note of this in his treatise *Confession Concerning Christ's Supper*. Luther maintained that the body and soul are in essential unity. Where the body is present, there the soul is present along with it. However, because of the fall, the essential unity between body and soul has been changed, resulting in their separation at death. This view allows for the fact that even though someone is buried, his or her soul exists in an afterlife.

Both 2 Corinthians 5:1–8 and Philippians 1:22–24 describe the separation of body and soul at the time of death. The "tent, which is our earthly home" refers to the mortal body. The "building from God" refers to the glorified body we will receive at the time of the resurrection at the Last Day. Paul teaches that to be at home in the body is to be away from Christ. But, to be apart from the body is to be in Christ's presence. One does not merely cease to exist as nihilism teaches.

The separation of body and soul is the mournful consequence of the first sin. God tells us that He gave the Commandments so that we may have life. In Eden, God gave Adam His commands to show him the way of life and to prevent him from hurting himself. Adam, with Eve's encouragement, chose to disobey God and brought this burden of death upon us all.

Read Romans 5:12–19 to see that all people bear the effects of death from the first man's sin. Some may ask, "Why should I be responsible for what one man did thousands of years ago?" God created Adam and Eve and gave them a free choice affecting the rest of the human race. It is important to note that Adam was not simply one individual, but a human being comprising and representing all humanity. The Hebrew term *adam* means "humankind." Adam comprised all humanity in himself, and therefore we all participated in the fall.

Some might regard Stephen's experience in Acts 7:54–60 as a near-death experience. The nature of Stephen's testimony is mysterious, but it is important to note that he described seeing Christ before the stoning started. Hence, it is not a near-death experience. Note Stephen's prayer and how Jesus, who is "at the right hand of God," stands to welcome Stephen.

Based on John 11:11–14 and 1 Thessalonians 4:14–15, some people believe in *soul sleep*, that the soul or spirit does not consciously enjoy the presence of Christ or the bliss of heaven after a Christian dies. However, read Luke 16:19–31 and Revelation 6:9–10 to see what these passages say about the state of the soul in death. Scripture describes people's souls as conscious or aware after death. *Sleep* in the New Testament, when describing death, is a euphemism that describes our rest in Christ (Hebrews 4:9–11; Revelation 14:13).

CHRIST THE LORD OF LIFE AND DEATH

Whether or not you believe near-death experiences actually occur, two fundamental truths should be noted: (1) you will face God when you die, and (2) all people will die (unless God miraculously intervenes). Because of the separation of the soul and the body at death, the soul lives on while the body lies in the grave. Scripture tells us that the soul meets God in the world beyond, standing before Him in judgment. Christ, who holds the keys of Death and Hades (Revelation 1:18), is the only way to the kingdom of heaven (John 10:9; 14:6). Therefore one's entrance into either eternal condemnation or eternal life is ultimately based on Christ.

Our Lord Jesus Christ knows our human weaknesses and even participated in human death. He died for you and for me, the ungodly, who were undeserving of such a sacrifice.

Christ is Lord over death, as His glorious resurrection shows. Such a victory has brought life to you, granting you the same hope of a bodily resurrection when Christ returns (Romans 6:9–10). Christ came to restore all things, including the disunity between our body and soul (John 5:25–29). Christ redeems you from death. He promises to raise your physical body anew so that you may enjoy eternal life with Him as a whole person.

Because of the limits of science and because the Scriptures do not directly answer many of our questions about near-death experiences, such incidents remain unexplainable. No doubt, research and interest in this topic will continue. But instead of focusing on the unknown, focus on what you can know: peace through Christ.

Christ was willing to suffer on our behalf (see Hebrews 4:14–16). The Book of 2 Corinthians associates death and life with two different ministries: that of Moses and that of Christ (3:7–18). Christ brought what Moses' ministry could not bring—life and glory. Death is confirmed in Moses' ministry, whereas it is annulled in Christ's ministry.

The Law condemns us under its demands. If the Law were the only covenant God gave us, there would be no hope. We would face God's wrath. But the work of Christ delivers us from the condemnation of the Law, thereby delivering us from death's dominion.

Christ, who holds the power over death, brought you from death to life through faith (John 5:24; 8:51). Death no longer has mastery over you, and you are now "more than conquerors" in Christ over death and its dominion (Romans 8:37). You have the hope of the resurrection in which Christ will raise you for future glory.

Death and resurrection are continual realities not only pertaining to Christ but also pertaining to you. His death and resurrection provide the basis for your own personal death and resurrection. The Christian life you live is one of continual dying and rising. As Christians, Christ abides with you by faith. The death of Christ is your death because its effects are "credited to your account." The forgiveness of sins won at the cross was achieved on your behalf and freely given to you. Moreover, you are being renewed through the power of Christ and His Spirit, putting to death the sinful nature and re-creating hearts and minds. The resurrection of Christ is your resurrection because, although it does not destroy the reality of physical death, it gives confidence and courage to face death knowing that the Lord Jesus Christ will raise you on the Last Day.

Before justification the old self cannot possibly please God. By participating in Jesus' death through our Baptism, the old self is put to death (Romans 6:3–14). After justification the new self lives the sanctified life by the working of the Holy Spirit (1 Corinthians 6:9–11). See also 2 Corinthians 4:7–18; Colossians 3:1–17; and 1 John 2:1. Therefore, the death and resurrection of Christ accomplish not only the justification of the Christian but also the sanctification.

Points to Ponder

Stories about near-death and out-of-body experiences circulate in popular literature, but what are we to believe? Circumstantial evidence and personal accounts can be convincing, or perhaps troubling, but what can we really know? And how can we be sure that Satan might not try to use such an experience to confuse or deceive us? Fortunately, our Savior has been through death and defeated it, and He promises not to lose any of us from His loving grip. Thanks be to God for this assurance in the face of our questions!

Words to Remember

The sting of death is sin, and the power of sin is the law. But thanks be to God, who gives us the victory through our Lord Jesus Christ. (1 Corinthians 15:56–57)

20

POPULAR MISCONCEPTIONS ABOUT HEAVEN

- Five-year-old Jenny came home from Sunday School with a puzzled look on her face: "Mommy, our teacher said that in heaven we'll all become angels. Will I have to wear those big wings?"
- Michelle was a high school honor student and was preparing excitedly for graduation evening. Her father had passed away tragically a few months before. Her mother assured her, "Your Daddy will be proud of you. I'm sure he'll be there to celebrate with you."
- Hoping to comfort a grieving friend, Terry said, "The Lord must have needed another angel in heaven. That's why He took your wife."

Examples like these are commonplace among religious people and even among Christians. Some misconceptions about the heavenly life are quite harmless, but others can be damaging to the faith. The Bible reveals all we need to know about heaven and urges us not to be deceived by human thoughts and imagination.

HEAVEN IS FOR EVERYBODY

We have all heard it: "We're all heading for the same place." Like three golfers who tee off together, one goes left, one goes right, one goes down the middle of the fairway, but all end up on the green. "If 'God is love'" (1 John 4:16), the thinking goes, "He must accept all of His creatures into heaven." This wishful thinking forgets about God and disagrees with God's plan of salvation.

God is love, but He is also holy and just. His plan is that only those who receive His love in Christ will be saved (John 3:16–18; 1 John 3:4–10). Unfortunately, even some Christians are swayed by the opinion that a loving God will not send sinners to a fiery hell. This view of Scripture and of Christ is inherently one-sided and inconsistent with the whole of the teachings of the Bible and of Christ Himself.

While there is one God, and we know that He loves all people, Scripture often speaks of pairs: believers and unbelievers, just and unjust, sheep and goats, angels and demons, God and Satan, heaven and hell.

The division between heaven-bound and hell-bound people is not always clear to us in this life. When will the division be clearly seen by all? Matthew

25:34–46 indicates that we will be able to distinguish believers from unbelievers only when Christ returns on Judgment Day.

At that time, He will clearly divide the righteous and the wicked from one another. He will base His judgment on each person's faith, which produces the righteous or unrighteous works described here. Note the description of the righteous: they are blessed by the Father with genuine faith (Matthew 16:16–17). In view of faith, they produced genuine good works. Good works were a consequence of faith, not the other way around. Without faith, unbelievers, then, produced no good works at all.

HEAVEN IS FOR GOOD PEOPLE

Many who realize that heaven is not for everyone fall into another trap—the belief that one earns heaven by being good. They mean those who are morally "good enough" but perhaps not perfect. Weighing the good against the bad, some will make the grade while others will not.

This seemingly reasonable thinking is wrong. No one is good enough to earn heaven (Romans 3:22–24). Everyone breaks God's Law (James 2:10). Paul explains that our righteousness, our right relationship with God, comes only through faith in His Son, Jesus Christ. James explains that breaking one commandment shatters the entire Law. This is similar to throwing a rock against one part of a window but shattering the entire thing. Paul and James both teach that we are saved by grace through faith, which results in good works (see Ephesians 2:8–10).

The curse of this belief is that the person who believes it must live with constant uncertainty: What is "good enough" to get to heaven? Martin Luther languished under this cloud of doubt and fear until he discovered the liberating Gospel of Christ.

How does anyone become good enough for heaven? Read Ephesians 2:8–9 and Romans 3:22–24. We are good enough for heaven only by God's mercy. God declares us righteous through faith in Jesus Christ, who paid the price for our sins, freeing us from the curse of condemnation and doubt.

What happens to the Gospel of Christ when we try to work our way into heaven? Galatians 1:6–7 says that if we reject God's Gospel of salvation in Jesus Christ alone, we have no Gospel at all and remain under the curse of the Law.

HEAVEN IS ON EARTH

Some who wish to discredit Christian belief in a real heaven assert a different heaven-related belief. Denying that there is any afterlife, and realizing that good and evil should in some way be rewarded or punished, they theorize that we must create our own heaven or hell on earth.

Such a belief denies that humans, unlike animals, are created in God's image with an immortal soul that cannot die (Genesis 1:27). It also denies the necessity of a final judgment on good and evil (Revelation 20:11–15), which the Scriptures, and to an extent even human experience, prove cannot be obtained "on earth."

Christians do experience a foretaste of heaven in their earthly life, but it is no substitute for the eternal life promised in the Bible.

HEAVEN IS MERELY A CONDITION

Space travel and powerful telescopes have not yet located a physical heaven "out there." From this, some have concluded that heaven must be merely a "condition" or state of mind.

Jesus emphasized that heaven is a real place by comparing it to a house with many rooms (John 14:2–3). God did not create us as mental or physical beings only. He created us body and soul. Therefore, He will save us body and soul. (See 2 Corinthians 5:1–10, where Paul compares the body to a tent or dwelling for the soul.)

To be sure, mysteries remain. Our resurrected and glorified bodies will be "spiritual" bodies like the body of the risen Christ. What kind of location does a spiritual body require? And where is this heaven located? The Scriptures speak of heaven as being "up." For example, Jesus ascended into heaven and will come down from heaven when He returns. Beyond that, heaven's location must remain a mystery.

FROM HEAVEN THEY SMILE DOWN ON US

Not infrequently when a loved one has died and is missing an important event, we hear it said that the deceased "is here" or "is smiling down on us today." This view of the dead having intimate knowledge of every affair on earth may arise out of wishful thinking or sentimentality, but God's Word does not support such a view.

Ecclesiastes 9:5 and Isaiah 63:16 say that a dead person has no knowledge of things on earth. On the other hand, Scripture does indicate that the martyrs in heaven do have some sense of what is happening on earth, or at least what happened while they were alive, and that the souls of the dead do express concern over the living (see Revelation 6:9–10; Luke 16:27–28).

God could, of course, give saints in heaven a special vision of pleasant things on earth. Jesus once related an illustrative story to emphasize that we should not expect communication between heaven and earth. In Luke 16:19–31, a rich man in hell requested that a messenger be sent to his brothers on earth, but the Lord did not fulfill his request. God communicates to us through His revealed Word, which contains all we need to know now.

Any claims that God communicates with individuals in other ways must be judged on the basis of what the written Word tells us.

Luke 16:29–31 points to Moses and the prophets (i.e., Scripture) as the way heaven communicates with us earthlings, but the Bible says little about what people in heaven may know about intimate, earthly affairs. Ecclesiastes 9:5 and Isaiah 63:16 seem to indicate that the souls of the dead do not possess omniscience—knowledge of all things—which is a divine attribute. However, Revelation 6:9–10 and Luke 16:27–28 suggest that they may have some knowledge as to events and behaviors on earth.

In Heaven We Become Angels

You may have seen cartoons where people in heaven have sprouted wings and are lounging on puffy clouds. Or perhaps you have viewed the classic movie *It's a Wonderful Life*, in which the bungling angel Clarence struggles to earn his wings. Many believe that we become angels upon entering heaven.

One cult claiming the name Christian goes even further. They teach that in heaven we can become gods. How absurd! Even becoming angels goes beyond what the Scriptures say. Angels are special creatures of God whose purpose is to serve His redeemed people. But in light of our discussion of angels in a previous chapter, would becoming an angel be a promotion or a demotion?

According to Romans 8:17, Christians in heaven have a unique title and position. Believers are "fellow heirs with Christ," inheriting with Him everything that belongs to God. For a human being, becoming an angel would be a demotion. Angels are only messengers, while believers are sons and daughters of God. In fact, the angels long to understand the promise of salvation for us in Christ (1 Peter 1:12). The divine Son of God assumed not angelic nature, but human nature —a real human body and a rational human soul.

We will, though, have opportunities to participate in some activities with angels when we are in heaven (see Revelation 5:11–14). Although we will never be angels, we will be close to God with everlasting innocence, righteousness, and blessedness, and we will continually praise and worship Him in heaven.

St. Peter Guards the Pearly Gates

The notion that St. Peter is the gatekeeper of heaven, admitting or rejecting applicants, often comes up in jokes or cartoons. But this teaching is misleading and damaging to some.

In Revelation, the Bible describes twelve "pearly gates," not one gate. Twelve angels stand at these gates (Revelation 21:12–13). Peter, as spokesman for all the disciples, is given the "keys of the kingdom" (Matthew 16:19).

Some have concluded from this that Peter would control the "pearly gates." The Bible explains elsewhere that the power to "open" heaven for others—the forgiveness of sins through the Gospel—is given to the whole Church and exercised through the pastoral office (see Matthew 18:18; John 20:21–23).

Who decides which people enter heaven and which will not? Jesus Himself decides who enters heaven (Matthew 25:34; Revelation 20:11–12). The "gatekeeper" is the door Himself, Jesus Christ. He is the only way to the Father (John 14:6). The manner of our entry into heaven does not seem important in the Bible. Neither is Peter responsible for our salvation. Our focus should always be on Him who is King of kings and Lord of lords.

As a student of God's Word, you should be able to sort out the truths and the untruths about heaven. Not all speculations about life in heaven undermine our saving faith, but even the "harmless" ones can detract from or trivialize what the Scriptures actually teach. They should not be encouraged.

The most damaging misconceptions are those that do not recognize Jesus as the only way to the Father and the glories of heaven. Don't be deceived by those high-sounding philosophies that "all religions are good" and "we're all heading for the same place." Stay grounded in the biblical truth that, though Christ died for all, heaven is for those who know Him as the one who rescued them from sin, death, and hell by His death and resurrection.

Points to Ponder

Our ideas of heaven are no substitute for God's plans, so let's be careful about what we do and do not know from Scripture. Those who belong to Christ will be joyously surprised and more than satisfied when they get there!

Words to Remember

As the heavens are higher than the earth, so are My ways higher than your ways and My thoughts than your thoughts. (Isaiah 55:9)

21

PICTURES OF HEAVEN

In an elementary school religion class, the teacher announced, "Our study today is about heaven. I want each of you to draw a picture of something you expect to see or do when you are in heaven." Pictures submitted included angels, a crown, a playground, a flower garden, and many others. The teacher later singled out Kevin's drawing for comment: "Why did you draw the picture of a man?" Kevin's reply surprised everyone: "Because the best part of heaven will be that I get to see Jesus."

Kevin got it right. The best part of heaven is to see Jesus face-to-face and be in His presence forever. The Scriptures, however, do add a number of grand and glorious "pictures of heaven" that increase our joy of anticipation and our determination to remain faithful to our Lord.

Biblical pictures of heaven are necessarily given in terms of our earthly experience and cannot fully describe the future life. Depictions of heaven in religious paintings or films must be viewed with care, since they are based on the artists' imaginations.

Read Romans 5:2 and 1 Corinthians 13:12, and consider what purposes such paintings or films might serve for you now. The attempts by artists or filmmakers to picture heaven should assure us that heaven is a glorious place in God's presence. However, any attempt to illustrate heaven surely fails in comparison to the glory we will experience in heaven as we enjoy the immediate presence of God and Christ.

PARADISE

The term evokes images of all that we think of as the good life and easy living. The word occurs only three times in Scripture and was used by Jesus Himself in two of those three times.

How much detail does Jesus give you about paradise in Luke 23:43? Notice that paradise is not described except for the fact that the thief and Jesus will be there together. Perhaps Jesus was drawing on common Jewish understandings from Scripture (see Genesis 2:8–10) that the final paradise will be like a garden.

Paradise naturally causes us to think of the Garden of Eden, where Adam and Eve lived close to God in a beautiful place. The advertising world has borrowed the word *paradise* to lure us to exotic places: resorts, golf courses, and South Sea islands. God's paradise will provide far greater pleasures—and without high prices, sand traps, or mosquitoes.

Paul cites a visit to paradise in 2 Corinthians 12:2–4. Why couldn't Paul tell us more about paradise from this experience? Paul himself does not seem to fully understand his experience. The purpose of it was apparently not to show him everything that goes on in heaven. It is quite possible that human language simply cannot express Paul's experience.

The word *paradise* originally meant a pleasure ground or park. The word *Eden* means "delight." You may picture heaven as a delightful park, but you will still be in for pleasant surprises when you get there!

THE FATHER'S HOUSE

Jesus Himself in the Upper Room gives a most endearing picture of heaven on the eve of His crucifixion. Jesus emphasizes the "homeyness" of heaven (John 14:1–3). The word given as *rooms* in the ESV is not easily translated from the original language. (For example, the King James Version uses the word *mansions*.) The typical construction of Israelite homes helps us understand the passage better. Israelite families usually dwelt in a collection of houses built around the first house erected by the head of the family. These homes were usually enclosed by a wall and shared a "compound" where the family members could work and play. This group of buildings was called "the house of . . ." followed by the father's name.

First Kings 12:21–26, describes the rivalry between King Rehoboam and Jeroboam, showing how broadly the ancient Israelites sometimes applied this picture of household/family. The house of David included the entire tribe or kingdom of Judah. The house of Saul included the entire tribe of Benjamin. Thus, a house implies completeness or fullness.

The word for "rooms" conveys with certainty that there is enough space for all in the Father's glorious presence. Our focus in this picture should be on dwelling with our loving Father, rather than on any particular kind of structure.

THE HOLY CITY

This picture of heaven, extremely meaningful to the believers of Jesus' day, becomes meaningful for us as we realize that we are the "new Israel" of which the Bible speaks.

Some people take Revelation 21:2–4 literally, but most Christians realize that Revelation is largely symbolic (e.g., certainly Jesus is not an actual lamb with seven horns and seven eyes as described in 5:6). Jerusalem epitomized glory and honor and power to the early Christians. The temple there stood for God's presence, His dwelling with His people. This must also be our focus.

Do we expect—as some do—that we shall be literally walking on streets of gold (not a very comfortable walk) or riding up to the New Jerusalem on some kind of vehicle?

A better thought: in the new Jerusalem, we shall be in the company of Abraham, Moses, Ruth, David, Isaiah, Mary, and other believers as God dwells among us.

"REST"

Jesus promised this rest to all who come to Him in faith. Read His beautiful promise in Matthew 11:25–30. True rest is being with Jesus and free of all earthly troubles. The rest and peace we humans crave begins on earth but is far from perfect until we reach the heavenly home. Ironically, the perfect life begins at death for believers.

Revelation 14:13 is often read at funerals. Why are those who die "in the Lord" called "blessed"? This promise mentions only that in heaven we are at rest from our earthly sufferings, but a believer's rest is more than relief from earthly suffering. The rest given to believers at death is being in God's presence (Ecclesiastes 12:7), where there is perfect relaxation and peace.

Rest in heaven is a perfect peace, but we should not equate this rest with inactivity. Human beings were made to be active. Adam and Eve in the garden were not simply swinging in hammocks. They were to tend the garden. In heaven we will be at rest, but we won't be couch potatoes. There, we will continually celebrate God's grace in Christ in song and worship (Revelation 5:9–14).

FOREVER WITH THE LORD

There are many unknowns about life in heaven, but we do know its most important feature.

When Christ returns for the final time on the Last Day, believers, both the living and the dead, will be "caught up" to join Him (1 Thessalonians 4:17–18). Our life with Christ in perfect, resurrected bodies will be eternal, which is the point Paul is making to comfort the Thessalonians and us. The Lord's presence with us on earth is real and powerful, but it cannot be compared with the joy of being with Him in heaven.

In Philippians 1:21–26, Paul contrasts his service on earth with his rest in heaven. He also wrestles over which he prefers. In the end, he trusts that God will decide the time for his departure. Paul concludes that whether in heaven or on earth, his life is one of service to his neighbor.

The Spirit's presence among us, and even within us, comforts and sustains us now, but we are still hounded by evil forces. Evil cannot exist in God's presence in heaven. God is light. God is love. "Forever with the Lord" is the essence of heaven!

The Crown of Life

In heaven, God's people wear crowns. These are variously described as a "crown of righteousness" (2 Timothy 4:8), a "crown of glory" (1 Peter 5:4), and a "crown of life" (Revelation 2:10). Even if these crowns are literal, they still have symbolic meaning, just like earthly crowns.

On earth, our instinctive desire to be recognized and honored is often thwarted. Others rule over us and sometimes oppress us. In heaven, we will be "on top of the world." All of God's people will be kings and queens. The King of kings will share His honor with us. Whether there are specific ways in which we shall share in His authority and lordship remains to be seen.

In biblical times, a crown was also given to athletes (1 Corinthians 9:25). How will our crown be superior to theirs? In the Olympic games and in athletic events during biblical times, winners were often rewarded with crowns of laurel. In a few short weeks, these would dry out and eventually have to be discarded. In contrast, our crowns are eternal.

I Shall Know Fully

One of the delights of heaven will be complete knowledge. Many of us have "God only knows" questions that we would like to ask once we are in heaven.

Read 1 Corinthians 13:12 and 1 John 3:2 to grasp how your mind will be improved and what sights will greet your eyes. God will share His knowledge with us, and we'll see Him as He is.

Like our bodies, our minds will somehow be glorified to resemble the mind of God. Most important will be our knowledge of God Himself, who now often seems far away and mysterious. It is possible that questions we have now may seem outdated and irrelevant in His glorious presence, but there is no comparison between here and now and there and then!

A Spiritual Body

God saves us in body and soul. At committal services in the cemetery, we often hear from 1 Corinthians 15 about the "spiritual body."

Although the words seem contradictory, Paul is expressing a deep, spiritual truth. Our real bodies will be resurrected like Christ's body (see Job 19:26; Philippians 3:20–21). How this will happen, we do not know. What we do know is this: what is resurrected will not be just "spirit," but our glorified, earthly frame.

In 1 Corinthians 15, Paul relates Christ's transforming work (Philippians 3:21; 1 Corinthians 15:45) to the "spiritual body" we shall have (v. 44). He says that our flesh and blood "cannot inherit the kingdom of God" (v. 50). However, our bodies shall be more than natural, sinful, perishable flesh and blood—they shall be "spiritual" because of His transformation. Our bodies will be like the glorified body of Jesus after His resurrection. To be glorified like Jesus—that will be heaven!

The pictures and descriptions of your future life in heaven are overwhelming. Ponder and reflect on them often. Let them sustain and comfort you when the going gets rough in your earthly life. Picture the glories of heaven, and you will want to remain faithful unto death and receive the crown of life!

Anticipating heaven's glories will draw you closer to your Savior, who reminds us that we must pass through much tribulation to enter into the kingdom of God (John 16:33; Romans 8:35–39). Through His own suffering and death on earth, Christ opened the kingdom of heaven to all believers. Look forward to spending an eternity with Him!

POINTS TO PONDER

God created us with imagination and some capability for abstract thought, but we are still finite beings. Scripture has many hints about what heaven and eternal life are like but often resorts to metaphors because the whole thing is so much more than we can grasp. Christians have a lot to look forward to, much more than we can yet know!

WORDS TO REMEMBER

No eye has seen, nor ear heard, nor the heart of man imagined, what God has prepared for those who love Him. (1 Corinthians 2:9)

22

QUESTIONS ABOUT HEAVEN

Joey sat watching his older brother play baseball. During a lull in the action, he startled his father with a question: "Will I be able to play baseball when I get to heaven? Mommy said that when we get to heaven everything will be perfect."

Joey had been handicapped from birth. Joey's father tried to answer carefully: "I hope so, but God hasn't told us for sure that there will be any baseball in heaven. I'm sure you'll have lots of fun things to do. We'll just have to wait and see."

We are curious creatures. Such questions about heaven abound, not only from children but also from adults. We need not ignore such questions. Neither should we become overly involved with them. The best approach is to deal with them cautiously, using insights from Scripture.

ACTIVITIES IN HEAVEN

What can we possibly do for all eternity in heaven? We are activity-oriented beings. Adam and Eve were active in the Garden of Eden before their fall into sin. Fishermen may dream of lakes and rivers, golfers may picture lush golf courses, scholars may think of books and libraries, and so on. But what should we realistically expect?

Earlier we read that worship will be an important activity. This worship may well include portions of the Sunday liturgical services to which we are accustomed. It is certain to be joyful.

What about other possible activities? Since food is so central to our earthly life, we are naturally curious about eating and drinking. The Bible does not discourage us on this matter.

Jesus implies that there will be some kind of eating and drinking in heaven (Matthew 26:29). The numerous parables and references to banquets in the heavenly kingdom suggest joyful feasting and drinking. And recall that Jesus performed His first miracle at a wedding feast!

When we are in heaven, we will have a "spiritual body." Will we eat and drink like Jesus did after His resurrection? Obviously there are mysteries to be resolved. Whether in eating and drinking or any other activity, one thing is certain: there will be no boredom in heaven!

Read Revelation 2:26–27 and 3:21 to see what other activities the saints will participate in. In both passages, Jesus states that we will rule with Him in heaven.

RELATIONSHIPS

Since relationships are so vital to our earthly life, it is only natural that we are curious about relationships in heaven. Human beings are created to be in happy relationships. Sinful selfishness wreaks havoc with our relationships now, but we can be sure that they will be perfectly restored in the glories of heaven. The Scriptures don't give us many details about relationships there.

Matthew 19:29–30 reveals that family relationships will be split in this life and that to come. Marriage, of course, is a blessing for earthly life and a necessity for the bearing and raising of children. This will no longer be necessary in heaven. Jesus' statement about marriage in Matthew 22:23–30 also answers a question from people who have been married more than once: "Which spouse will I be with in heaven?" Apparently, sexual attraction or gender differences will not be a factor. We could probably think of heaven in terms of "one big happy family."

Read Acts 2:42–47, where heavenly relationships are best foreshadowed. No one will be poor, needy, hungry, or sick. The Word and Sacraments, so essential here on earth, will no longer be necessary—we will be in the immediate presence of God and the Lamb. Unity and love will continue to be expressed.

RECOGNIZING AND KNOWING ONE ANOTHER

At Christian funerals we hear of a grand and glorious reunion. Will we recognize one another in heaven? The Scriptures provide only clues and hints, but they are all positive.

Paul makes a broad statement about the full knowledge we will have in heaven (1 Corinthians 13:12). Full knowledge means to know and understand as God now does and we do not. We can expect mysteries to be solved and our many "Why?" questions to be answered.

At Jesus' transfiguration, Moses and Elijah appeared and were easily recognized by the three disciples. They probably were not wearing nametags! This at least suggests that in heaven we, too, will recognize the believers from biblical times and others who have gone before us into glory. Mysteries remain, but we should not doubt that our knowing as God knows us includes recognizing and enjoying our loved ones.

PETS

Will there be pets in heaven? Will that precious dog, cat, or bird be there for us to enjoy as we did on earth? This is another question to which the Bible gives no direct answer.

Several animals or animal-like creatures are pictured as being in heaven or coming from heaven. Read Revelation 4:7; 5:6; and 19:11 to see what animals are listed. The lion, ox, eagle, lamb, and horse, mentioned as animals or as animal features, serve as symbols of heavenly characteristics. For example, the lamb stands for Christ, who offered Himself for our sins. These passages neither prove nor disprove the place of animals in heaven.

Contrary to what evolutionists try to tell us, there is a huge gap between humans, who are created in God's image, and animals created for man's use. We do know that "the resurrection of the body" speaks only of humans. The sentiment that there may be a special "pet heaven" is not taught in the Bible.

Can God possibly re-create a special pet or even create new pets for our enjoyment? We know that with God, all things are possible. Adam and Eve enjoyed animals in the first Paradise before they fell into sin. We do well to leave the whole matter of heavenly pets in God's hands. If they do not appear in glory, it will in no way detract from the glory.

DEGREES OF GLORY

Will the residents of heaven enjoy varying degrees of glory? On this subject God's Word again provides little information but indicates that God does plan some "rewards of grace" (see Daniel 12:3; Luke 19:16–19).

Some sects or cults, such as the Mormons, strongly encourage members to work for a higher status in heaven (see *Comparative Views on Life After Death*). However, the Bible does not encourage us to think of different levels of heaven. Although Paul does once refer to knowing someone who was "caught up to the third heaven" (2 Corinthians 12:2), he does not encourage us to base a doctrine on that unusual experience. The experience seems to have taken Paul's acquaintance beyond the visible firmament, and even outer space, into the very presence of God. Since God exists apart from His creation, so it would seem that this man might even have been taken out of creation. His experience was so profound and so personal that he was prohibited from revealing all the details.

On the other hand, God made Adam and Eve different. He does dispense special gifts to believers on earth (1 Corinthians 12:11) so God has no problem creating us different from one another. Angels have "ranks" in heaven (e.g., Michael and Gabriel are called "archangels"). We should not imagine that everyone in heaven will appear the same or melt into some amorphous celestial unity.

Jesus emphasized that we should never think in terms of power over others (Matthew 19:28–29; 20:23). Special positions in heaven would have to be positions of grace. Jesus did not appear to be anxious to elaborate on "degrees of glory," so there is little point in speculating beyond what He revealed.

We have also learned that in heaven all believers will reign with Jesus as kings. Jesus used earthly terms, such as "thrones" and "kingdoms," to describe spiritual realities that are still beyond our comprehension. We do well to wait and see how these special honors are experienced. Above all, there can be no spirit of competition for higher glory among heaven-bound people. Jesus made this plain (Mark 10:42–45).

Your basic attitude as you look forward to the glories of heaven should be one of humility, according to 1 Peter 5:6. We are not to seek honor, but trust that God will bestow honors in His way and His time.

Curiosity about heaven will always be with us. This is not bad. God does not fault you for being curious about the unknown things of heaven, but He does ask you to let it be controlled and limited and to keep your focus on the sure things He has revealed in His Word. Meanwhile, He gives us work to do here and now.

The important questions about heaven are answered. The way to heaven—most important of all—is clear and certain. The kingdom of heaven is open to all believers in Jesus. He atoned for their sins by His sacrificial death on the cross and His victorious resurrection. The Bible's pictures of heaven, many of them in symbolic language, portray a future life of joy and honor that has no end. This is the heaven God wants you to enjoy. Already you have a taste of that joy as you live your new life in Christ by the power of the Holy Spirit. Your worship and love foreshadow what will be perfected in heaven. As a stranger and pilgrim on earth, you enjoy your earthly blessings but always live in joyful anticipation of that glorious future God has planned for you as His gift through Jesus Christ.

POINTS TO PONDER

God richly blesses us as we live here on earth, but He has much more in mind for our life with Christ in heaven. Think of how a world-class symphony orchestra's music compares to a grade school band. The grade school band may be good but is probably a little off-key from time to time. Meanwhile, the orchestra is in tune, in sync, and playing glorious music. There is really no comparison between the orchestra and the children's band, and there is no comparison between heaven and what we know now.

WORDS TO REMEMBER

I press on toward the goal for the prize of the upward call of God in Christ Jesus. (Philippians 3:14)

23

THAT OTHER PLACE

Little Julie came home with a disturbed look on her face: "Mommy, I saw two guys arguing on the street, and one guy told the other one to 'go to hell.' Isn't hell a terrible place to be?"

Her concerned mother tried to explain: "He must have been very angry and didn't know what else to say. Maybe he doesn't really know what hell is."

This little incident points up a general ignorance that prevails concerning the seriousness of hell. Even Christians often need reminders or refreshers on this point. The Bible is clear and explicit about the reality of hell. We cannot think of heaven without being aware of "that other place."

HELL

Hell is one of those four-letter words we hear bandied about glibly and carelessly. Perhaps some people have no understanding of the horror of hell. Perhaps others do not believe it exists.

We seldom hear serious discussions about hell even among believers. Perhaps not even from the pulpit. Why is this so? Even believers may not take the reality of hell seriously. Also, hell is difficult to talk about if you believe that someone you know might go there. Fear of ridicule for believing in such "old-fashioned ideas" may keep us from speaking (or preaching) about hell.

THE REALITY OF HELL

Expressions like "war is hell" may indicate that for some people, hell is nothing more than intense suffering on earth. Even some who believe in a real heaven cannot accept a real hell. God is love, the argument goes, and could not punish anyone eternally. But this argument overlooks another important attribute of God.

The God of great love is also righteous and just and cannot close His eyes to sin and unbelief (Deuteronomy 5:7–15). Christianity that has been influenced by the New Age movement (itself influenced by Hinduism) often minimizes or rejects the concepts of God's righteousness and justice.

Read John 3:18, and consider how these words of Jesus overturn those who argue that "God would never send anyone to hell." God does not force people to go to hell, but He does *let* them go there if they reject His love and forgiveness in Christ.

Rather than argue "hell versus no hell," we do well to examine what God in His wisdom and for our good has revealed to us in His Word. Unpleasant as the subject may be, the Scriptures are clear on the matter. The Bible uses the word *hell* or its equivalent over sixty times. Even Jesus, loving and forgiving as He is, did not hesitate to describe hell.

Jesus speaks bluntly about the reality and horror of hell in Matthew 25:41–46. Those who go to hell are cursed. Hell was originally prepared as a prison for the devil and his angels. It is eternal and fiery.

In His love and concern for people, Jesus warns against unbelief and its consequences. We, too, should warn others of hell. God has revealed the horror of hell for the sake of both unbelievers and believers. Frankly, the teaching about hell should strike fear in the hearts of unbelievers and make them ready for the Gospel (Matthew 10:28).

Believers, or Christians, need to be reminded of the reality of hell for a twofold purpose. As believers, we should realize that (1) we were headed for hell because of our sins (Ephesians 2:3), but that (2) we are rescued from hell through hearing and believing the Gospel of Christ (Ephesians 2:4–7; Romans 10:13–14).

WHAT, WHERE, AND WHEN

As with heaven, the Scriptures can speak of hell only in human terms and pictures. Spiritual things are still beyond our comprehension, so God uses words that we can understand. We do know that the essence of hell is total separation from God's love and care. Though unbelievers do not receive God's Spirit, God does not totally abandon them during their earthly life. He still shows mercy to them in many ways. In hell, residents will learn what it is to be totally without God's love and care.

Speaking through Peter, God calls unbelievers to repent of their sins and be baptized into Christ for the forgiveness of their sins (Acts 2:38–39). This promise of forgiveness through Baptism, incorporation into Christ, and the gift of the Holy Spirit is for all people, including infants and children.

The Scriptures refer to hell using terms that are not always easily translated or understood (see Appendix 3). The Scriptures depict hell as separation from God's gracious presence, in eternal fire (Matthew 25:41), utter darkness, and intense physical and spiritual agony (weeping and gnashing teeth; see Matthew 8:12). The image of flames is most commonly used today. Five times, the Book of Revelation graphically refers to being thrown into a "lake of fire." How literally should we take these images? Since we are dealing with spiritual mysteries, caution is certainly in order.

Some have argued—perhaps out of wishful thinking—that suffering in hell cannot be everlasting. They have advocated what is known as "annihilation." Already at death, some say, the human person goes out of existence completely. This, of course, ignores all that the Bible says about the immortality of the soul created in the image of God.

The Bible contrasts everlasting death with everlasting life. Both are eternal—without end. Read again what Jesus says in Matthew 10:28, and then read 2 Thessalonians 1:8–10, which speaks of hell as "eternal destruction." *Destruction* is not easily defined. Words like *incapacitated* or *ruined* come to mind, but they seem more passive than *destruction*. Destruction is not annihilation; hell is destruction that lasts forever, as well as total separation from God's love and care.

Mark 9:47–48 describes the endless suffering of hell. Because the human soul is immortal, hell begins at death—just as heaven begins at death for believers. Recall Jesus' story about a rich man who had died and found himself in hell. He pleaded to Abraham for his brothers who were still living on earth (Luke 16). Clearly the wicked enter hell right away.

Read John 5:28–29 to see what it says to those who believe that death and the grave are the end and that there is no resurrection. Endless suffering is like a wiggling worm that suffers in the flames but never dies.

As with heaven, the exact location of hell is difficult to define. It is not beneath the ground as some ancient pagan religions described it. Again, these are spiritual things beyond our comprehension. The Bible does hint at general directions: heaven is up; hell is down. But these may simply be examples of God working with people's existing ideas about the universe, not road maps to heaven and hell. The Apostles' Creed states that Jesus "descended into hell" and "ascended into heaven." We do well to leave it at that.

Degrees of Punishment

There is some indication—though no details—that in hell some will receive greater punishment than others.

Read Matthew 11:23–24 to see which unbelievers can expect greater punishment (whatever that may be). Those who have had the greatest opportunities to know Jesus and rejected Him—like those in Capernaum where Jesus lived—can expect the greatest severity of hell.

Why Hell?

Unpleasant as the subject is, hell is real. To deny this is to question the truthfulness of Jesus Himself. But why do you think God has revealed this so emphatically? The doctrine of hell is explicit and uncompromising so that unbelievers will repent and believe, and so that we Christians proclaim the Gospel of salvation to rescue them from hell (see 2 Corinthians 6:2).

Hell is little understood. Many have serious doubts about its existence; others blatantly deny that there is a hell. Don't be swayed by this so-called wisdom of the unbelieving world. Understand the biblical teaching that the "wages of sin is death" (Romans 6:23a). This is much more than physical death. Death, we have seen, is eternal separation from God's love and care in a place called hell.

God, in His love for us sinners, has provided an escape from the tortures of hell: "The free gift of God is eternal life in Christ Jesus our Lord" (Romans 6:23). Thank Him daily for that gift. Remember, too, that God is "not wishing that any should perish, but that all should reach repentance" (2 Peter 3:9). The horrors of hell should cause you to increase your prayers for the lost and your zeal to reach them with the saving Gospel of Christ.

Points to Ponder

Words and metaphors only go so far, and however awful we think hell might be, the reality is much worse. Fortunately and amazingly, God wants everyone to be saved for eternal life in Christ, and He makes this offer to all.

Words to Remember

Whoever believes in the Son has eternal life; whoever does not obey the Son shall not see life, but the wrath of God remains on him. (John 3:36)

24

LIVING FOR HEAVEN

When Tony went to work in a rough-and-tumble lumber mill in the Northwest, he knew it would be a largely unfriendly environment for a Christian. When he returned home after several months, his pastor expressed his concern for Tony, "How did you fare? They probably made it hard for you as a Christian." Tony seemed rather unconcerned, "It wasn't bad. They haven't found out yet that I am a Christian."

Tony, like many believers, needed to be reminded that heaven-bound people cannot blend in comfortably with the unbelieving world. Our earthly life must reflect that we are citizens of heaven. God in His wisdom foresaw this need and provided for it in the Scriptures. The life in heaven is a continuation and perfection of our spiritual life on earth. In view of the glories of heaven, we need not make the mistake Tony made. God provides the resources needed to help us bear witness to our heavenly Savior (1 Peter 2:10–12).

Baptized into Christ, you are on the road to heaven. But how should you see your life now? As God's holy people and royal priests (1 Peter 2:9), we are temporary residents on earth, passing through on our way to heaven.

With a view toward heaven, we can pinpoint six areas in which a Christian's attitudes and actions reflect a heaven-centered life.

"LET US WORSHIP AND BOW DOWN" (PSALM 95:6)

Heaven is pictured as a worshiping community. Saints, angels, and elders voice their praises to God. It is the dominant activity in heaven.

Revelation 7:9–12 points us towards the dominant theme of all worship, whether on earth or in heaven. The dominant theme for worship is thanking and praising God our Father for salvation through Jesus Christ, given to us by the Holy Spirit.

Worship is the first and natural response of all who receive the love of God that comes through Jesus Christ. What are we to think of those who have no desire or very little desire to worship God seriously?

Jesus expects heaven-bound people to worship "in spirit and truth" (John 4:24). Worship must be directed to the only true God—Father, Son, and Holy Spirit—and must come from the heart. In John's Gospel, the truth is always associated with the person and teachings of Jesus.

"Born Again to a Living Hope" (1 Peter 1:3)

We may wonder why God has told us so much about the glories of our future life in heaven. He wants us to be hope-filled people on earth. Hope points to your future but gives joy for the present. Christian hope is not mere wishing, such as "I hope it doesn't rain tomorrow." Christian hope is a sure thing.

The Book of 1 Peter declares the fact, the bedrock truth, that is the basis for our hope. Our hope is based on the reality of Christ's resurrection from the dead. According to Peter, our new birth (1:3) through the Word (1:23) occurred at our Baptism into Christ's resurrection (3:21). The sure hope we have of heaven is a motivating and sustaining force as we live in an imperfect world.

Read 1 Peter 1:6–9, and consider the situations in which you find your hope most helpful. The hope that is ours through our Baptism into Christ helps us in times of suffering and disappointment. With Christ and in Christ there is hope for the future.

In 1 Peter 3:8–17, the apostle writes about suffering. In endurance and suffering the door is open to speak of our faith in Christ and to pray that others will come to faith (evangelism). The road to glory is not always a glorious road, but it does lead to glory. In this hope, God's people can live and rejoice!

"Set Your Minds on Things That Are Above" (Colossians 3:2)

If the view of heaven provides a living hope, it must also affect the way you live before you get there. Your mind-set should be one that gives priority to things that are spiritual and eternal. Jesus' miracles show that He is concerned about our temporal needs of food, clothing, shelter, and health, but He often warned against giving priority to them. Heaven is a treasure much more valuable than anything we might find on earth (Matthew 6:19–21).

We necessarily experience some tensions here: How much time and money to invest in temporal things? How much to "lay away" for a rainy day? We must begin with the basic principle that "if we have food and clothing, with these we will be content" (1 Timothy 6:8). But beyond that, how are we to distinguish between needs and wants? We know, too, that what we invest in evangelism and world missions bears fruit for eternity, while material things are short-lived. Handling this tension of the earthly versus the heavenly requires the wisdom of a Solomon!

In our lives as stewards, we need to balance our focus on earthly and heavenly concerns according to God's priorities. What works for one Christian may not work for others because of different circumstances or opportunities involving stewardship matters. This struggle requires much prayer and reflection on God's Word. Through His grace, God strengthens us in our vocations as we choose, plan, and decide.

Matthew 6:33 tells us what we should always keep before us: "the kingdom of God and His righteousness." We must resolve that spiritual things have top priority in our lives and trust God to provide the material things we need.

"Love One Another" (1 John 4:7)

Another mark of God's heaven-bound people is genuine Christian love that will be perfected in heaven. Chapter 13 of 1 Corinthians reminds us that love will continue there even after faith and hope are fulfilled. That loving community must have its beginning among Christians on earth.

According to Acts 4:32–37, did the first Christians live up to this expectation? The early Christians clearly understood and practiced Christian love. Sharing material blessings seemed to come naturally for the first Christians as they appreciated God's love for them. You can find examples that could be drawn from modern life as well.

It should also be noted that the saints in Jerusalem later fell on hard times, and offerings had to be gathered to support them (2 Corinthians 9). God grants us generous hearts and thoughtful minds like the Christians in ancient Jerusalem and Corinth as we work together toward the goals of His kingdom!

Jesus emphasized that His followers are to be a loving community in the eyes of the world (see John 13:14–15). Genuine love shows that we belong to Jesus and want to love as He loved. (The world sees some of this but probably not enough.) We realize, of course, that we are not heaven-bound because of our deeds of love, but we do deeds of love because we are heaven-bound.

Showing love can be challenging and difficult, so what kind of motivation do we need for this behavior? God's love to us in sending His Son to be our Savior is the true source of our motivation and gives our love authenticity. His love for us in Christ overflows in our love for our neighbor (1 John 4:19).

Advent People

"Waiting and watching" is the posture of God's heaven-bound people. We are Advent people waiting for the second coming of the Lord and His ushering in of the final phase of His kingdom. The time may come sooner than we think!

Consider whether or not you can honestly pray the prayer in Revelation 22:20. Not many people are praying for Judgment Day to come today or tomorrow, but why not? When the Lord Jesus comes, at the end of time, we get to go home with Him to heaven!

The time of Jesus' second coming cannot be known. Matthew 24:36 and Acts 1:6–8 assure us of His return, but also affirm that we will not know in advance the time of His coming. God knows the time but says it's not for us to know. He wants us to live as Advent people, alert and watching every day. He calls us to proclaim the Gospel throughout the world while we wait, watch, and pray.

The signs of the end are all around us: wars, earthquakes, increasing immorality, teachers of false religions, and so forth. The end of time will come soon, but *soon* is a relative term and simply emphasizes that God's heaven-bound people must live every day as Advent people expecting Him to appear at any time.

EXPECT SURPRISES

Our God is full of surprises, and we can be sure that He has kept the greatest surprise of all for the end. The glimpses we have of heaven, wonderful as they are, are necessarily given in terms of our earthly experiences and understanding. Therefore, they are incomplete revelations.

In 1 Corinthians 2:9, the apostle Paul tells us that the glories of heaven are beyond our present understanding. God already surprised us with the likes of Christmas, the transfiguration, and Easter. The greatest surprise of all is the Gospel itself—that He would sacrifice His own Son to redeem sinners like us. Expect more surprises when you get to heaven!

As you travel the road that leads to the glories of heaven, welcome God's reminders that the earth is not your permanent home. Recognize your weaknesses and failures as you strive to keep the focus on heavenly things. Daily confess your faults to God. Take advantage of the forgiveness and strength He offers in His Word and Sacraments.

Jesus' death and resurrection gained heaven for you. Through the Gospel, God's Spirit increases your desire and ability to lead the heavenly life now. Though perfection is not possible in your earthly life, growth in faith and Christian life is possible and is expected by your loving God. Pray for His strength to grow more and more like the heaven-bound person He calls you by faith to be. Your worship, love, joy, hope, and Advent attitude will surprise even you!

POINTS TO PONDER

The more we understand about spiritual matters—heaven, hell, our sin, and what Jesus has done for us—the more we are amazed at God's grace. And God uses this to change us. Not only can we not look back, but we also bubble over in joy, peace, and relief as He changes us, prepares us, and uses us to reach others.

WORDS TO REMEMBER

Set your minds on things that are above, not on things that are on earth. (Colossians 3:2)

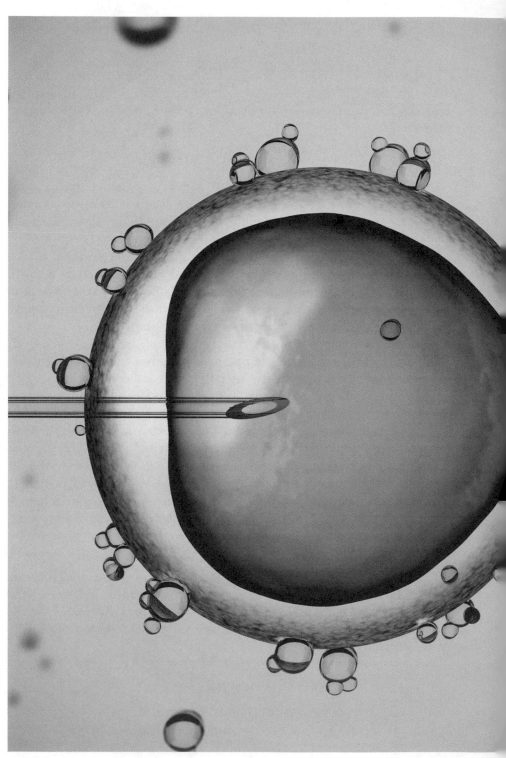

PLAYING GOD
Redesigning Life

INTRODUCTION

Your scientists were so preoccupied with whether or not they could that they didn't stop to think if they should.

—From the 1993 film Jurassic Park

At a Rotary Club presentation a few years ago, I listened in amazement to the ranting of a science fiction writer about the benefits of human cloning. Speaking from his self-created world, he joyfully anticipated the day when technology would make it possible to clone designer bodies without brains so that his brain could be transplanted into a new and youthful body whenever he needed one. When I questioned him about the ethics of such a venture, he brayed about how some people are simply too fearful to face the future and all the wonders technology can provide.

What this writer failed to understand is that it is not the technology that troubles me. It is the people who might use it, people so enthusiastic for the latest thing that they haven't considered the implications. For many tech-crazed people, "right" means getting it made and getting paid for it, and "wrong" means getting second place in the race for the future.

Though technology changes constantly, human beings don't change. The Bible records how people have always misused technology and misused their strength with fatal results. This part of our study will help you understand the God-pleasing use of technology. It will provide you with sound guidelines and wisdom not only for this life but also for the life to come.

25

AND YOU'LL BE LIKE GOD

Your eyes will be opened, and you will be like God.

—*The serpent to Eve (Genesis 3:5)*

Mary and John show their special parking pass to the guard. The metal gate swings open, and they enter the lower-level parking area of the BioMed Plaza. As they walk to the first floor, they see a coffee shop, floral shop, toy and department stores, and specialty stores for prospective parents and even for those who are planning their death or funeral.

The only access to the second floor is by appointment, requiring a special identification card imprinted with their genetic code and appointment time. After they swipe their card through the genetic scanner, the elevator door opens. They enter the elevator and arrive at the second floor. Stepping out, they see the following agencies: Bundles of Love Fertility Clinic, Clone-Genics, StemCell Bank, and Terminal Choices.

John says, "Biotechnology is wonderful, but is this going too far?"

Mary says, "Look at those signs. They have made-to-order babies that can be reproduced in test tubes, as well as eugenic and cloning laboratories. Why, people can even clone themselves to generate their own replacement tissues or organs." She points. "Look at that last sign, 'Terminal Choices.' It looks like a mortuary, an assisted-suicide facility, and an abortion clinic wrapped up into one."

John says, "Who would have imagined? Looks like all things are now possible."

Though the BioMed Plaza viewed by Mary and John is fictional, all the biomedical technologies it offers are available today to varying degrees. Have you ever found yourself awed by modern medical procedures? by the potential that biomedical technologies offer? This section will evaluate some of the procedures made available by recent technological advances.

How might the BioMed Plaza tempt Mary and John in the same way that Adam and Eve were tempted by the fruit of "the tree of the knowledge of good and evil" (Genesis 2:8–9, 15–17)? In both cases, the "fruit" is within the grasp of humans, and they imagine that it holds boundless, godlike potential for them. Scholars have noted that another way to translate "the tree of the knowledge of good and evil" is "the tree by which good and evil are known." In other words, God set up the tree to be a moral boundary marker. It was good to eat the fruit of the other trees in the garden but evil to eat from this tree.

Mary and John entered the BioMed Plaza with the best intentions. Can good intentions protect them in their medical decisions? Solomon addressed this issue more than once (Proverbs 16:2, 25; 21:2, 30). Good intentions are important, but they cannot safeguard against evil. As an English proverb warns, "The road to hell is paved with good intentions." From the Lord, Mary and John need a clear understanding of right and wrong.

New Tech, New Toys

Biomedical technology has changed humankind. These changes can be helpful or harmful. Occasionally, they may be both. Medical advances may create, sustain, alter, or destroy human life.

Biomedical technologies that *create* include those referred to as Assisted Reproductive Technology (ART). A few examples of this technology are in vitro (in glass) fertilization, artificial insemination, and direct egg-sperm injection (injecting one sperm directly into one egg). The ART of in vitro fertilization may also result in the destruction of embryos during their freezing and thawing, and in many cases it creates surplus embryos who face an unknown future.

Biomedical technologies that *sustain* involve artificial means, such as the use of respirators, feeding tubes, kidney dialysis, and pain-control therapies. When these medical technologies are abused with the intent to kill, they no longer sustain life while providing comforting, palliative care, but rather *destroy* life. Such is the case in the state of Oregon, for example, where assisted suicide is legal.

Look over the biomedical technologies mentioned in the prior two paragraphs. How common are these techniques in your community, and how widely do you see them publicized or advertised? ART is the work of specialists. The techniques listed in the second paragraph are used at many reproductive clinics, available in most metropolitan areas. You probably know someone who has used one of these techniques. Did they benefit from these techniques? When technology is used well, the results can be a great blessing.

Biomedical technologies that *alter* a human life include sex selection, gene replacement therapy (replacing a "bad gene" with a "good gene"), sperm and egg donation, cloning, use of spare frozen embryos for stem cell research, and organ transplants. Consider how these techniques might alter—and possibly disrupt—human life. Cloning and embryonic stem cell research, for example, will result in the *destruction* of human embryos.

Biomedical technology is an extension of our natural lives. But it is also a means to an end. The technology can be used for the common good of society; however, as suggested by the BioMed Plaza, it can also be used merely for profit or to fulfill personal needs and ambitions.

Biomedical therapies tend to cater to human emotions. We choose them to comfort ourselves. What we want—the human desire to improve ourselves—is apt to become the norm, the standard of right and wrong. We may feel positive about the benefits, but we are using the technology to transcend the Word of God.

How might emotions affect the use of biomedical techniques such as ART? An infertile couple may turn to ART to overcome their feelings of disappointment or to meet expectations about having children. The drive to have children may so possess them that they may neglect options like embryo adoption or adopting an infant or child.

THE TOWER AND THE ARK

There are many biomedical technologies that serve humankind in a God-pleasing way to correct various diseases and injuries. However, we must recognize that biomedical technology can become our idol.

God's Word reminds us that humans are dependent new creatures in Christ. We are not morally independent to create a "tower of Babel." Christians struggle with the proper and improper use of biomedical technologies, especially regarding beginning- and end-of-life issues. Christians are encouraged to avoid using technology for self-serving purposes. We should approach the use of biomedical technology in service to God's Word (Colossians 3:17).

To grow in your understanding of these issues, you need to understand what God teaches about the use of technology. For example, God condemned the tower of Babel in Genesis 11:1–7. The builders of Babel laid the foundation of their tower and city in human pride. They ignored God's command to "fill the earth and subdue it" and instead sought to conquer heaven. Humankind was "playing God."

Biotechnology is a way for humans to control human life using science and nature as their instruments. This represents a shift in the stewardship of God's good gifts from "dominion" to "domination."

Reflect on the use of technology described in Genesis 6:13–16. Here God commands the use of technology to save Noah, his family, and the animals. Remember, God is not opposed to technology. He wants us to use technology for His purposes rather than for our own sinful purposes.

"Playing God" is nothing new. Examine the Lord's words to Adam before and after the fall (Genesis 2:16–18; ch. 3). Adam and Eve intentionally tried to elevate themselves to God's level, overruling His Word about what was right and wrong. Through a lie, Satan also set himself as judge over God's Word and His intentions. Commanded by the Lord, Adam and Eve were not to eat of the tree of knowing good and evil, or they would die a physical death and be separated from Yahweh. Satan tempted Eve with these words: "Did God actually say, 'You shall not eat of any tree in the garden'? . . . You will not surely die. . . . God knows that when you eat of it your eyes will be opened, and you will be like God, knowing good and evil" (Genesis 3:1, 4–5).

Read and reflect on the First Commandment in Exodus 20:1–6. How does technology tend to become an idol? When people put their trust in technology or those who develop technology, they may forget that life truly depends on God rather than man. Science as savior is one of the sins of modern life.

How foolish for humankind to trample the Word of God in the rush for personal gain and greed! Self-glorification and independence are the gods of all sinners. This is Satan's playground, which leads to our isolation from God.

As people of the trinitarian God, we have the whole Law given to us in the Ten Commandments for holy living. God wrote this Law on our hearts at creation. He gave His commands to us on two tablets of stone when He led Israel out of Egypt. Through these commands, He calls us to live as wise and loving parents, just as He is a wise and loving Father to us.

God calls parents not just to create life but also to nurture and sustain it through His Word (Genesis 18:19; Deuteronomy 6:5–8; Ephesians 6:4). If parents abandon the standards of God's Word in order to bring forth life—using destructive biotechnology—how will they ever pass along God's standards for their children?

Any technology that would destroy the unborn, directly or indirectly (e.g., by freezing an embryonic human being), violates the Fifth Commandment and places our selfish desires above God who, like a dear Father, provides for us but also preserves us. As Paul writes, "And whatever you do, in word or deed, do everything in the name of the Lord Jesus, giving thanks to God the Father through Him" (Colossians 3:17). This sets apart the idolatrous motive of the builders of the tower of Babel from the righteous motive of Noah, the builder of the ark. The technologies in both cases were good and useful, but one served self as god while the other served the triune God to His glory.

GUIDED BY GOD HIMSELF

It is very difficult to discern the proper or improper use of biotechnology. But through prayer and meditation on the Word of God, His Spirit provides an answer (Isaiah 65:24). As baptized Christians, we are comforted in our difficult decisions because God's grace is sufficient for us in all the challenges of life (2 Corinthians 12:8–9). As you face life-and-death choices, remember the choices your heavenly Father made for you in Christ.

Ephesians 1:3–5 declares that God chose us in Christ to make us holy. He adopted us as His children. We can always be sure of God's ultimate will and purpose for our lives, no matter what loss or disappointment we may face.

As redeemed Christians, we are given the eternal righteousness, innocence, and blessedness of the risen Christ. Baptized into His death and resurrection, we use and apply technology in service to the Word of God. Perhaps one of the best summaries for guidance on using technology is found in Hebrews 12. God's Word directs us to look to Jesus, the Author of our faith. He will "perfect" or complete us by His grace. When we face suffering, we know that we face it with Him.

Your trinitarian faith, which holds to the words and promises of Jesus Christ, will equip you to work through a key question regarding the use and abuse of biotechnology: "Where does a Christian draw the line?"

Trinitarian faith is God's gift through Holy Baptism. It treats all human beings as persons created in the image of God. This faith holds to the words and promises of Christ, who gives to us His undeserved love. This *agape* love does no harm to its neighbor (Romans 13:8–14). As Christians we are to "fear and love God so that we do not hurt or harm our neighbor in his body, but help and support him in every physical need" (Luther's Small Catechism, Fifth Commandment). This applies to unborn, newborn, and adult human beings.

POINTS TO PONDER

Advances in science and technology can raise questions of right and wrong as the advances are put into use. These questions become more personal when they involve biotechnology or medical matters. Where would you go for truth and discernment, and why? The Bible is God's Word, and God is the final authority. We need to turn to Him rather than to false alternatives.

WORDS TO REMEMBER

And whatever you do, in word or deed, do everything in the name of the Lord Jesus, giving thanks to God the Father through Him. (Colossians 3:17)

26

In the Beginning, God Created

Bob and Joan received a referral to Bundles of Love Fertility Clinic at the BioMed Plaza. Since they each carry the gene for cystic fibrosis, they were referred to Dr. Smith's clinic for in vitro fertilization. The main purpose of this referral was to test all the in-vitro-produced embryos for the cystic fibrosis gene. The test is called "preimplantation genetic testing." If an embryo contains a cystic fibrosis gene from each parent, the embryo will develop into a child with cystic fibrosis. Dr. Smith explained that all embryos carrying the disease (one gene contributed by one parent) or exhibiting the disease (one gene contributed by each parent) would be destroyed. Only the disease-free embryos would be placed into Joan's womb.

Joan commented to Dr. Smith, "Right now, my husband and I feel all right with this because embryos really aren't human beings. They don't have arms, legs, or a beating heart. They aren't aware of their surroundings. An embryo is no more than a blob of cells."

As they left the BioMed Plaza, Bob said, "Joan, I'm not sure about this. Is that tiny embryo just a 'blob of cells,' or is it truly a human being? What about our faith? Are we in danger of playing God by choosing which embryos will live and which will die?"

As they reached the car, Bob recalled a few words from the Bible quoted in a pro-life Sunday sermon: "When I was being made in secret, intricately woven in the depths of the earth. Your eyes saw my unformed substance" (Psalm 139:15–16).

Compare Joan's description of the unborn child as a "blob of cells" to the practice of abortion, and then to King David's description of the unborn in Psalm 139:13–16. David writes in awe of the reproductive process designed by the heavenly Father. Joan, in her zeal to have a healthy child, distances herself from the process.

Bob and Joan might rationalize or justify a decision to reject an embryo with the gene for cystic fibrosis. They might argue that cystic fibrosis is a terrible disease and that any loving parent would spare a child from such suffering. But even if medical technology gives them the power to make such a choice, do they have the moral right to make that decision?

DEFINING LIFE

Is a human-procreated zygote (a unicellular embryo) a human being with potential or a potential human being? This is the most central ethical issue for ART.

Many scientists believe that an embryo doesn't have the same moral status as a newborn or infant because it lacks the possibility of *sentience* (being aware of its surroundings). Also, they point out that each cell within the embryo hasn't "decided" what it will form. Lastly, the high rate of natural mortality of embryos within the womb assures these scientists that they are simply following the example of nature by choosing which embryo will live.

However, some pro-choice organizations and many politicians argue that a human being's life begins at implantation (a period of about six days after fertilization, when the embryo attaches to the wall of the uterus).

Even though single-celled organisms like amoebas are very small, scientists regard them as living beings. Why do you suppose they might classify an embryo differently? A scientist might argue that an amoeba has reached the fullness of its development, whereas an embryo is only at the beginning of this process.

Some embryologists (experts in the process of prenatal human development) have argued that each human being begins at fertilization, when the genetic material from the woman's egg and the man's sperm are united. The process of development continues in the uterus until birth. Hence, conception and in utero development are part of a continuing process that has a specific purpose: birth.

Science confirms that at fertilization the genetic union of sperm and egg causes procreation (a new human life). Everything needed to mature a human being exists at fertilization. From that point on, it is simply a matter of development.

Doctors usually divide human development into two periods: prenatal (before birth) and postnatal (after birth). According to embryologist Keith Moore, birth is merely a dramatic event *during* development, resulting in a change in environment. Development does not start at birth or stop at birth. According to Dr. Jim Russell, the brain does not complete its neurological development until around the age of thirty!

As Dr. Diane Irving points out, scientists know when human life begins; the question is when does the life of a *human being* begin. Since all body cells are given human life by the Lord God Creator, the correct scientific language for the developing in utero human is a human being, not merely human life.

Why are the terms *human being* and *human life* important, and how do they differ? Organs used for transplants might be described as human life since the cells are human and are alive. But they differ greatly from an embryo, since they have no development as a human being. (We will address the issue of cloning a human being from living human tissue later.)

A human being has a body and a soul. In the most simplistic language, a human wife and a human husband procreate according to God's will, creating another human life of equal value and dignity. This is a scientific and theological fact. It is also the moral basis for our life together as humans.

God Defines Life

Some scientists define the moral status of a human being based on possession or lack of possession of certain "rational attributes," such as sentience, or "biological attributes," such as a nervous system. This establishes identity on the basis of what a human being has and not on the basis of what a human being has been given by God in Christ at conception. Attempting to define the beginning of a human's life on the basis of rational or biological attributes or location (in the womb or out of the womb) is arbitrary.

For example, according to the National Institutes of Health, the Human Embryo Research Panel of 1994 reported that the embryo is not a human being because it is not aware of its surroundings (i.e., nonsentient). Readers should recognize that sentience is poorly defined by science. Sentience is a philosophical concept that has been imposed on the scientific data. Since a so-called lack of sentience qualifies an embryo as a nonhuman being, some scientists use this as permission to experiment on an embryo or destroy it.

Readers need to know that more recent research has suggested that embryos are able to respond to pain after only about twenty weeks of development, meaning that they are aware of pain. Some researchers are even investigating how embryos respond to music or voices while still in the womb, implicitly recognizing that the embryos are aware of this part of their surroundings. In this realization they are two millennia behind Scripture, which records that John the Baptist responded to Mary's voice while in the womb, only six months after conception (Luke 1:36–44).

How might the sentience rule affect other groups of people: the mentally ill, the severely mentally disabled, Alzheimer's patients, and the permanently unconscious? This rule could be used to deny human rights to these groups by arguing that they are subhuman and undeserving of protection.

The arbitrary and capricious character of the rules about sentience and development show themselves through another example: the mortality rate of embryos. Some scientists argue that the high rate of natural mortality of embryos in the uterus (approximately 30–70 percent) demonstrates that the embryo is a nonhuman being because it dies before implantation. But since when does death define whether someone is a human being? What percentage of human adults die? A full 100 percent! (Although with a few miraculous exceptions recorded in the Bible). Does that mean human adults aren't human beings?

What are some problems with defining humans based on death? According to Romans 5:12, as a result of the fall into sin, death has become a consequence of human life from which we cannot escape. The mortality rate of embryos should not become an argument that embryos aren't human. It should instead remind us of the far-reaching consequences of sin, which corrupts and destroys life at every stage of development.

If the embryo is viewed as a nonhuman being, scientists are permitted to use it as they wish—the end justifies the means if a "nonhuman" is destroyed. However, the Law of God speaks clearly: "You shall not murder." We are "neighbor" to the embryonic human being (Luke 10:36–37).

If you consider an embryo a human being, then you will be guided by that belief. If you consider it to be only a potential human being, then you will be guided by that belief. Whatever your idea is about the moral status of the embryonic human being, you will find yourself basing your decisions on that idea. But what does God think?

The Lord said to Jeremiah, "Before I formed you in the womb I knew you, and before you were born I consecrated you" (Jeremiah 1:5). Some say that this is a special case that cannot be applied to human conception in the present-day world. Yet the Scriptures testify in other places that God knew us before the foundations of the world were created (Ephesians 1:4).

Read Psalm 139:13–16, and reflect on its meaning for defining human beings and life. Note that a human being begins with God, with His handiwork, and not simply the human decision to have sexual intercourse. Truthfully, the wonder of it all is beyond human knowing.

Another important passage assisting the Christian in understanding that the unborn are human beings is found in Exodus 21:22–23. Note the words about "life for life." The baby in the womb was regarded as a child.

The Hebrew word for "child" is *yeled*. Other passages that use this term help us understand how the Scriptures viewed life. For example, in Genesis 21:12, Ishmael was at least fourteen years old when the Scriptures referred to him as a *boy*. In Genesis 37:2, Joseph was at least seventeen years old when he was referred to as a *boy*. In 2 Chronicles 10:8, 10, 14, Rehoboam began his rule over Judah at the age of forty-one (2 Chronicles 12:13). Before his reign, he rejected the counsel of the elders and received advice from *young men* described as Rehoboam's contemporaries and peers. The same Hebrew word—*yeled*—is used for all these ages. This suggests that regardless of the stage of development of an individual, the biblical authors and the Lord who inspired them viewed that individual as a human being, a person.

Based on the passages listed above, how might you answer people who use development as the basis for deciding when an embryo/fetus is a human being? Simply put, the Bible doesn't permit such a basis for evaluating a human life. Age and development are not factors for defining a human being.

Look up Isaiah 7:14; Luke 1:31, 41, 57; and 2:6–7. According to these passages, how does the Bible describe what is in the womb? The terms are consistently "child" and "baby." God views the life in the womb as a child or baby, using the same terms to describe that life after the child is born. This leaves no room for the development argument put forth by some scientists.

Made Man

One of the most profound testimonies that the unborn are human beings is learned from the incarnation: God taking on the flesh of a human being in the person of Jesus Christ, God's only begotten Son. The Second Person of the Trinity was "born in the likeness of men" (Philippians 2:7).

Although Jesus' conception is very special—that is, by the Holy Spirit—He became like one of us in every way. He passed through all the stages of life—zygotic embryo, embryo, fetus, newborn, child, and adult—so that "He might become a merciful and faithful high priest in the service of God, to make propitiation for the sins of the people" (Hebrews 2:17).

When the early Christians summarized what the Bible teaches about who Jesus is, they stated that He "was incarnate by the Holy Spirit of the virgin Mary and was made man" (Nicene Creed). According to the early Christians, then, when did Jesus become a human being, and what made Jesus a man? The answer to both questions is conception. Each person begins at conception, not at a later stage of development.

Read 1 Timothy 2:5; Luke 24:39; and Matthew 26:38, and consider why the Bible emphasizes this aspect of Jesus' person. Jesus didn't treat the human body as an empty shell. He became *man*. The incarnation of Jesus shows how God values you as a person, body and soul. He became like you in every way, yet without sin (Hebrews 4:15), so that He might redeem you in every way.

Points to Ponder

"In the beginning, God . . ." Issues of conception, birth, old age, and death can be complicated and emotional. Frankly, the world does not value life as God values life, and we face tension between these competing values. Regardless, God is Creator and Lord of Life. What does this mean as we face the rationalizations and pressures of secular values that prefer death?

WORDS TO REMEMBER

For by Him all things were created, in heaven and on earth, visible and invisible. (Colossians 1:16)

27

IN SEARCH OF THE PERFECT CHILD

Joe and Sue received their special pass by registered mail for the Bundles of Love Fertility Clinic at the BioMed Plaza. As they stepped from the elevator, Dr. Love greeted them warmly and led them to his office. Joe and Sue sat with him and explained their desire to have a "normal" child, that is, one who would be free from any genetic disorder. The doctor assured them that their needs would be met.

Joe said, "We have been unable to have a child through normal sexual means for the past several years. Sue has been told that her eggs are not good enough for fertilization. We will have to seek a child through egg donation."

Dr. Love replied, "We can help you select, in a very general way—weight, IQ, hair color, athletic ability, blood type, eye color—the child of your choice through our egg donation computer catalog. We can usually determine gender by selecting from your husband's sperm one that will produce a girl or one that will produce a boy. The former is 95 percent successful, while the latter is 75 percent successful."

"Wow!" Sue said. "That means we can plan the decor of the nursery ahead of time."

"You can really determine the baby's hair color?" Joe asked.

"Remember," Dr. Love said, "choosing characteristics of your child is nonspecific. We can only get you in the ballpark."

"By the way," Sue asked, "what is the average cost for one in vitro cycle for making our baby?"

"The average cost for one IVF cycle is about $15,000." Dr. Love said. "It could be more and it could be less. Since we have to go to an egg donor, that additional cost will depend on the education, IQ, and professional level of that donor. In some cases, the undergraduate academic institution that she graduated from may be important and, perhaps, add to your cost. The range is $5,000 to $10,000 or so. Sex selection will cost an additional fee. Will any of this be a problem?"

"Nothing's too good for our baby," the couple said in unison.

Dr. Love said, "In addition, a legal agreement will have to be drawn up to assure that you own any spare embryos, since the egg donor is the biological mother of the child you will bear in your womb."

As Joe and Sue were leaving the BioMed Plaza, Joe seemed troubled by all of this. He said, "While we were sitting there, I thought to myself that we Christians should be content in anything and everything. Are we trying to satisfy ourselves by searching for the perfect child? Should we just trust in the Lord and try not to control so much? Is this 'making' a child or is this 'begetting' a child like the Bible describes? The barrenness issue is very tough to deal with in the face of all of this Assisted Reproductive Technology."

FERTILITY

The following paragraphs about ART are not meant to judge the situations in which it is used appropriately or inappropriately nor to bind the Christian's conscience. This section is about getting the facts straight about different techniques for conception.

Infertility is defined as the inability of a married couple to conceive and bear a child after one year of unprotected sexual relations. About 10–15 percent of all married couples are infertile. Approximately 35–40 percent of infertility issues are related to females and the same percentage to males. Approximately 20 percent of infertility issues are related to both husband and wife, while a very small percentage of couples are infertile for unexplained reasons.

Consider the emotional and personal aspects of infertility. In Genesis 30:1–24, Rachel and Leah felt great disgrace when they experienced infertility. Rachel blamed Jacob, and Jacob blamed God. The two sisters even gave their servants to Jacob as surrogates to bear children for him. (This was legal and acceptable at that time in the Middle East.) The entire situation caused considerable difficulties for the family.

A couple today may choose to conceive and bear a child through several artificial methods. A child may be artificially conceived either within the woman's body or outside her body. There are two main reproductive procedures that may create a child within the woman's body. The first is called artificial insemination (AI). This medical procedure requires the recovery of male sperm from the husband, placing them directly into the woman's reproductive tract. The second artificial method of conceiving a child within the woman's womb is called gamete intrafallopian transfer (GIFT). Herein, a concentration of sperm and usually no more than three eggs are injected together into the upper end of the woman's fallopian tube with the intent that fertilization will occur at that location.

The most commonly used artificial method of making a baby outside the woman's body is called in vitro fertilization (IVF; *in vitro* means "in glass"). Direct egg sperm injection (DESI) is less frequently used. In the former process, male sperm and female eggs are removed and cleaned. Usually six to thirty-five eggs are recovered from a woman. Millions of sperm may be removed from the man. Using the man's sperm, the woman's eggs are fertilized in a petri dish. In general, no more than three fertilized eggs are placed into the woman's uterus at one time. If there are spare embryos, they are frozen in liquid nitrogen at about -321° F. The second artificial procedure, direct egg sperm injection, involves the isolation of one sperm, which is injected directly into the woman's egg in a petri dish. The resultant zygote is placed into the woman's womb. In all of the artificial procedures described, a couple may also choose to use donated sperm, donated eggs, and a donated womb (called a surrogate womb).

Read Genesis 2:22–25; Exodus 20:13; and Leviticus 18:4–6. How would these biblical guidelines help you determine whether making a baby in a petri dish accords with God's will? Clearly God didn't create us for this type of procreation. The thoughtless death of embryos that results from this procedure and the possible complication of family relationships contradict God's Word.

Legal agreements are also frequently drawn up to address the issue of frozen spare embryos. Couples must decide in advance who will have custody of these frozen embryos in the case of death or divorce. In addition, if a sibling or other relative donates her eggs to her sister, a legal agreement must be drawn up to decide who has custody over any spare embryos, since the donating sister or relative is the biological mother. The same approach would apply for sperm donation, since the donor would be the biological father.

Reflect on the legal agreements involved in the use of fertility technology. These agreements are custody agreements, just as in a custody battle or an adoption agreement. These agreements suggest that people understand that something far greater than property is involved. Actually, human beings are at stake.

In some cases of surrogacy, elective abortion clauses are added. In the laboratory setting, sperm, eggs, and the resultant embryos created in the petri dish are graded regarding their ability to either fertilize or implant. Only those embryos that look viable to the "naked eye" are kept for implantation or freezing. Read Genesis 16:1–6. The biblical story of Abraham, Sarah, and Hagar reveals the awkward feelings and responses people have under these circumstances. Couples who choose a surrogate birth face considerable difficulties.

A woman decides to donate her eggs to her sister and brother-in-law because "God teaches us that this is the loving and caring thing to do." However, the loving and caring thing to do in Christ is to leave procreation to the Lord and not to the egg donation of a sister. In addition, this may violate the Ninth and Tenth Commandments regarding seeking what doesn't belong to you, in this case, your sister's eggs or womb. God's Word is clear that the procreation of a child is God's work through the mutual sexual love of a husband and wife (Genesis 1:27–28).

BE FRUITFUL

The Lord God brought man and woman together as one-flesh, sexual beings. Before and since the fall of Adam and Eve into sin, the Lord's command to Adam and Eve (which includes all humankind) has been to be fruitful and multiply (Genesis 1:28; 9:1). This is procreation, commonly known in the Bible as "begetting." A married couple's primary intention as one flesh is their sexual union, their mutual love, and if it is God's will, the procreation of a child.

Oliver O'Donovan writes that the biblical term *beget* describes our ability to procreate another human being, not by our power of will or intention but because of who we are. The creation of a child outside the mutual sexual embrace described in the Bible separates the one-flesh union from the intentional act of sexual intercourse and places it within the context of the laboratory.

Couples must guard against violating the First, Fifth, Ninth, and Tenth Commandments in their desire to conceive. When the quest to conceive a child becomes an obsession for self-fulfillment, the First Commandment is violated. If embryos are frozen, couples need to know that 30–70 percent die in the thawing process. This violates the Fifth Commandment. If sperm and egg are received via donation, then the Ninth and Tenth Commandments are violated. Some theologians would include the Sixth Commandment about adultery (remember the custody agreements necessary for these procedures!). In addition, this quest for a child by any means violates the one-flesh union and the marriage vows to remain faithful to God's Word and to each other until death.

Some Assisted Reproductive Technology, such as artificial insemination, seems to be within the one-flesh union, as the child is conceived within the reproductive system of the wife. Other types of ART that make a child outside the body of the husband and the wife are subject to idolatrous abuse. In these cases, the married couple tends to be "producers" of a child. Their embryos are rated according to viability; spare embryos are frozen, which may cause their premature death; thawing of spare embryos often causes death; the financial cost of making a baby outside the womb may drive the husband and wife apart; and lastly, their parenting is based on personal control and fulfillment.

Procreation may not be possible because of fertility issues, but constructive alternatives are available. The couple may turn to the old proven method of adoption or to the newer method of embryo adoption to build their family. These can become a win-win situation that "rescues" born or unborn children from an uncertain fate. And, with adoption, there is no need to resort to ART methods of problematic ethics.

CONTENT IN CHRIST

Following the original sin of Adam and Eve, barrenness became a terrible stigma and emotional trauma. Over the centuries, this has not changed. However, the Lord never condemns those who are barren, but rather brings them comfort and consolation through His Gospel of mercy and compassion. Some stories of barrenness in the Bible are the following: Abram and Sarai (Genesis 15:4; 16:1–2); Rebekah (Genesis 25:20–21); Rachel and Leah (Genesis 29:31–30:24); Abimelech's wife and female slaves (Genesis 20:17–18); Manoah's wife (Judges 13:1–24); and Hannah (1 Samuel 1:1–20).

Desire and determination can be great strengths. Through prayer and patience, Abram and Sarai have a child and keep their vows to the Lord. Ultimately, God fulfills His greatest purpose through them: Jesus, the Savior of humanity, is born from their line.

Infertile couples are encouraged to search the Scriptures, praying and learning all that they can about making a child outside the one-flesh union. The emotional trauma of barren couples needs attention from all members of the Body of Christ (1 Corinthians 12:12–26). Remember, the love of God in Christ "does no wrong to a neighbor" (Romans 13:10), which includes the unborn.

In this life, perfection is a laudable yet ever-unattainable goal. That's because each of us derives from the flawed raw material of sinful men and women—each of us except Christ. Jesus was conceived by the Holy Spirit. Though He partook of His mother's human nature, He did not inherit her sin. As the Son of God, He was the perfect child, entrusted to us so that we, through Him, might again trust the perfect love and forgiveness of our heavenly Father.

Philippians 3:4–14 shows Paul seeking that which has been given to him by God's grace through faith—the promise of the resurrection of the body and its union with the soul to live in the eternal blessedness of heaven with Christ. Paul knows that by God's grace, heaven is his home now but not yet. Knowing this by faith, Paul continues to pursue this heavenly end in Christ.

The trinitarian faith of barren couples holds to the resurrected Christ and His promises. Jesus knows the desires and emotional trauma that infertility generates. Since the Word of God does not address the specific use of Assisted Reproductive Technology, couples are encouraged to examine their motives for making a child through the cross and resurrection of Jesus Christ.

The Lord Jesus Christ is the Author and Creator of all life, especially a human being's life. He died so that those who are created in the mutual sexual love of a husband and wife would be baptized and raised in the instruction and discipline of the Lord (Ephesians 6:1–3). Hence, through the love of God in Christ Jesus, Christian couples that are barren receive wholeness through the resurrected Christ.

The couple that is childless has a child, for the child that was conceived by the Holy Spirit and born of the Virgin Mary is born for them. In Him, infertile couples have their being and their life. In Christ, all couples, whether barren or fruitful, live first and always the life of Christ in the world.

Is the wholeness of God's people received in Christ without heartache? Of course not (Philippians 3:10–11). Consider the human desires that Christ experienced growing up in Nazareth. Consider that He was never able to take a wife or have the joy of fatherhood. He knew the ache of empty arms as surely as He knew the pain of pierced hands. You can entrust the future of your marriage and family to Him.

POINTS TO PONDER

"In the beginning, God . . ." Issues of conception and fertility can be complicated and emotional. We can survive the confusion, though, by returning to the fundamental truth: God is the Creator and Lord of Life. What does this mean as we face options and false hopes thrust upon us by medical technology and secular values?

WORDS TO REMEMBER

"Knowledge" puffs up, but love builds up. If anyone imagines that he knows something, he does not yet know as he ought to know. But if anyone loves God, he is known by God. (1 Corinthians 8:1–3

28

THE IMMORTAL CLONE

Mr. and Mrs. Johnson arrive at the BioMed Plaza for their appointment at CloneGenics. A drunk driver killed their seven-year-old daughter recently while she was riding her bicycle. The doctor assures them that he can clone their daughter, but that she will probably have a different personality, interests, and hobbies. Other than similarity in looks, the clone will be a different person. The Johnsons don't care.

Before the cloning process begins, the Johnsons agree to undergo a psychiatric evaluation and genetic profile. If they are approved, their daughter will be cloned. Three cloned embryos will be implanted in a surrogate womb. The Johnsons agree to pay $200,000 to cover the procedure, healthcare costs, and legal agreements. Everything has been approved. It's a go!

As the Johnsons leave the BioMed Plaza, they discuss their office visit. Mrs. Johnson turns to her husband and says, "Will this really be our child or merely a younger twin of our daughter? And how will this cloned child deal with the fact that she is a replacement?"

Mr. Johnson says, "I recall hearing our pastor say, regarding the use of cloning technology, 'Everything is permissible—but not everything is beneficial. Everything is permissible—but not everything is constructive. Nobody should seek his own good, but the good of others.' Are we being masters of our life or servants to God's Word?"

The couple hasn't come to grips with the fact that the cloning of their daughter will result in a different person. Although the child will have the same genetic makeup, the nurture and experience of the child will be different. Further, cloning technology is extremely new, but the motives pushing for this technology are not new. The desire for godlike control is almost as old as humanity, and it almost always leads to unexpected complications.

MAKING COPIES

According to *Stedman's Concise Medical Dictionary*, human cloning means transplanting the chromosomes from a human cell into a human egg from which the genetic material has already been removed. You don't clone a person. You clone a person's genetic material, the DNA that is responsible for a person's physical looks.

It is important to review the prevalent method if humans were to be cloned: (1) an egg is removed from a woman; (2) the nucleus containing the woman's genetic material is removed without damaging the egg; (3) a somatic cell, such as a skin cell, is removed from the person being cloned; (4) this cell is set aside so that it becomes inactivated, that is, it no longer "recognizes" itself as a specialized somatic cell, but just as a cell with forty-six chromosomes containing the sex chromosomes, either an XX if a woman is going to be cloned or an XY if a man is going to be cloned; (5) the inactivated somatic cell is brought in contact with the cell membrane of the anucleated egg (without a nuclear DNA), after which a slight electrical charge is applied, causing the body cell to fuse with the egg cell; (6) the forty-six chromosomes enter the egg, causing the egg to "think" that it is a zygote or fertilized egg; (7) this cloned zygote is placed in a surrogate womb so that in thirty-eight to forty-two weeks either a clone female or male is born.

The resulting human clone may be compared to an identical twin of the person from whom he or she is cloned. While a clone may look like the person from whom he or she is cloned, the clone will be different in his or her behavioral and social skills.

Some people have wondered whether a clone will be a human being and have a soul. Yes, a clone will be a human being and have a soul. If the answer is "No!" because no sperm are used, then Adam, Eve, and Christ are not human beings with a body and a soul, and we know this isn't true. The more important question is this: "What about the salvation of the cloned person?"

Consider the following case: A husband and wife decide to use cloning technology to have a "child" that will come from the husband's cells. The husband is thirty-five years old; this means the husband will essentially be thirty-five years older than his cloned "twin."

Some families will seek to use this technology to "resurrect" their domestic pet. Some scientists are already using cloning technology to save endangered animal species such as the bald eagle, the Bengal tiger, and the like. The company that assisted in the cloning of the first cat, called Copy Cat (C.C.), is Genetics Savings and Clone.

PARENTING

Consider this scenario: Marion is sitting on a bed holding a photograph of her lost son, whom she hopes to replace with human cloning technology. She has had a few inches of his somatic skin cells preserved in liquid nitrogen so that when the cloning technology is perfected, she will be able to bring him back, at least in terms of his looks.

Reflect on Marion's wishes and her plan. Christians must return to the basics of what we should do, what we shouldn't do, and how we are to live the life of Christ in the world. The Lord established marriage as a one-flesh union between husband and wife. If it is God's will, a couple may be blessed with a child through sexual procreation or adoption. Viewing cloning from the doctrine of marriage and parenting, the cloning of self, that is, the husband or wife, violates the Word of God, especially the Ninth and Tenth Commandments about coveting. Of course, when these commandments are violated, then they all are broken, since God is the author of them all.

James 2:8–11 explains what happens to the Law when one part gets broken—the whole Law shatters. It's like throwing a rock through a window in an attempt to break a small corner. Instead, you shatter the whole window.

The "producing" mentality of cloning is seeking to control destiny and turn procreation into an industry. This mentality also gives way to eugenics. *Eugenics* is crass social hygiene, as it strives to mate the "best" humans. All other people are eventually eliminated. In this way, only good, productive individuals in society are reproduced, assuring that the best genetic characteristics will be passed on from generation to generation.

Eugenics, by its very nature, emphasizes human prejudice and creates classes of human beings. As a result, it brings into question the rights or even the humanness of those who lack the proper genetic makeup.

Between 1927 and 1972, more than eight thousand children and young teenagers were forcibly sterilized at the Lynchburg Colony for the Epileptic and Feebleminded in Virginia. The state claimed that the children had hereditary defects that could potentially be passed on to their offspring. In fact, the children were simply poor and ill-educated and were considered to be a burden on the state. Today, the Repository for Germinal Choice in Escondido, California, is a eugenic sperm bank that seeks the generation of the most genetically productive people by using sperm donated by persons with a high IQ.

Eugenics marks some people for extinction because they don't measure up to social standards of excellence. The most horrifying example in history is Hitler's Final Solution; his desire to create a strong, healthy, vigorous Aryan people was influenced by U.S. eugenic policy and sterilization laws, which had been declared constitutional in 1927.

Eugenics is with us already through Assisted Reproductive Technology. For example, sperm donated by Nobel laureates, Ivy League school graduates, and others with high IQs and other special academic or athletic abilities are available for a significant fee. This approach to procreation exchanges the natural for the unnatural, that is, the sexual one-flesh union for the asexual reproduction of "self." The cloning of "self" exacerbates the move away from the biblical world of the one-flesh union and procreation as God's work to child manufacturing and production.

The effort to make better people through eugenics actually leads to a lack of respect for human life as people with preferred genes receive preferential treatment. Other people might lose certain rights, undergo sterilization, or even be killed.

The most sinful god is the god of self. Satan tempts Christians by emphasizing that cloning would bring fulfillment of the Lord's command to "be fruitful and multiply." Satan may tempt us to use this technology to escape the pain of infertility, to replace a dead loved one, or to create youthful spare body parts. But even the youngest legs cannot outrun the accusations of God's Law.

According to Romans 3:23, every person is born sinful and imperfect. Read 1 Samuel 17:4–7 and 1 Kings 11:4–6, and think about how God sees a person. Does stronger, faster, or smarter necessarily make a better person? These accounts tell of the downfall of the strong and the wise. Although physical strength, speed, and genius are blessings, only God can make a person good.

Children are not commodities; they are human beings made in God's image! Have you ever heard a comedian joke about disciplining a child, "I brought you into this world. And I can take you out!" While this statement is intended to be humorous, imagine the consequences of our throwaway mentality applied to "replaceable" human beings.

YOUR ETERNAL FAMILY

Christians are saved by grace through faith (Ephesians 2:8). Through the death, resurrection, and ascension of the Lord Jesus Christ, we have been saved from sin, death, and the power of the devil. Having baptized us into Christ's death and resurrection, God enables us to have no other gods before Him. We belong to God. He is responsible for us and promises us greater blessings than this life could ever promise.

Compare the "promise" of cloning with God's promises (1 Corinthians 15:42–49). Cloning holds out false comfort. It can't replace a lost loved one. It can't give immortality. These blessings will only come from God in the resurrection. In the resurrection, everyone in Christ will be reunited and enjoy the eternal blessings of the Lord in heaven (1 Thessalonians 4:13–18).

Christians respond by faith to His good gifts of creation, redemption, and sanctification. Sin distorts and compromises this relationship. By the grace of God, Christians are called to remain faithful and true to the Word of God that is given to us through the Author and Perfecter of our faith (Hebrews 12:1–3). Cloning technology is not true to the Word of God regarding procreation and parenting. It creates a tower of Babel situation that Satan uses to separate and isolate a married couple from their marriage vows, from each other, and from their Redeemer.

Marriage is a gift given by the Lord God. Procreation of a child is a gift given by the Lord God. By His grace, married couples that struggle with infertility will "fear, love and trust in God above all things." While it is sometimes difficult to know which Assisted Reproductive Technologies can be used to the glory of God and in service to His Word, cloning technology clearly violates the one-flesh union and parenting commands given by the Lord God. As baptized children of God, we never face the frustrations and disappointments of life alone. Our heavenly Father knows our troubles and agonies. He walks with us, promising never to leave or forsake us.

POINTS TO PONDER

Many people today believe they have the right, and sometimes even a responsibility, to use medical technologies to select which babies live and which are killed, to provide suicide options for those who wish to decide when to die, and to engineer a better population by choosing which genders, attributes, and characteristics to include or delete from the gene pool. Why might we think we have this right? Just because technology makes it possible? Consider the original sin of Adam and Eve, the sin of wanting to be God. In contrast, Jesus called His people to be salt and light in this world, so we can't sit on the sidelines.

WORDS TO REMEMBER

"All things are lawful for me," but not all things are helpful. "All things are lawful for me," but I will not be dominated by anything. (1 Corinthians 6:12)

29

THE STEM CELL REVOLUTION

Teddy suffers from Parkinson's disease. His geriatrician and neurologist referred him to the BioMed Plaza StemCell Bank. The bank specializes in growing tissues and organs from spare frozen or cloned human embryos and in growing adult stem cells from umbilical cords and placentas. Unused embryos from Bundles of Love Fertility Clinic and those created at CloneGenics are frozen and kept for those couples who want embryonic stem cell tissue and organ production to cover the future possibility of tissue or organ transplantation.

After Teddy arrives at StemCell Bank, they wheel him to their laboratory for blood evaluation to determine what spare frozen embryonic stem cells will be compatible with his body. They don't find a compatible match. To avoid this rejection problem, Teddy will undergo "therapeutic cloning." They will create embryos that have been cloned from his skin cells. In essence, they are cloning Teddy to save him or, at least, to buy him some time.

Teddy's five-day-old cloned embryos will be destroyed to remove and isolate dopamine-producing nerve cells. These isolated cells will be injected into his brain to treat his Parkinson's disease, especially those terrible tremors. An appointment is set up for the surgical transplantation of the dopamine-producing stem cells into a specific area of his brain. It will take place in two weeks, but Teddy will have to wait about eight to twelve weeks to see if he receives some relief or a cure from the tremors.

Leaving the BioMed Plaza, he recalls the words of a hospital chaplain who expressed his reservations regarding the use of this biotechnology: "Do you not know that your body is a temple of the Holy Spirit within you, whom you have from God? You are not your own, for you were bought with a price. So glorify God in your body" (1 Corinthians 6:19–20).

SUCH GREAT POTENTIAL

Stem cells are cells that have the ability to divide indefinitely, giving rise to specific cells or tissues such as those for the kidney, heart, bone marrow, muscles, and so on. There are two sources for stem cells. Adult stem cells (ASC) are found in the adult organism (e.g., in the bone marrow, skin, intestine, umbilical cords, placenta). These ASC replenish tissues in which cells often have limited life spans. Embryonic stem cells (ESC) are derived from the inner cell mass of a four- or five-day-old human embryo/blastocyst.

ASC are taken from consenting adults and do not involve the destruction of an embryonic human being. ESC involves the destruction of an embryonic human being who is unable to give consent. This is a violation of the Nuremberg Code, but you may never hear this in the news media or public conversation.

Some ethicists believe that exercising the will determines what is good (pro-choice). Cloning embryonic stem cells violates the pro-choice principle because it gives no opportunity for choice to the clones who will be used for therapeutic purposes. The "sacred" will of one person is simply preferred over the will of another.

While ASC can be taken from consenting adults, ESC acquisition requires two processes involving embryonic human beings. First, ESC may be recovered from embryos that have been created by in vitro fertilization and then frozen. These frozen embryos are either abandoned or made available for donation by their parents.

A second possible origin of ESC is through a process called therapeutic cloning. This uses the same process of cloning described in the last session. This process is performed to eliminate organ and tissue rejection (since you would be cloning your own DNA) but also uses a developing embryo called a blastocyst.

Consider the following scenario: Company A makes cloned cells and then sells them to Company B to take them apart and use for therapeutic purposes. Company A may argue that it doesn't actually destroy the embryos; it simply creates them (like the Bundles of Love Fertility Clinic in the earlier story). Company B may argue that these embryos exist anyway; why not put them to therapeutic use? (Like the StemCell Bank in another earlier story.) By dividing the process, the companies seek to escape responsibility while maximizing efficiency and profitability.

Therapeutic cloning is being promoted over and against reproductive cloning. The scientific process is the same in both technologies, with one major difference: therapeutic cloning destroys the embryonic human being at about the fifth day to recover stem cells, whereas reproductive cloning allows for the complete gestational development of the cloned human being. Since society has trouble with the idea of making clones but less trouble with destroying embryos, scientists and politicians promote therapeutic cloning. Because the embryo in both cases isn't considered a human being from such a perspective, killing it makes little difference to those involved in this research.

Life or Tool?

Christians justified by God (Romans 5:1) are called to holy living. The Ten Commandments serve as our guide. In addition, we have learned from the Scriptures that an embryo is a human being, endowed with a body and a soul. Therefore, people who seek to clone themselves to produce cells or tissues for therapeutic purposes forget that this does not honor God with their bodies (1 Corinthians 6:20). Let's take a closer look at these principles.

Deliberate destruction awaits embryonic human beings created for their stem cells. Such destruction also awaits spare frozen embryos created and then abandoned by infertile couples. The Fifth Commandment says, "You shall not murder." God forbids us to take the life of another person wrongfully.

The unborn embryo is a human being, created by God to be His own and live under Him in His kingdom. Even if a person clones himself or herself, these clones are human beings who deserve care and nurture with God's Means of Grace—His Gospel, Holy Baptism, and the Lord's Supper.

In what ways would the use of cloning technology to alleviate Teddy's tremors (above) violate God's Word? Adult human cloning violates the First and Fifth Commandments. It uses technology to create an exact copy of yourself, intending either to create a child—which is really your identical twin—or to create an embryonic human being for destruction to recover stem cells that can be used to grow specific cells, tissues, and organs.

Some people may argue, "God gave us the technical ability to clone. Shouldn't we use that ability?" However, just because you have the ability to do something doesn't mean you should use that ability. Adam and Eve had the ability to eat the fruit of the tree of the knowledge of good and evil, yet God specifically told them that it was not theirs to eat. If a soldier has the ability and technology to destroy thousands of human lives, does that mean God wants him to use that ability? Civilization depends on thoughtful restraint of our bodies, wills, and technology.

Consider the following statement: "If you lose the honor and respect for the embryonic human being's life, you will lose the honor and respect for all human beings, regardless of their age and developmental stage." While some people may restrain their destruction only to embryos, logic and expediency will drive many other people to a lack of respect for all human beings. We see this social trend already at work through abortion and euthanasia.

DEPEND ON THE LORD

Christians are dependent human beings. God in Christ brings us into a covenant relationship through Holy Baptism and the pure Gospel of Jesus Christ. This places a Christian not only in a relationship with the Lord God but also with the Body of Christ, the Holy Christian Church on earth, the communion of saints.

God has made dependence a constant aspect of human life, beginning with conception. Conception can't take place without parents. The embryo can't develop without its mother. A baby depends on its parents/family for food and shelter. Although as adults we may attain considerable independence, a person cannot start a family without another person. In old age a person must depend on the help of others in order to maintain life. God designed us for caring and mutual interdependence.

Christians need to see the use of medical technology to help correct or care for a debilitating physical ailment in view of their birth into a human family and Baptism into the communion of saints. The wanton destruction of spare human embryos or their creation via cloning and subsequent destruction turns this dependent covenant relationship into an independent, self-serving relationship.

God's care for us in Christ enables us to care for all human beings, regardless of their location or developmental status. Human life and its creation, redemption, and sanctification are blessed gifts from the Lord Jesus Christ. Living the life of Christ within this covenant calls into question any biotechnology that causes humankind to make independence their destiny.

Paul's Letter to the Galatians describes a situation where people sought salvation through a routine medical procedure (circumcision). In Galatians 5:1–6, Paul tells the Galatians where they will find true freedom, as well as salvation.

The Galatians believed they could save themselves through circumcision. Paul warns them that they are trusting in their own works, works that in the end cannot save. True independence/freedom comes through entrusting your life to Christ. Why not let the Maker of heaven and earth, the Savior of the world, bear your burden? Ironically, depending on Christ is the path to genuine independence.

In the sight of God, frozen and created embryos have a living purpose: to be His own and live with Him in His eternal kingdom forever. Christians view the sanctity of a human being's life through the cross of Jesus Christ. The cross says that Yahweh is in control. By His Holy Spirit, we are enabled to fear and trust in God above the use of technology that may lead us into the sin of idolatry through cloning and petri dish abortions of embryonic human beings.

Christ freely gave Himself for you. He served you in love by fulfilling the Law of God for your salvation (Galatians 5:13–14). God is the Author and Creator of human life. His *agape* love, given to us in Christ, bears, believes, hopes, and endures all things. This love never fails. Manifest in the cross of Christ, this love helps Christians see through the temptation of correcting afflictions such as Parkinson's disease, Alzheimer's disease, and spinal cord injuries through cloning technologies.

POINTS TO PONDER

Driving beyond the headlights means that a person is driving in the dark too fast to be able to avoid hitting anything that might come into view. Bio-engineering, selective abortion based on gender or other characteristics, genetic manipulation to enhance desirable attributes, and embryo destruction to benefit research agendas are all examples of driving beyond the headlights. How would you bring God's Law and Gospel to bear on this?

WORDS TO REMEMBER

Do you not know that your body is a temple of the Holy Spirit within you, whom you have from God? You are not your own, for you were bought with a price. So glorify God in your body. (1 Corinthians 6:19–20)

30

THE VALLEY OF THE SHADOW OF DEATH

Bob is suffering from Lou Gehrig's disease. Bob is fully competent; however, he is in the end stage of this disease, which causes him to lose control of all of the muscles in his body. A ventilator breathes for him. A feeding tube nourishes him. He receives morphine to manage his discomfort. He could be kept alive for several months, perhaps several years. At least he's able to live at home.

However, as a result of his increasing muscular weakness and general wasting, he has decided that life is not worth living. Bob doesn't want the disease to "get" him. He wants to die on his own terms. Therefore, he is contemplating a visit to Terminal Choices at the BioMed Plaza for information about their assisted suicide program. He's thinking about asking his physician to turn his ventilator off. He also wishes to donate all of his usable organs so that others may benefit from his death.

Even though he has a Durable Power of Attorney for Health Care (proxy directive) and a Do Not Resuscitate order, the family is divided over what he wants to do. They recall a few words from the pastor: "If we live, we live to the Lord, and if we die, we die to the Lord. So then, whether we live or whether we die, we are the Lord's" (Romans 14:8).

Some might take these words to mean that it doesn't matter whether we live or die. However, the apostle's point is that no matter what state we are in, we belong to the Lord. We are subject to His Law and are recipients of His blessings in Christ.

What help can a Durable Power of Attorney offer to a Christian family? Durable Power of Attorney for Health Care (proxy directive), known as Medical Power of Attorney in some states, gives authority to a trusted individual to make decisions when a person lapses into incompetence regarding his or her medical care. This provides comfort and direction for loved ones who are entrusted with care and treatment.

THE NEW FACE OF DEATH

A few decades ago, when a person was dying at home, at a hospital, or at a care center, loved ones surrounded him or her. Much of our current technology and health care directives were not in common use. Medicine was primarily low tech, with a majority of sick people dying quickly of acute illness. According to Dr. Robert D. Orr of the Christian Medical Dental

Society, 90 percent of North Americans today die slowly from debilitating disease (organ failure, malignancy, dementia, etc.). Because of the use of high-tech interventions and because families are often unavailable to care for dying relatives at home, perhaps 70–75 percent of people die in institutions.

Considering these changes and the continuing pace of change, does medical technology always improve people's lives? Though technology has lengthened our lives, it has also prolonged the suffering and increased the isolation of many people. We thank God for technology, but we also pray that He would grant us greater wisdom in how we use technology.

According to the American Medical Association, persons who are dying need only two things: good symptom control (palliative care) and human presence. The ministry of presence is emphasized by The Lutheran Church—Missouri Synod's Commission on Theology and Church Relations in a publication entitled *Christian Care at Life's End.*

At the end of life, care is emphasized over cure, and being a servant over being a "fixer." Pain management is given a top priority in patient comfort care. Yet sometimes pastors or family members fear giving too much pain medication. They fear that such pain medication could suppress the patient's breathing, with possibly fatal results.

Family members and pastors must learn about the "principle of double effect," which is when an action expected to have a bad effect (e.g., refusal of treatment leading to death) is lawful only if the intended good effect (alleviation of pain) is not one that immediately or directly follows from the action. The good effects of pain drugs outweigh the risks of their effects on respiration, blood pressure, pulse, and heart rate. According to Dr. Orr, concern about respiratory suppression from narcotics is greatly exaggerated. Pain stimulates breathing above normal, causing rapid, shallow breaths. The application of pain drugs brings a person's respiration back to a comfortable level. Breathing is normal (15–20 breaths per minute) and deeper when pain is managed appropriately. Managing pain is not an "all or nothing" approach. The good effect—managing pain with the careful application of narcotics—outweighs the bad effect of respiratory suppression.

Though it is often very difficult to predict when a patient will die, it usually becomes clear when he or she is "dying" (e.g., organs are shutting down, increased weakness is observed with a decrease in oral intake, rapid pulse, and cold and mottled extremities). A family's anxieties over the dying process can be lessened by (1) their presence, (2) medical explanation that all these symptoms are normal, and (3) the presence of an experienced caregiver such as a nurse, pastor, or chaplain.

Dr. Gilbert Meilaender noted that the refusal of treatment doesn't mean the refusal of life. Wisdom can help us recognize when it's appropriate to let a body rest from treatment.

When might people think of death as a solution? Paul describes death as an enemy (1 Corinthians 15:20–26). This is certainly true. We shouldn't "make our peace with death." Instead, as Christians, God calls us to make our peace with Him (Isaiah 27:5). More pointedly, He calls us to receive His peace offered through the life, death, and resurrection of His Son. For those in Christ, death is a defeated enemy and eternal life is their hope and blessing.

UNNATURAL DEATH

Secular views of dying and death, especially suffering at the end of life, are strangely contradictory. For example, many secular thinkers view death as the ultimate terror that must be avoided at all costs by the exaggerated use of medical treatments that are doomed to fail. Others, however, may view a human being's life as so broken and the quality of life as so pathetically poor that such life isn't worth living.

Sin gives people the false impression that they are in control of their living and their dying. Many think of death as simply a part of living. Satan may use two other secular doctrines to make them complacent about death: (1) the principle of utilitarianism, that is, seeking the greatest good for the greatest number of people, and (2) the theory of natural Darwinism.

Both of these views lead to the sin of idolatry and ultimately deny that we are finite, sinful human beings whose physical death is not natural. Both ideas can be used to justify keeping a person alive at all costs (even if the art of medicine says treatment is useless and excessively burdensome) or to end a person's life via some form of euthanasia or assisted suicide.

In contrast to these ideas, "God is God" (Exodus 3:14). God forbids us to take the life of another person (murder, abortion, euthanasia) or our own life (suicide or assisted suicide). He assures us that He is in control. He is the one whom we should fear, love, and trust above all things.

Read Deuteronomy 32:39, but don't receive this passage fatalistically (as though whatever happens is God's will). God permits us to make decisions, even life-and-death decisions. However, as our Maker and Judge, He can overrule our decisions. Life and death ultimately belong to Him.

We are to care for those who are ill and at the end of their earthly lives. We are called to be kind and compassionate to one another, to forgive one another, and especially to bear one another's burdens. The Word of the Lord God declares this to be meet, right, and beneficial for Christians living the life of Christ in the world.

ALIVE IN CHRIST

The Lord God creates a human being's life. In the beginning He made our first parents by His Word, and we human beings were perfectly made. But our bodies and souls are now corrupted by sin.

God is God. His Son, Jesus Christ, the Savior of all humankind, has restored to us His perfect love and righteousness by His grace through faith. For daily bread, life, and breath, we depend on Him. He takes responsibility for us, caring for us through His Means of Grace, the Gospel, Holy Baptism, and the Lord's Supper. God created us not just "by His will" but "on account of His will" (see Revelation 4:11). He desires to be with us and enjoy our fellowship.

Healing for the sick and dying begins with repentance and faith, knowing that in our suffering, God in Christ forgives our sins by faith alone. Hence, we go to the cross of Jesus Christ not to learn how to deal with suffering at the end of life but to know that by faith alone our suffering is not in vain.

Remarkably, Paul says that we can rejoice in our suffering (Romans 5:3–5). This is not meant sadistically. We can rejoice because we know that our suffering is not the end for which God created us. He will sustain us in the midst of it so that we may partake of all He has for us in Christ.

God is in control of our lives. Comfort for the dying and their loved ones comes from the God of grace. We rejoice knowing that in our dying, God's Word declares that we are new creatures in the resurrected Christ. "If a man dies, shall he live again?" (Job 14:14). Job says, "And after my skin has been thus destroyed, yet in my flesh I shall see God, whom I shall see for myself, and my eyes shall behold, and not another" (19:26–27).

Holy Baptism states that our identity is in Christ. Since we have been baptized into His death and resurrection, we, too, live a new life in Christ (Romans 6:4). Comfort care begins with the cross of Jesus Christ and continues throughout our earthly life until we stand before the Lord in our heavenly home. "Cast your burden on the LORD, and He will sustain you; He will never permit the righteous to be moved" (Psalm 55:22).

Whether one is baptized as an infant or later in life, Baptism works forgiveness of sins, rescues from death and the devil, and gives eternal salvation to all who believe this, as the words and promises of God declare (Romans 5:1–14; 1 Peter 3:21). Baptized Christians know that God calls them His children and that they are not alone but that Christ walks with them, bringing the hope that is in Him. Baptism tells us that we are in Christ and that physical death is a gain.

POINTS TO PONDER

Abortion, assisted suicide, and euthanasia are too frequent and on the increase in many parts of the world, and those who oppose such practices often meet apathy, derision, or outright hostility. Christians are surrounded by a culture of death, but we know the Lord of Life. How can we support and encourage one another, and how can we share God's love with a world that seems so intent on death?

WORDS TO REMEMBER

Be faithful unto death, and I will give you the crown of life. (Revelation 2:10)

Photo: © Andrey Kuzmin/Shutterstock, Inc.

Bioengineering, Artificial Intelligence, and the New Gnosticism

Although the stories in this section on "Redesigning Life" are fictional, the science behind them is expanding at breakneck speed and moving into areas undreamed of only a decade or two ago. This research and development is driven by a profit motive, scientific curiosity, national security, ideology, or, in some cases, ego and pride. Inevitably, questions follow about the propriety of the science and its uses.

Several years ago, for example, DARPA (the Defense Advanced Research Projects Agency) requested proposals for research into how the human body responds to infection or injury. The idea was to develop technologies to help soldiers survive on the battlefield. But if someone were to develop such technologies, would they be used to save a soldier's life or simply to keep him alive and in action to fight for a few hours longer? Is the soldier a person or a tool? The research opens up complicated, difficult-to-discuss questions about its potential and its possible uses.

In a different area, scientists have been working for years to develop advanced computing capabilities, including artificial intelligence. Occasionally you will see authors speculate that it is only a matter of time before we will be able to replicate part or all of a human mind, that machines (i.e., computers) will become so advanced that they can replicate themselves or in some sense take on a life of their own, or even that machines will someday become more advanced than their inventors (humans) and will take over the world. It is certainly true that computational systems (computers and their sensors) are becoming steadily more advanced. However, no computational technique or capability has been able to replicate personality, free will, or sentient behavior, much less the spirit or soul of a human being on any level, or even suggest how such a thing might be accomplished. Scientists can't even agree how to define some of these concepts!

Examples of bioengineering and related technologies come to mind in other areas as well. Scientists are working to develop artificial retinas that hold the potential to restore the sight of many people who have lost their sight, and primitive versions of these devices are into clinical trial. New generations of curative and performance-enhancing drugs are in development, and old drugs are finding new uses. DNA mapping of the human genome provides a starting point for developing new gene-based therapies for previously intractable ailments.

The science associated with each of these areas of development has its own risks and potential downfalls. And often, what scientists discover also underscores just how much we do not know. For example, when the human genome was mapped, scientists confidently wrote that much of the human DNA was identical to that of other organisms, even worms, and that about 80 percent of the DNA was surplus, dormant, and served no useful purpose. And they cited this as baggage that accumulated as humans evolved from less advanced organisms. But they were in for a surprise. Subsequent research discovered that this "dormant" DNA was actually functional and played crucial roles in turning biochemical processes on and off during the development of each cell. We still do not know what all of the DNA does, but now we know that what we don't know is really large, rather than assuming that we have it all figured out.

Other parts of this study discuss the scientific method and why someone would feel motivated to push the state of the discovery in their investigations. However, important questions of motive, ethics, morals, and values will accompany scientific research as long as scientists do research. And these questions point us to a spiritual divide, of sorts, between a path that fulfills a God-ordained vocation and a path that leads elsewhere.

Consider some of the motives suggested in the fictional "Redesigning Life" stories. On a basic level, these motives emphasize fulfilling our selfish desires to the extent that effects on our body are no longer as important as our desires, and the effects on our soul even less so. We see this in action in people who abuse performance-enhancing drugs or use other science or technology for selfish advantage or pleasure at the expense of their health. This reflects the corrosive effect of ignoring God's Law, as people yield to the temptation to sacrifice their own bodies for the sake of their desires.

The old Gnosticism taught that the physical body was corrupted and unimportant and that spirit and self were all that mattered. Today we see a resurgence of this heresy in a new Gnosticism that makes mind and body subservient to an enhanced, pleasured self. Scripture plainly points us in a different direction, though, as we realize that Jesus died for our mind, body, and soul (all of each person) and rose from the dead so that we can look forward to the bodily resurrection to life with Him (1 Corinthians 15:42). This is the kind of enhancement that counts!

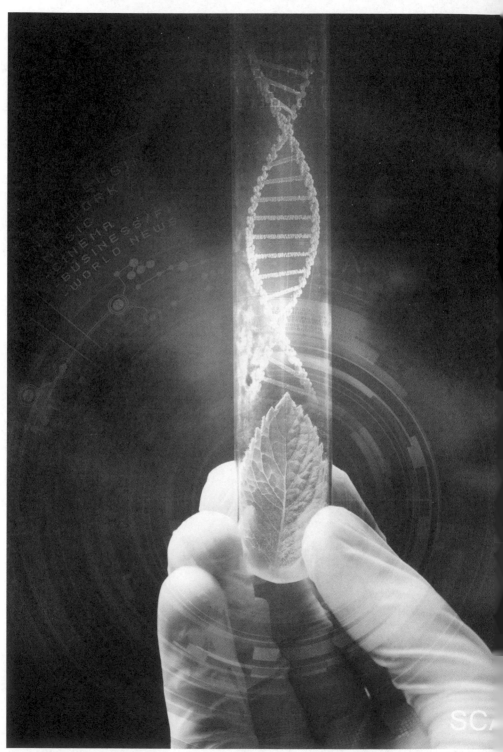

SCIENCE AND THE SAVIOR

The Calling of a Scientist

When we grab our umbrella on the way out the door, we take the advice of a scientist about the weather. When we buy prepackaged food, we buy into someone's research about microbes. When we kick back to enjoy the game, we enjoy the benefits of the latest in telecommunication.

Modern science began as a rare and specialized discipline. Today, science and scientific ideas touch our daily lives and govern numerous types of work. See if you can find your place in the following list:

Aeronautics	Engineering	Meteorology
Agritech	Forensics	Nursing
Anthropology	Genetics	Pharmacology
Archaeology	Geology	Physics
Astronomy	Histology	Psychology
Biology	Immunology	Robotics
Chemistry	Kinetics	Telecommunications
Computing	Manufacturing	Transportation
Ecology	Mathematics	Zoology
Economics	Medicine	

Modern science has grown to touch every field of study and every occupation. But amid all this knowledge and technology, something is being lost: meaning, morality, and our immortal souls. The children of modern science are in danger of fulfilling the apostle

Paul's words: "Claiming to be wise, they became fools" (Romans 1:22).

We are learning that knowledge is a poor substitute for goodness. Technology eases some burdens of humanness but aggravates others. No matter how intelligent we grow, we cannot outgrow our weaknesses. Simply put, we never outgrow our need for God.

The following discussions will help you explore some of the issues, facts, and myths about modern science and the Christian faith. It will teach you to appreciate science as a blessing from your Creator. It will also help you see scientists at their greatest potential as the great astronomer and mathematician Johannes Kepler saw them, as "priests of the highest God in regard to the book of nature."

31

GOD'S INTENTIONS FOR SCIENCE

Nonreligious people typically see science as something that humans decided to do for themselves, without any guidance from God. For them science shows the authority of human reason and rejects God's Word as outmoded superstition. This may be called *autonomous science*. It creates a sense that human beings can figure everything out for themselves, without God's guiding hand.

They see advances in agricultural science and industrial food processing as providers of their daily bread—not God. They look to pharmaceuticals, not to God, as the source of healing and health. In effect, they see science as a source of secular salvation, saving us from hard work, pain, and illness by the wonders of technology and medicine. For example, in highly secularized Europe, one could reasonably argue that faith in science is more prevalent than faith in God.

Faced with a confident secular rejection of God, Christians sometimes conclude that science is a dangerous thing, since it encourages human beings to play God, supplanting His roles as Provider and Savior. Some feel tempted to conclude that science was not part of God's intention for human beings. They conclude that science epitomizes the prideful rejection of God's sovereignty and the desire to be "like God" in knowledge and power (Genesis 3:5). In other words, the fact that unbelievers embrace science as a way of rejecting God encourages some believers to reject science. But should these go hand in hand? Education and knowledge in and of themselves do not undermine faith. In fact, the Lord encourages us to pursue knowledge (Proverbs 23:12, 23). However, pride that comes with success can undermine faith.

Believers rightly perceive the danger that science can become a tower of Babel (Genesis 11) and that faith in human ingenuity and power over the natural world can supplant faith in the Creator and Savior of that world. However, we must not fail to consider the idea that God can have different and better intentions for science.

AUTONOMY AND HUMILITY

Excessive confidence in science reflects a misunderstanding of what science is. Ultimately, science provides a collection of instruments, not only physical but also intellectual ones, such as theories and formulas. These instruments are very useful for explaining, predicting, and even controlling natural things.

But first, it should be noted that something can be useful without being true. A scientific theory can make the right predictions without being an accurate model of reality. For example, in about AD 150, the Egyptian scientist Ptolemy wrote his *Almagest*, which provided an ingenious method for computing the orbits of the known planets. The model assumed that all planetary motions must be circular. However, single circles could not account for retrograde motion, wherein planets such as Mars appear to move backwards. So Ptolemy proposed that planets are going around smaller circles (epicycles), which are themselves going around a larger circle (the deferent). This allowed him to chart planetary motions with surprising accuracy. Yet scientists today agree that there are no epicycles and that Ptolemy's model of the solar system is mistaken. We may conclude that today's theories, which seem useful and plausible to modern scientists, may also be seriously in error.

Some scientific claims made today are regarded as established facts that cannot be legitimately questioned. One scientific claim that some may question is the theory of evolution. All theories should be treated as theories, even when they are widely accepted and respected. For more on evolution, see appendix 1 at the end of this book.

Second, when scientific results are held to be certain, the claim usually depends not strictly on science but on a prior worldview. For example, the statement that the human genome project has traced the complete blueprint for humanity rests on the assumption that we are nothing but material entities, like rocks or minerals. Christians should be aware that there is a spiritual dimension to humanity that transcends the physical characteristics studied by natural science.

Consider this claim: science has proven that there can be no miracles. However, as we discussed earlier in this book, science cannot disprove the existence of miracles or a spiritual aspect to life. Science studies events in nature, which may be open to both natural and supernatural causes.

Most scientists today assume methodological naturalism, according to which scientists should investigate nature as if God had nothing to do with it. With this frame of mind, nothing is allowed to count as scientific evidence for a miracle or spiritual existence. Science simply cannot investigate something already rejected by its starting assumptions!

But this does not show a lack of scientific evidence for miracles or spiritual beings, providing we allow a more open picture of science that follows the evidence wherever it leads. On a more open model of science, one may see that a supernatural explanation is sometimes more likely than a natural one. Suppose you knew that various jars at the wedding at Cana (John 2:1–11) had been filled with plain water and, as they were in plain view, you knew they had not been tampered with. Then someone drew wine from the jars. Naturally, water does not turn into wine in such a short period or without the addition of other materials, including grapes. This would be good evidence that a miracle occurred.

The confidence that miracles or spiritual existence are impossible does not come from science at all. It comes from the view that nature is a closed system. However, for Christians, nature is an open system in which God can intervene. Water may naturally stay water, but the Lord of nature, through the same power He used to create water, can turn water into wine.

Third, powerful scientific instruments do not necessarily improve life. And even with good intentions, technology leads to unforeseen problems. Radiation can be used to treat cancer but can also produce it. The overuse of antibiotics has produced more virulent strains of bacteria.

Today, tyrannical regimes use science to develop deadly chemical and biological weapons. Even in the West, deadly agents such as anthrax weapons were developed during the Second World War and now may have fallen into the hands of rogue nations. This requires the development of antidotes and safety procedures, also done by means of science.

Even when a good result is intended, there can be bad consequences. The consumption of fossil fuels for heating and transportation has generated pollution and may be causing "global warming," although this area of research has become politicized. Mechanization, laborsaving devices, and industrialized fast food—all the products of science—are important factors in increased obesity and a decline in health and fitness, although the role of poor choices must not be ignored. Computerization has granted much convenience but may be bad for our eyes and wrists and certainly exposes our data to the dangers of worms, viruses, and identity theft.

Believers sometimes overemphasize the failures of science. Science can be misused, but it can also be a means of serving our neighbor. For example, early scientists like Robert Boyle (1627–91) saw chemistry as a means of providing inexpensive medicines for the poor. Probably the most important advances for public health have been the provision of clean drinking water and the sterilization of medical instruments, both of which depended on scientific discoveries.

Some of the most important blessings of science seem quite humble and yet have saved and improved the quality of countless lives. Safe disposal of waste, pasteurization, antiseptics, and the development of vaccines have been wonderful achievements. Compassionate scientists have also developed numerous technologies to assist those with impaired senses and those who cannot walk or use their limbs. And they have even developed partial replacements for body parts that are no longer functioning, such as artificial hips and artificial valves for the heart. Although the Internet is also open to abuse, it has allowed valuable communities to form that are not bound by geographical location or the problems of transportation.

Both believers and unbelievers tend to suppose that science is a purely human institution. Having an inflated sense of human goodness, unbelievers often exaggerate the blessings of science. Having an understanding of original sin, believers often fixate on the abuses of science. Both can learn from the biblical record.

THE LIMITS OF SCIENCE

Science does not threaten Christians. But science that views itself as disconnected from God does threaten Christians and everyone else! The idea that scientists can find ultimate truth by their own reason denies the true relationship between God and humankind. Frustration will follow when science is viewed as a means of engineering a heaven on earth. We need to remember that the fall into sin has affected all of our abilities, including our reason. Even when our logic is correct, we tend to use it for corrupt goals.

In the late nineteenth century, there was enormous confidence that improvements in the quality of life were guaranteed by scientific innovations in technology. Indeed, this scientific pride was so great that some, following Karl Marx, thought they could devise a scientific method for organizing society.

Then came the First World War, in which the very latest technological innovations were used to kill millions of people in horrific ways. The Soviet Union attempted to use Karl Marx's ideas, leading to a brutal totalitarian regime marked by mass purges and exile to labor camps of millions of "antisocial elements," that is, people who would not conform to the system.

Genesis 11 (the story of the tower of Babel) shows us that human reason is a poor substitute for God. Humans cannot by their own reason or strength reach up to God, because God is righteous, all-knowing, and all-powerful, and we are not. All attempts to use science to create a Utopia, a heaven on earth, ultimately fail. When God confused the language at Babel, He revealed the cacophony of conflicting, selfish voices that underlie humanity.

History has repeated itself. Two world wars, death camps, and totalitarianism shattered the nineteenth-century idea of inevitable scientific progress. Each of these horrors used science to dehumanize entire populations. This led to skepticism about human reason and our current "postmodern times," where there are many competing worldviews and groups but no basis for consensus and peace. In this time of confusion, we must come to our senses and confess our sins to God. For "if we confess our sins, He is faithful and just to forgive us our sins and to cleanse us from all unrighteousness" (1 John 1:9).

King David confesses a basic truth about the human condition in Psalm 51:3–6. Sin is not just a problem out there in an uncooperative world that needs to be fixed by technology. It is within us, in our desires for power, wealth, and control of others, and above all in our desire to be our own gods. The truth is that we are by nature sinful from conception and have no power of our own to change this. We are enemies of God and cannot approach God or become godlike by anything we do, including the exercise of our reason in science. Since we are infected with sin, sin manifests itself in any attempt to create a heaven on earth. Our failure is inevitable, but fortunately we are saved by God's grace and can now have the more realistic goal of doing what we can to serve our neighbors out of love.

Autonomous science assumes a utopian result because it denies the fundamental truth that even the most enlightened scientists are infected with original sin, a problem that cannot be solved by pills, surgery, or psychotherapy. The idea of science as salvation proposes that evil is only in the world or in social institutions and that we can fix all these problems with human ingenuity. But the truth is that evil is within us and is liable to corrupt all human projects.

These prideful abuses of science make some Christians shy away from appreciating the value of science. But there is a legitimate vocation (calling) of scientist. A *vocation* is a station of work that God calls us to as a means of providing for the needs of others. From the sixth day of creation, we see that God is not a micromanager. He delegates responsibility to human beings. After God created our first parents, He appointed them as stewards of the rest of creation (Genesis 1:28–30). Likewise, He gave Adam the task of classifying and naming the kinds of animals (2:19–20). Even after the fall, human beings are still stewards of their natural environment, though now the task is more difficult (3:17–19).

The commission to be "gardeners" of Eden is sometimes called the "cultural mandate." Culture can be defined as what humans do to nature to make it suit their purposes. Vocations are means of making cultural products to serve our neighbor. Science provides powerful ways of controlling nature (making cultural products) for the benefit of others. This is why there is a legitimate vocation of scientist.

When scientists or others use science as a means of harming others, they are no longer serving their neighbor. But this shows that they are acting outside of their true vocation, not that there is something wrong with the vocation itself.

A vocation is an office instituted by God. How would understanding science as a vocation help prevent some of the dreadful abuses of science we mentioned earlier? All such offices are bound by God's Law and are aimed at curbing sin and providing for our neighbors' needs. Seeing science as a vocation would help us keep science in perspective as a gift to limit evil and help others, not to increase evil and harm others. Seeing science as a vocation would also help us focus more on what our neighbors need and less on making a profit by producing services they might like but that are really unhelpful.

MASKS OF GOD

When it comes to salvation, all vocations are equal. They are all equally irrelevant! What work could we possibly do to "help" God? As a vocation, science has nothing to do with salvation. God does not need our vocations, but our neighbors do.

God sets us free to serve those around us. Martin Luther explained that in this service we are nothing less than "masks of God" (*larvae dei*); we are the visible means through which God provides for others. What is more, there is much that God wants us to do to serve others (Ephesians 2:10).

Ephesians 2:8–10; Romans 12:4–8; and 1 Corinthians 12:12–26 speak to us about vocations, including the vocation of scientist. Vocations have nothing to do with salvation. Vocations are directed at works, and we are saved by grace, not works. But vocations are so important to God that He has created good works for us to do in advance (Ephesians 2:10) so that we may aid our neighbor.

The scientist is revealed as merely one part of the Body of Christ, which contains many elements, all of which are needed for the body to function, and all of which contribute something of distinctive value. God calls all people to help right where they are and with the gifts they have, and that includes the scientist. The scientist is no better or worse than any other member of the Body of Christ but plays an important contributory role in a wider project that includes those who supply scientists with their needs and those who benefit from scientific results.

It may not always be easy for a Christian to be a scientist (for example, one might work at a lab that has chosen to perform research one believes is unethical), but Christians who are scientists can place their confidence in Christ and do what they can to help others and witness to their faith, just as all Christians are called to do.

The fact that God uses us as instruments of His providential care is all the more remarkable because we are still in a fallen state. Even Christians, freely saved by Christ's righteousness, retain the old Adam and remain sinful. Yet God can work through sinful human beings to provide for others.

Even when scientists have sinful motives of greed or lust for fame, their discoveries may still benefit others. Although a medical scientist might develop a wonder drug to make himself wealthy and famous, the drug itself may be used to benefit many people. By contrast, the scientist who is a Christian is set free to serve and may develop the drug for a better reason. In gratitude for what Christ has done in saving us, a Christian may gladly and freely serve others as a scientist.

Read Genesis 50:15–21, where the story of Joseph gives us an example of how God provides (see especially v. 20). Joseph's brothers were used by God to place Joseph where he could save many people, including his own family, from starvation. We all experience failure, and scientists may experience it more than most because of the exacting demands of their profession. However, we must remember that God is in charge and that even when we fail, intellectually or morally, God can work through failures to bring success.

These events in Joseph's life prefigured the life of Jesus Christ (see John 11:47–53). God used the leaders in Jerusalem who demanded the crucifixion of an innocent man, Jesus, in an action that redeemed all humankind. Thankfully, God's love does not falter as ours does, but His love endures forever.

We should be comforted by the fact that our salvation does not depend on how we use our gifts and also by the fact that there are many different ways God can use us to achieve His ends. We may now be more willing to encourage talented young people to become scientists in service to others. If we feel that science may sometimes be abused, we can encourage more Christians to become scientists so they can be salt and light in the scientific community (Matthew 5:13–16).

In our individualistic age, we tend to think that everything we do is a choice, but vocations are really sent to us by God. Although we can choose whether or not to follow the vocation and how we will follow it, the calling comes to us through our gifts and circumstances. We do not create it by our own choice.

Today we think of everything as a choice, not only food and clothes, but also beliefs and lifestyles. This way of thinking seduces us into thinking we have everything under control, that we are in charge. But ultimately, God is in charge (see 1 Corinthians 7:17–24). He sends us vocations by the gifts He equips us with, the circumstances we find ourselves in, and the neighbors who live beside us. Those people need help, and if we can help them, that is our calling. It may mean crucifying some of our ambitions and desires (vocations are crosses), but as the old self is killed, a new self will appear in Christ, and we are rewarded with a sense of satisfaction in a job well done. We may be tired and overworked, but there is a legitimate sense of achievement and fulfillment in faithful service to others.

Thanks be to God for the vocation of our Lord Jesus Christ. The heavenly Father called Him to create us anew through Baptism in His name. He perfectly fulfilled His calling so that He might atone for the sins we commit in our callings. Through Christ we live and work to the Father's glory and the good of all.

POINTS TO PONDER

In the Sermon on the Mount, Jesus called His disciples to be salt and light. We live this out mainly through the vocations (plural!) He gives us. Vocation is more than a job or an occupation or a relationship; it is a divine calling that God uses to reach and serve those around us. And this is not something we contrive; it is something God prepares in advance for us to live!

WORDS TO REMEMBER

For we are His workmanship, created in Christ Jesus for good works, which God prepared beforehand, that we should walk in them. (Ephesians 2:10)

32

SCIENCE SERVES OUR NEIGHBORS

The stereotype of the "mad scientist" expresses the fear that scientists may be so consumed by their desire to know how things work, and to make things happen, that they lose good judgment and act unethically. Mary Shelley's *Frankenstein* (1818) highlights the lack of concern for basic moral values that may arise when human life is viewed merely as an object of experimental investigation. Frankenstein is, of course, science fiction.

But today we see scientists engaged in stem cell research, disregarding questions raised about the God-given value of all human life. We hear of scientists paid by tobacco companies to create the false impression that there are no significant health risks associated with smoking. We see pharmaceutical scientists developing more and more drugs that are aggressively marketed. Some of this marketing tempts people who do not need the drugs to demand that their doctor (another scientist) prescribe them. Against better judgment, he or she sometimes does just that. All of this makes us wonder whether science can really be a moral enterprise.

What other kinds of moral dilemmas might scientific activities raise? According to some critics, much of science is inherently immoral because it attempts to play God. They question whether science is really about helping others or about glorifying the powers of the scientist and providing products we would really be better off without but find almost impossible to resist. Others see science as amoral, a powerful instrument that can be used for good or evil. Scientists themselves sometimes excuse work that they know will be used unethically, saying they are only "concerned with the truth" and how that truth is used is someone else's business. The idea that science is a vocation that falls under God's Law is virtually absent. The idea that scientists are citizens and brothers and sisters of all other human beings is not considered often enough.

SCIENCE AND MORALITY

As we discussed earlier, humans have been given a "cultural mandate" to subdue the earth. One of the ways they can do this is through the vocation of science. We have also noted that the world is no longer perfect. It is a fallen world afflicted with disease, discomfort, drudgery, and poverty. Many of the early scientists saw their work as a means of easing those consequences of

1. For example, Robert Boyle became interested in chemistry partly because he hoped to make inexpensive remedies for the many ailments affecting the poor. To scientists such as Boyle, science was conceived within a moral context as necessarily serving the needs of fallen humanity. It was not directed at harm or selfish gain, nor was it viewed merely as an instrument to be used in good ways and bad.

Viewing science as a vocation can help restore its moral dimension. Most vocations are offices instituted by God through the order of creation and preservation. As a result, they fall under the "left hand" kingdom of God's Law. The fact that the content of scientific theories is devoid of morality does not make scientific office holders exempt from God's moral law, anymore than accountants stop being human beings or citizens because they only study numbers. In a community, we must be concerned about how our work is used by others. Scientists are called to work with others to help their neighbors, and they are not doing that if their results are being used to harm others.

We need to be careful. All vocations are under God's Law. Some ways of finding cures or laborsaving devices may indeed be immoral. Furthermore, the unnecessary or excessive use of some of these items may reflect poor stewardship and do more harm than good. Efficient, reliable transportation, for example, is a great boon of scientific technology. Yet there are also many inefficient vehicles that drain resources and produce unnecessary pollution. While humans are given dominion over creation, it is a dominion of stewardship, not a license for wasteful greed and practices that poison the air, earth, and water.

The vocation of scientist can help provide an ethic for environmental care. All human beings are called to be stewards of their natural environment. Scientists have a special responsibility, though, because they understand better than nonscientists how that environment works and because they can control and adapt it for good and bad purposes. Nature is not to be worshiped as if it is a god or to be trashed as if God had not made it. Nature has value in its own right as part of God's creation and value for human beings as a precious resource to be husbanded.

Gardeners do not leave nature to its own devices, nor do they exterminate all life to make a pavement. They nurture living things and use them to provide food for our bodies and beauty for our eyes. Likewise scientists intervene in nature but should do so to meet needs and beautify the environment, not to despoil it.

Scientists are not called to be gods, usurping God's lordship over life and death. Stanley Jaki (1924–2009) called for "the middle road" approach in science; it is important to consider the implications of his "middle road" for scientific ethics. When scientists treat human life as a disposable, experimental item, they act outside of their vocation. For example, the Nazi scientr gaged in hideously dehumanizing experiments. In one, they placed prise in a refrigerated room and lowered the temperature progressively to find at what point a human being would die of hypothermia. Another horrit idea, discussed earlier, is cloning human beings to provide "spare parts" for other human beings. Such experiments violate Kant's requirement that we should never treat human beings as simply a means to other ends. Although scientists are called to mitigate the consequences of the fall, not all ways of doing this are morally acceptable.

Scientists may be tempted to see an unfortunate human being as a way of testing a hypothesis, even without that person's knowledge or consent. Should unwitting humans be exposed to the fallout from a nuclear bomb test to see what the effects of radiation might be on human beings? Should a patient who might recover from a disease in a few years without treatment be an involuntary guinea pig for any and every medicine designed to acceler- ate recovery? When human beings are treated as no more than experimental subjects, the personal is reduced to the impersonal, and human dignity is violated.

Many scientists pursue highly ethical research from which numerous human beings benefit. For example, geneticists have discovered the specific causes of such hereditary diseases as cystic fibrosis and Tay-Sachs disease. Modern germ-line therapy can do nothing to stop original sin. But it can prevent offspring from suffering some of the temporal consequences of sin.

Ethical science has produced countless devices that help disabled people function more effectively by compensating for weakened, broken, and un- responsive limbs. Our sight and hearing is much improved, ligaments are replaced, and prosthetic limbs extend our control. Voluntary subjects coura- geously try new drugs that may lead to important cures for serious diseases. New scopes, cameras, and lasers allow specialized operations with an accu- racy and safety level undreamt of only a few years ago. All of these advances help people continue in productive work and better enjoy the life God gave them.

One Calling among Many

The vocation of science provides more power to human beings than many other vocations. But we must remember Lord Acton's warning that all power corrupts. We need to be aware that science should be constrained by strict guidelines. Since the content of science is the operation of the natural world, and this is a world of "what is," not "what ought to be the case," sci- entific theories and results cannot themselves tell us how scientists ought to behave. In other words, science has nothing to do with how science is used. But the scientist is an office holder in his vocation, and the Law of God binds ces. This is true not only for the believer who accepts the validity of s Law, but also for the unbeliever who does not.

Fundamentally, scientists are no more important than anyone else. They may serve as our intellectual "eyes" when attempting to peer into the secret workings of nature, and they may be the ones who direct the "hand" of those who manufacture and use scientific technology, but "the eye cannot say to the hand, 'I have no need of you!' " Scientists may be the intellectual heads of modern society while others are called to walk along paths shaped by science, but "the head [cannot say] to the feet, 'I have no need of you'" (1 Corinthians 12:21).

In a body, all the parts are interdependent (1 Corinthians 12:14–26). There is no use having a brain without a heart to pump blood to the brain or without lungs to provide oxygen to be transported by the blood. Likewise, scientists have a role to play only in relation to others. Some may regard scientists as the brains of society, but scientists rely on others to bring them raw materials for their experiments and to provide the food, housing, clothing, and transportation that science has helped to improve. They rely on sound government, which protects all legitimate callings through law enforcement and the military. And scientists would be useless if there were no other people who benefited from their results or who could use their results to serve still others.

Fundamentally, we need to see that scientists are not a secular priesthood set apart from others. Scientists are members of the community and are not granted superhuman privileges. The doctrine of vocation helps us by pointing out that vocations are *reciprocal.* For example, as there is a vocation of parent, so there is a vocation of child. As there is a vocation of scientist, so there are various vocations that thrive by the use of scientific products and generate profit. Agricultural scientists develop hardier crops and various pesticides, but they are not superior to the farmers who use their products to grow corn. In fact, the agricultural scientists work with farmers, bakers, truck drivers, retailers, and marketing advisers to bring us our daily bread. Instead of seeing vocations as competing for prestige and preeminence, we can see them cooperating to fulfill God's providential plan.

In our modern age, scientists seem to stand out because of their specialized knowledge and power. They can seem like secular magicians who can do things other people cannot. When it comes to plumbing and building, however, the average theoretical physicist or organic chemist is no better off than the average postal worker. Such a person relies, or is well advised to rely, on the vocations of plumber, architect, and construction worker. We need constantly to remind ourselves that specialized knowledge in one area is not godlike knowledge of all areas.

In any vocation, there is a temptation to see the work as an
In *The Great Divorce* (1945), C. S. Lewis describes a painter who
career trying to capture glimpses of heaven but then became intereste
paint and the artistic process for its own sake. Likewise scientists can
wrapped up in the machinery of their work that they lose sight of any G
pleasing goal.

Some years ago scientists developed a bovine growth hormone that increases the milk yield of dairy cows. Not only were there (perhaps unfounded) concerns about the safety of the milk, but also the product seemed curiously unhelpful in a time of milk surpluses! To see science as something to be done for its own sake falls short of seeing it as a wonderful gift for enhancing our ability to help others.

Many computer users complain that computer scientists spend too much of their time developing flashy features and too little on improving reliability, security, and ease of use. The pharmaceutical industry also produces an inordinate number of drugs for mental and physical conditions that might be remedied by alternate means (e.g., diet and exercise). These drugs sometimes have side effects at least as bad as the original ailment and are often over-marketed and overprescribed. As a result, many people end up taking drugs they do not need and in combination with other drugs, which may lead to dangerous interactions. Scientists who pander to the consumer society's insatiable desire for quick fixes do not serve the needs of their neighbors but tell them what their "itching ears" want to hear (2 Timothy 4:3). A most tragic case, for example, is the overprescribing of Ritalin for unruly children, which evades serious questions about whether the behavior is truly unruly or only inconvenient curiosity, or if parental neglect and abuse might be part of the problem. There may also be health risks from children taking such drugs for a protracted period of time.

Scientists can refocus their work by remembering that they should be most concerned to provide for their neighbors' needs, not their wants. They should also see their primary goal as supporting existing and useful vocations, rather than further weakening them by providing a scientific surrogate.

UNITED IN CHRIST

Where scientists have acted outside their office, harming others or despoiling God's creation, they need to know that God's forgiveness is for all people. Where scientists have elevated science above God's moral law, the Word gives sight to the blind so that they understand where they truly stand in God's creation and in society. Intellectual sight is not the same as spiritual sight. This is because "the natural person does not accept the things of the Spirit of God, for they are folly to him" (1 Corinthians 2:14). And spiritual insight is never received through our sinful human wisdom, but only through

om. "Has not God made foolish the wisdom of the world? For
ᵥe wisdom of God, the world did not know God through wisdom,
ᵤ God through the folly of what we preach to save those who believe"
ᵢnthians 1:20–21).

Christ is so much more than a wise man or a moral compass. He is for us
ᵢsdom from God—that is our righteousness, holiness, and redemption. By
His death for our sins, He has overcome death. Through His rising to life, He
gives us new life, hope, and genuine unity, an eternal bond of love and grace
with our Maker.

Science does provide intellectual enlightenment. But reason does not
save, and intelligence in the service of greed, ambition, pride, and arrogance
only exacerbates evil by making it more potent. The spiritual enlightenment,
which shows us our true condition, makes us depend on God, and the desire
to serve others in humility comes only from God, not from our autonomous
intellectual development.

Not only does the Gospel bring spiritual sight, but it also brings spiritual
gifts that enable us to have a proper concern for one another. Scientists trans-
formed by the Gospel cannot view themselves as cut off from other humans.
They must see themselves as part of a united body in which they play one
role among many that have equal dignity, even though they differ in worldly
status. For "God has so composed the body, giving greater honor to the part
that lacked it, that there may be no division in the body, but that the members
may have the same care for one another" (1 Corinthians 12:24–25). As a result of this unity, there is a sense of appreciation and compassionate concern
for others. United by Christ, we are not competitors, jockeying for advancement in the world's eyes. We don't live to get ahead by elevating ourselves
and putting others down. We are "fellow passengers" invested in a common
project, as Stephen Carter points out in his book *Civility* (Basic Books, 1998).

It is because of this common project that there can be no justification for
using another being for the benefit of only some members of the community.
In the community created by the Gospel, "if one member suffers, all suffer
together" (1 Corinthians 12:26a). Further, great scientific achievements are
not a reason to create an elitist separation of scientists but are beneficial to
the whole: "if one member is honored, all rejoice together" (1 Corinthians
12:26b). For all, including scientists, are called to humility. "Live in harmony
with one another. Do not be haughty, but associate with the lowly" (Romans
12:16).

What creates unity is ultimately not us but Christ, for in Him "the whole
structure, being joined together, grows into a holy temple in the Lord" (Ephesians 2:21). The building is not made by sinful human hands but by Christ,
in whom we are "being built together into a dwelling place for God by the
Spirit" (v. 22).

Legal restraint curbs our selfish desires only because we want to be warded for good behavior or to avoid punishment for bad behavior. Suc "enlightened self-interest" helps keep order, but if a scientist believes he or she can benefit from unethical behavior that won't be detected, what will hold that person back? Conscience may help, but conscience is corrupt since the fall, and we engage in all sorts of self-deception to suppress it. The Gospel provides a sense of gratitude and love of neighbor that makes us want to do the right thing. Christians—scientists or otherwise—no longer see themselves as special or others as inferior but seek to do what they can to hold the Body of Christ together and to draw others to it.

Points to Ponder

The vocation of scientist can serve its neighbors in many wonderful ways, but it needs guidance and moral boundaries. Actually, this is true for any vocation. Fortunately, we have the privilege of knowing the living God. How should knowing God make a difference in how you perform your vocation?

Words to Remember

You were called to freedom, brothers. Only do not use your freedom as an opportunity for the flesh, but through love serve one another. (Galatians 5:13)

33

SCIENCE AS SUB-CREATION

Science "creates" so many products that some people see scientists as creators in the same sense that God is the Creator. For example, God said, "Let there be light" (Genesis 1:3), and there was light. Scientists have figured out how to generate and direct electricity to create artificial light for when the sun goes down. God said, "Let Us make man" (Genesis 1:26). Now life scientists can use germ-line therapy to prevent mankind's offspring from acquiring a hereditary disease. Others are proposing to make people through cloning.

If humans can be cloned successfully, will scientists be their creators? And if so, does this mean that the clones are made in the image of the scientists and not in God's image? If scientists can manufacture a person, can they own that person? It seems to some that there is less and less room to affirm God as Creator.

Some now claim science has shown that even humans are not made in God's image, but do they really understand what this means? They argue that the examination of human and animal genomes shows that humans are fundamentally similar to other species. They cite this as proof that humans have simply evolved by the undirected processes of random mutation and natural selection. Thus humans have no special dignity, being made in the image of what modern-day scientists Richard Dawkins and Daniel Dennett call respectively the "blind watchmaker" and "Mother Nature."

But if human beings are not made in the image of God, they are not like God and do not have any special powers. This seems an odd conclusion for some scientists to reach, since the ability to do science is something that distinguishes human beings from all other creatures on earth.

Why is it that other creatures, such as chimpanzees, who share so many genes with humans, do not develop theories, design instruments and experiments, make predictions, and offer explanations to make sense of or control the world around them? In fact, God created humans to have charge of the creation (see Psalm 8:4–9). This distinguishes humans from all other creatures.

CREATIVITY

Creation is an ambiguous word. Before God created the universe, there was no other thing in existence except God Himself. So God created the universe without drawing on any other created thing. He also created human

beings in a special way, in His own image (Genesis 1:26–27). Th.
creation, and scientists are not capable of primary creation. When
"creates" something, he or she is harnessing or rearranging forces or
als that already exist. The product may be highly novel, and would no
existed without the scientist's ingenuity, but it was assembled from pree.
ing elements. Scientists, therefore, engage in secondary creation. They ta.
the elements of primary creation and rearrange them in various useful ways.

J. R. R. Tolkien (1892–1973), the famous writer of *The Hobbit* and *The Lord of the Rings* trilogy, said that humans are "sub-creators." God uses them in His continuing providential care of the world to create cultural products that benefit others.

Suppose that someone claims that a scientist/inventor (e.g., Thomas Edison) created electrical current and incandescent light. Although scientists can make light where there was none, what they have done is set up an electrical current and a conductor using existing materials. Electricity consists of electrons, which already existed. The electric cord contains copper and is coated in plastic synthesized from oil, which already existed. The glass, filament, and thread of the bulb were likewise derived from preexisting sources. Not only that, but if there had been no natural light of the sun to begin with, such scientific work would have been very difficult to do! Only God creates the original resources. Scientists recombine them in clever ways to produce new technologies. In a sense, though, we always plagiarize from the original author, God.

Humans might use their subcreativity to produce machines that can themselves "create." A cleverly programmed computer can "create" output such as spreadsheets or slide shows. Complex computers at manufacturing facilities can now generate products. As a result, some laborers have found themselves replaced by machines. Some worry that computers will make human labor or even human thinking obsolete.

However, computers have even less creative power than humans. Human creativity involves imagination, foresight, and planning. Humans can develop a blueprint for a complex structure before building it. Human creativity is goal directed and intentional. Computers passively implement human goals. They have no goals of their own. Computers engage in tertiary creation. They are made in the image of humans but not in the image of God. Our being "like God" does not mean we are at the same level as God. In a similar way, the fact that computers can behave like humans does not mean they have the same level of creative capacity as we do.

Some chess programs do seem to be very smart, because they appear to learn from their previous games and gradually increase their play level. However, these programs contain two sets of rules: rules that currently guide their behavior and higher-level rules used to modify the weights of the lower-level

onse to success or failure. If a lower-level rule leads to a win, it is
gher preference and is more likely to be used in the future; if it leads
, it is given a lower preference and is less likely to be used.

al of these rules were developed by the programmer, not by the pro-
ns. More important, it is only the programmer who has the goal of pro-
ucing a successful program. The program is not trying to win; it is not glad
when it does or sad when it does not. People, unlike programs, are agents
who act for personal reasons because of something they want to do. Computers cannot act in these ways, though science fiction makes much of the
possibility that computers may someday become sentient.

Humans are also different from computers in that they have a will. Computers are completely deterministic devices, even when invoking statistical
or variable techniques. Given their programming and input, they inevitably
produce a particular kind of output. Human beings, on the other hand, can
make choices and may produce highly individual work. When computers
"create," what they create lacks their influence. This is also true of everything
humans develop. For example, Albert Einstein had an active will, but his theory of relativity does not.

The human will demonstrates incredible creativity, which honors the
Lord who made it. However the human will is likewise a disappointment.
Because of the fall into sin, the human will and creativity are thoroughly cor-
rupt and dishonor their Lord (Genesis 6:5–6).

What happens when humans interfere in the production of human life?
If scientists clone human beings, would the clones lack a personal will and
only be made in the image of man? Here it is important to remember that
humans who have not been cloned—such as you and me—are not the direct
creation of God. Today God creates indirectly, working through means such
as parents. God creates new human beings through the natural reproduction
process, which He established at creation. The fact that human activity is
involved does not mean that the offspring are only made in a human image.

Human reproduction unites cells containing information that already
existed and that stems from God's creating work. So if scientists clone humans, they may modify what unaided nature would do (secondary creation),
but the scientists will not be the source of the original information that specifies the physical and spiritual characteristics of humans. There is every reason to think that a human clone would still be made in the image of God and
have a personal will and foresight.

As we discussed in an earlier chapter, human cloning is morally problematic because it treats the clone as a product manufactured for the purposes of the person who requests cloning. It is true that natural reproduction
also produces people who did not ask to be born, but they are not produced
in accordance with a preconceived template solely to serve the whims of the
person who makes them or who asked for them to be made.

Motives for cloning are often corrupt as well as illogical. For exa. some people would like to replace a son or daughter who died young. even though a clone would be genetically identical, it would not be the sar. person. And if it is impossible to re-create the same person, why not "replace the son or daughter with another child conceived naturally by the parents of the lost child or with an adopted child who needs loving and nurturing parents? With cloning there is a disturbing desire to be in control, to see the child as a means to some end of ours and not as another human being and a gift from God who is called to serve His purposes. To the extent that cloning attempts to exploit a clone, it fails to meet a basic standard or morality taught by our Lord: "Whatever you wish that others would do to you, do also to them" (Matthew 7:12).

Since such exploitation violates God's Law and God's Law binds all vocations, there is no such vocation as the vocation of human cloning.

Humble before Our Maker

Human beings should never be viewed as manufactured products. A spiritual danger of human cloning is that the scientist falsely sees himself as a god (Genesis 3:5), as a primary creator, and that what the scientist creates is seen as being less than a human being, as simply technology, like a computer. The great German philosopher Immanuel Kant (1724–1804) asserted that we should never treat other human beings as a means to our own ends. As our Creator, God has the right to "use" us in this way. He not only has the right, but He also has a good and perfect will in the exercise of that right (Romans 8:28; 12:2). Through our vocations we are means of His creating work. We are not the Creator. Other human beings are not our creatures. They have dignity equal to our own. For they, like us, are made in God's image.

Even without cloning, we are often tempted to treat other human beings as inferior, as means to our ends.

Perhaps the most obvious example of this is slavery. Britain, the United States, and many other nations throughout history have found it convenient to claim that other people were inferior, or even less than human, existing to provide a higher standard of living for the beneficiaries. There are disturbing cases of parents who attempt to fulfill their own ambitions vicariously through their children, pressuring them into activities that may not suit them.

In a scientific context, fetal stem cell research is premised on the idea that the fetus is not a full human being but a disposable biological resource that can be used to find cures for other human beings. Christians should oppose any and every attempt to treat other human beings as inferiors, since all people have the same worth before God.

atheists are tempted not only to view scientists as primary creators but to hold that these scientists are uncreated beings! This is not because they think scientists are like God, existing from eternity, but because they think scientists are the products of the blind, undirected process of natural selection. This thinking results in an odd contradiction. At the very same time that a scientist's creative gifts of imagination, foresight, and planning are exalted, it is maintained that the scientist came from a process devoid of imagination, foresight, and planning!

The basic problem for the evolutionist's account is that it undermines confidence that the scientist's faculties are reliable. If we are the product of blind, undirected causes, then the natural conclusion is that we are lacking in foresight and direction. And yet scientists themselves plan experiments and make predictions, activities that require considerable foresight and intentionally directed action. As C. S. Lewis repeatedly pointed out, it is a bad idea to try to use reason to discredit reason: either the attempt fails, or, if it "succeeds," it undermines any basis for saying it did succeed! Evolutionists cannot hope to convince us by argument that their theory is true if their theory implies that argument is not to be trusted.

In his book *Miracles* (1947), C. S. Lewis refuted the evolutionary naturalist's picture of life. He demonstrated that when we argue logically, we see in advance that a conclusion must follow. For example, if we assume that A = B and that B = C, we can also know that A = C.

What Lewis pointed out was that logical thought and morality are quite different from natural physical processes. Natural (undirected) processes (1) simply occur, (2) are not trying to get anywhere, and (3) could have been otherwise. In contrast, logical thought specifies (1) what we ought to believe, (2) how we can use it, and—if the argument is valid—(3) what conclusion must follow.

Like logic, the "oughts" of morality do not arise from the facts of natural science. Our access to logical and moral thought reveals a realm that stands over nature and can never be derived from it. But for naturalists, all we can claim is that one event happens to follow another event, and natural events do not have goals (e.g., the boulder tumbling down the hillside is not trying to reach the valley below).

In our moral thinking, we see that things ought to be done in certain ways. But in the naturalist worldview, all we learn is what is done, without an investigation of whether it should or should not have been done. It is a logical fallacy to argue that because something is the case, therefore it ought to be the case.

Atheists exaggerate human creativity, putting us on the same level as God, but they belittle it too, reducing us to machines. A Christian contribution for understanding human creativity is to affirm what Stanley Jaki

(1924–2009) called "the middle road." Scientists are not God. also not merely manufactured products or the result of chance. H made in the image of God, so we do have special abilities to imagine, and plan. These special abilities give scientists a wonderful means of s others and also the potential to enslave and harm them. Therefore, scien are no more (or less) important than other human beings. All people in ever useful vocation are created in God's image and called to serve Him. Scientists should therefore pursue "the middle road" that accurately reflects the true relationship between all humans and God.

In the case of genetic engineering, there is much merit in germ-line therapy to prevent a child from receiving an otherwise inherited disease. This approach respects both parent and child and merely attempts to use a sophisticated version of preventive care. Some Christians might oppose this, but scientists would fall short of what they can legitimately accomplish by neglecting this approach. On the other hand, other scientists are tempted to abuse their power to develop enhancements and so-called "designer babies." This is sinful because some people are selecting this design for their own purposes and therefore treat the designer baby as an inferior. They do not see the child as a gift of God but as a made-to-order product.

GOD'S CALLING

The deification of science is a pathetic attempt to usurp God's vocation and leads some humans to dehumanize their fellows. We are like God in certain respects but lack His power, wisdom, and knowledge. And since the fall, we lack original righteousness and stand condemned.

But thankfully our salvation does not depend on our being just like God. The central message of Holy Scripture is that works, including scientific works, save no one. Paul asks, "Then what becomes of our boasting? It is excluded. By what kind of law? By a law of works? No, but by the law of faith. For we hold that one is justified by faith apart from works of the law" (Romans 3:27–28). We did not have to attain a certain level of goodness or intellectual enlightenment to receive this gift. Salvation is a free gift of love. "But God shows His love for us in that while we were still sinners, Christ died for us" (Romans 5:8).

Salvation is by grace, and we are not called to perfect this world by our works. Such perfection is found only in heaven, and for now we are called to do what we can to serve and witness to our neighbors. A scientist who despairs of finding cures for all diseases can find comfort in this. Dying of disease may be horrible, but it may also be an escape from this vale of tears. Our hope is not in making this earth a heaven but in the One who draws us and others to His heaven.

...derful, free gift of salvation is available to all. Since Christ died ... all people, we can see that all people are equally important in ...es. From this perspective, we can see how wrong it is to treat others ...inferiors, as experimental subjects, biological resources, or subversives ... need "reconditioning" to suit the purposes of the state. For as God loved ..., so we are called to love others, unconditionally, regardless of their sins, whether or not we like them or they suit our purposes. Indeed, "We love because He first loved us. If anyone says, 'I love God,' and hates his brother, he is a liar; for he who does not love his brother whom he has seen cannot love God whom he has not seen. And this commandment we have from him: whoever loves God must also love his brother" (1 John 4:19–21).

What surpassing love Jesus shows for you, your brothers and sisters, and even His own enemies! While we were still sinners and hostile toward God, Jesus laid down His life for one and all (Romans 5:8–11). Despite your sin, no matter what your calling, Christ loves and treasures you. He displayed this love on the cross. He continues to display this love through the blessings He gives through His Church, the creation, and the good works of all.

Scientists can show the love of God by focusing on technologies that respect the full humanity of those who are helped. Good examples are the sophisticated adaptation of computers so that they can be used by blind and paralyzed people and speech synthesizers for those who otherwise cannot speak. At their best, scientists provide the means to "Open your mouth for the mute" (Proverbs 31:8) and thereby show how God spoke up for us by sending Christ to die on our behalf and to serve as our advocate before God the Father when we had no power to defend ourselves.

Brotherly love cannot, however, be compelled from someone, but is a fruit of faith. When we see Jesus as our Savior, we see our own sinful condition accurately and can no longer see others as inferior. Indeed, as C. S. Lewis once said, we are "fellow patients in the same hospital," and if some have an advantage, it is not because they need treatment any the less but because they know the doctor, Jesus Christ. The "sinners club" includes all of fallen humanity, including the most brilliant scientists. "None is righteous, no, not one" (Romans 3:10). But God in Jesus Christ has "appeared once for all at the end of the ages to put away sin by the sacrifice of Himself" (Hebrews 9:26). The payment is complete, requiring nothing further on our part, and is made available to all through faith.

Seeing everyone as a sinner levels the playing field. If we are "fellow patients in the same hospital," none of us has an inherent advantage over anyone else. Our only hope is the doctor, Jesus Christ, and as He sets scientists free from bondage to sin, they will, in gratitude, be motivated to do what they can to help their fellow patients along life's way.

From this perspective, scientists should not see other huma. or themselves, as insignificant by-products of a natural process that have them in mind. Rather, because God redeems us all, the task of th entist is to use his or her special gifts to reflect the love God has showe on us. Scientists who minister to the bodily needs of others have wonderf. credibility when they share the Gospel.

Points to Ponder

Our tendency to want to be God, our most basic sin, turns up in surprising ways. This is why it is so easy to drift away from pure Law and Gospel and into some kind of theology of glory or a salvation by works. It can also turn up in revering a vocation such as science (or our own vocation) rather than revering God. Let us pray that God would protect us from such error, whether subtle or flagrant!

Words to Remember

When I look at Your heavens, the work of Your fingers, the moon and the stars, which You have set in place, what is man that You are mindful of him, and the son of man that You care for him? Yet You have made him a little lower than the heavenly beings and crowned him with glory and honor. You have given him dominion over the works of Your hands; You have put all things under his feet. all sheep and oxen, and also the beasts of the field, the birds of the heavens, and the fish of the sea, whatever passes along the paths of the seas. (Psalm 8:3–8)

34

HOW THEOLOGY GAVE BIRTH TO MODERN SCIENCE

Many people have heard and believe that science and Christianity are in an irreconcilable conflict. Andrew Dickson White (1832–1918) made a very influential defense of this thesis in *A History of the Warfare of Science with Theology in Christendom*, published in 1896. White portrays the Christian Church as dogmatic and oppressive, clinging to outmoded superstition in the face of experimental evidence. He portrays scientists as enlightened, liberated thinkers who will usher in a new era of peace, prosperity, and tolerance. Many support White's conclusions by arguing that Luther opposed Copernicus's heliocentric model of our planetary system and that the Roman Catholic Church opposed Galileo because of conflicts between science and Scripture.

At the same time, some assume that science does not fit well with orthodox Christianity because of the latter's reliance on supernatural miracles, especially the incarnation (God's becoming man) and the resurrection. Science, it is thought, must investigate the natural world as if God's actions were undetectable. The idea is that science can only investigate natural causes of natural effects, and so divine activity in the world is beyond the concern of science.

Some scientists take a view called "methodological naturalism." They proceed in their work as if there were no God at work in nature, but they are free to believe in nature as a matter of faith. Others hold to "philosophical naturalism," according to which nature is all there is. This view denies miracles and the existence of God.

Some argue that scientists are inevitably drawn to philosophical naturalism. Others argue that it is all right for a Christian who is a scientist to be a methodological naturalist. They deny that God may allow both believers and unbelievers to know that a creator is at work in nature.

THEOLOGY YIELDS SCIENCE

Recent work in the history of science thoroughly discredits Andrew Dickson White's "warfare" thesis. Numerous contemporary works show that Christian theology was actually a major impetus to the rise of modern science. As Nancy Pearcey and Charles Thaxton argue in their book *The Soul of Science* (Crossway Books, 1994), there are indeed many non-Christian re-

ligions and worldviews that are antithetical to science. For pa
spiritual is entirely within nature, making investigation of the na.
sacrilegious. Polytheism implies that events are governed by inde,
capricious local deities, undermining any basis for believing in unifor.
ural laws. On the other hand, Stanley Jaki points out in *The Savior of Sci.*
(Eerdmans, 2000) that Christian theology contributed the idea of a transce.
dent, rational Creator who made humans in His own image.

What does *transcendent* mean, and how does the fact that God transcends His creation make scientific study of nature permissible? *Transcendent* means "above and beyond" or "not contained." It is to be contrasted with
immanent, which means "dwelling within." These are both qualities of God
(Psalm 139:7–10; 1 Kings 8:22–23, 27; 4:29–34). The fact that God is transcendent means that we are not somehow desecrating His abode by examining nature. God is at work within creation, and in that sense He is immanent
and transcendent at the same time.

Since God is rational, we can expect that, even in its fallen state, the
universe contains rational laws and, even in our fallen state, our reason is
attuned to discovering those laws. Here it is important that our reason is
like the reason in nature, because the two have a common source in God.
Although He says, "So are My ways higher than your ways" (Isaiah 55:9) and
there are mysteries of faith we cannot fathom, we are nevertheless equipped
to understand much about how God's world works.

Modern science did not appear until the late-sixteenth century. Someone
might ask, "If Christian theology was so congenial to science, why did it take
so long for science to develop when the Church had already existed for about
1,600 years?" Peter Harrison argues in his book *The Bible, Protestantism, and
the Rise of Natural Science* that one main answer is found in medieval Scholasticism. The Scholastics had a tremendous veneration for ancient texts, not
merely Scripture, but also the classics of the Greco-Roman world. Aristotle
(384–322 BC) was viewed as *the* philosopher, and it was standard practice
to explain natural events by showing how they fell under the Aristotelian
scheme of science.

Scholastic science relied on preconceived metaphysics and supposed it
could anticipate nature's operation. But if one thinks one knows what nature
must be up to, one is discouraged from actually investigating nature. Why do
an experiment if you already know the result?

At the same time, following the allegorical approach to interpretation of
the Bible used by some Early Church Fathers, allegory was likewise used to
interpret the natural world. Allegory interprets things as symbols. It places
emphasis on discovering the higher truth that stands behind an object or an
action. For example, allegorists interpreted Jesus' freeing of the doves during
the cleansing of the temple (John 2:12–22; some translations have "pigeons")

. He frees our souls. They concluded this because in ancient
, a dove represented the soul or spirit. Allegorists would focus so
ʌy on the symbolic potential of something that they would fail to
er the thing itself.

For the allegorist, animals were created by God to teach us moral lessons,
ʌich were described in various stories called "bestiaries." Insights of ancient
writers were held in high regard, and the figurative meaning of an animal was
not something that could be detected with the naked eye. It was therefore
thought more profitable to study the ancient authorities than to make careful observations of animal behavior. As a result, incorrect views were often
retained. For example, St. Ambrose suggested that in Christlike manner the
pelican wounds its breast to feed its starving young. This is touchingly pious
but scientifically inaccurate.

An allegorical approach to the natural world presents an obstacle to genuine scientific understanding. Allegories encourage one to indulge in speculation about what things might be for or what they might mean, distracting
one from the more basic scientific task of finding out what caused them and
how they work.

The Reformation made a decisive contribution to the emergence of
modern science. The reformers realized that allegorical interpretations of the
Bible were speculative. For authoritative Church doctrine, what matters is
the plain, natural meaning of the text. By careful study, Martin Luther realized that the Medieval Church had obscured the plain scriptural teaching of
justification by grace alone because the Medieval Church had not focused on
what the Scripture actually said.

The change from an allegorical to a "natural" method of interpreting
Scripture was carried over to the natural world. Now what mattered was discerning the patterns that God had literally inscribed in nature. The forefront
of modern science included Lutherans, such as Tycho Brahe (1546–1601),
Johannes Kepler (1571–1630), and Joachim Rheticus (1514–74). For Kepler,
scientists were "priests of the highest God in regard to the book of nature,"
called to "think God's thoughts after Him." Contrary to the "warfare" theory
about science and theology, Luther encouraged Rheticus to explore Copernicus's theory at Wittenberg. And recent scholarship suggests that the Catholic
Church opposed Galileo because his views conflicted with Aristotelian philosophy and scientific observation, not because he contradicted Scripture.

A literal approach focuses science on accurate description and measure-
ment. This allows precise predictions, testing, and an increasing ability to
control and regulate phenomena. Facts are not everything in science, but
they do form the data that a scientific theory attempts to explain, and the
more accurate the facts, the more scientists can conform their theories to
reality.

The Book of Nature

Even after the fall, humans have the ability to make sense of God's
ation. When the best minds of the Scholastic era thought they should lea
about creation by reading the ancients, they were closing their eyes to th
book in front of everyone's eyes. This book of creation is not mute, and we
do have the gifts to read what it says. As the psalmist writes, "The heavens
declare the glory of God, and the sky above proclaims His handiwork. Day
to day pours out speech, and night to night reveals knowledge. There is no
speech, nor are there words, whose voice is not heard. Their voice goes out
through all the earth, and their words to the end of the world" (Psalm 19:1–
4). The Lutheran Church—Missouri Synod's Commission on Theology and
Church Relations publication *The Natural Knowledge of God in Christian
Confession and Christian Witness* explores some of the implications of such
understanding.

The psalmist tells us that God's creation contains "speech." Nature is
more like a book than a cake. In a cake, various elements are stirred together
randomly in an appealing form, which nonetheless does not say anything. A
book, however, contains specifically arranged information that derives from
an author's mind and communicates to the book's reader.

The speech of the natural world consists in part of the mathematical regularities that govern its operation and which can be "read" by highly trained
scientific minds. Scientists are encouraged to believe that such regularity ex·
ists to be discovered and hence that the search for regularity is not a waste of
time, as it would be if chaos were the ultimate reality.

The Reformation helped human beings use their God-given faculties to
discern the clear messages that God Himself had provided, both in Scripture
and His other book, the book of nature. But in order for a book to be read
and its message discerned, one must suppose that the book has an author.
Methodological naturalism pretends that we can read nature on the assumption that the message was inscribed by nature itself. But without God, the
blind, undirected processes of nature can only produce an incoherent and
meaningless text.

It is important to combat the view quite prevalent today that a Christian
who is a scientist should have no problem being a methodological naturalist.
Methodological naturalism closes nature to the source of its intelligibility
and yields a muted nature, incompatible and quite different from the one
described in Scripture.

Some theologians argue that our rational faculties are so damaged by
the fall that we can no longer understand God's work in creation without the
regeneration of saving faith. They then argue that, because scientific results
must be accessible to all scientists, regardless of faith, these results will not
include pointers to the divine. But if the consequences of the fall were as se-

this, surely we would be unable to understand this theological truth! In any case, this skeptical view does not agree with the scriptural teach-ing of the natural knowledge of God. "For His invisible attributes, namely, His eternal power and divine nature, have been clearly perceived, ever since the creation of the world, in the things that have been made. So they are with-out excuse" (Romans 1:20). It is clear that this knowledge is available to un-believers—this is why they are "without excuse"—so it cannot be maintained that it falls outside the realm of scientific knowledge, because it can only be discerned through the eyes of faith.

People often cannot see God's work in nature because sin makes them turn away from God in enmity (Romans 1:18–25). Unrepentant sinners then seek to suppress the truth that they really know; they deceive themselves by exchanging truth for more comforting lies. It is not that unrepentant people cannot see God's work in nature, but that they will not see it.

Not only is it possible to see God's handiwork, but Christians are also called to study God's "other book." Kepler had trained to be a pastor but felt unable to go into the ministry. His mathematical brilliance suited him to as-tronomy, but he wondered if it was God pleasing. The Reformation doctrine of vocation showed Kepler that one could be called to astronomy. And the "priesthood of all believers," together with the idea that nature was a book, showed him that one could be a "priest" in the book of nature, seeing the whole universe as a kind of temple where study would glorify God.

If scientists see themselves as priests, they know that they serve in a temple built by someone much greater than themselves. They cannot expect to acquire infallible and ultimate knowledge, but they can be confident that God has provided a meaningful "text" in nature that we are able to read. The idea of "thinking God's thoughts after Him" reminds us that some of God's thoughts are higher than our thoughts; nonetheless, there are coherent truths to discover.

TRANSCENDENT AND INTIMATE

Scientists are not saved because they view their work in a certain way. The majority of Christians who are scientists do follow methodological natu-ralism because, since the Enlightenment, this is how scientists are trained. In many areas, the approach is successful because scientists are only studying the immediate or proximate causes of things and not their ultimate explana-tion. Whether scientists choose to consider God's work in nature or not, it was God's supernatural intervention in our world in the incarnation and res-urrection of the Son of God that saved all of us from our sins, including the sin of closing our eyes to God's messages for us. In case there was any doubt that God was the author of the natural text, the author appeared as a character in the story, with a divine and human nature united in the person of Jesus Christ. He lived, died, and rose again in the same history that we all inhabit.

This is problematic for religions such as Islam, which maintains that its god is wholly transcendent and would not dirty himself by becoming man. Islam insists that Allah is entirely other than us, that he would not and could not be like us, and so there is no "middle man," such as our mediator, Jesus Christ. This view raises a very serious problem of how such a god can communicate with human beings at all. And even if he did, how could we know if anything such a god said transcended our powers of understanding? Why suppose that such a god cares about human beings in particular when he has done nothing to identify with their affliction?

Christianity comforts us because it tells us that God became man to identify with our suffering, to show that He meant to save us, and to present God in a form we can relate to and understand.

Viewing science in a biblical way, as a priesthood in the book of nature, does not save anyone. It simply teaches what the vocation of science is really about: reading the inscriptions and traces that God has left behind in creation. But ultimately such priesthood is intended to show ways of serving our neighbors. It does not serve God, and it does not save us.

For salvation, the only priest that matters is Jesus Christ, who was "made like His brothers [fellow humans] in every respect, so that He might become a merciful and faithful high priest in the service of God, to make propitiation for the sins of the people" (Hebrews 2:17). God is not an aloof high priest who is unable to understand the weaknesses and temptations of human beings, including scientists.

Scientists are tempted to claim they know more than they do or to claim that their work has nothing to do with God. They may see their work only as a means to power, fame, and wealth. But there is comfort in Christ, for He shows His complete solidarity with human affliction. "For we do not have a high priest who is unable to sympathize with our weaknesses, but one who in every respect has been tempted as we are, yet without sin" (Hebrews 4:15). The perfect life we could not lead has been lived by Christ. The perfect payment we could not pay has been paid in full by His death on the cross for all our sins.

The priesthood of science is simply a priesthood of one vocation among many. God confers no special honors on scientists; they simply take their place with all other vocations. And no matter how often they succeed, scientists can save no one by their work. By contrast, Jesus is the High Priest who sacrificed Himself once and for all to pay the price for all sin and to save us all. Scientists can be comforted that they do not need to function as saviors. They are freed to imitate Christ's sacrifice by allowing their old selves to be crucified so that the new selves in Christ can better serve their neighbors through scientific work.

Christians who are scientists know they do not have to construct meaning. Meaning is out there and God-given, waiting to be discovered. Einstein said that the most incomprehensible thing about the universe is that it is comprehensible. But this should not surprise Christians. Even after the fall, the universe and the human mind reflect the rational design of the Creator. Although the story went wrong, as C. S. Lewis once said, God provided the "missing passage" that makes sense of it all.

Scientists do not have to make the world fit together correctly. The world already fits together because it was created through Christ and is still held together by Him (Colossians 1:16–17). This assures the scientist that there is meaning behind and beyond this world, giving work a purpose now and hope for life in eternity.

POINTS TO PONDER

Children are born with a natural curiosity, and we have the opportunity to carry this curiosity forward into our adult vocations. This curiosity can be inspired and lead to praising God, or it can be self-serving. And it can make our vocations a joy or a burden. If we see colorful clouds in a beautiful sunset, for example, we can stop and admire God's artwork and colors, or we can scowl at the clouds and wonder if the weather will change. The difference is to recall that God is in charge and holds it all in His hands, freeing us to relax in the vocations He gives us to enjoy.

WORDS TO REMEMBER

The God who made the world and everything in it, being Lord of heaven and earth, does not live in temples made by man, nor is He served by human hands, as though He needed anything, since He Himself gives to all mankind life and breath and everything. (Acts 17:24–25)

35

Science, Beauty, and God's Handiwork

Many materialists believe that beauty is an accident. These materialists can be called *reductionists*. For them, blind, inarticulate matter is more fundamental than any of the apparent "wonders" it has generated. They believe that the ultimate reality is undirected and random. What lies behind so-called eternal truths of order and rationality is chaos. What lies behind so-called goodness and love is a reality devoid of value or concern. Beauty is a mirage, an arbitrary preference. In place of the true, the good, and the beautiful, these reductionists see the unstable, the indifferent, and the illusory. Behind meaning itself is unmeaning. To use Daniel Dennett's phrase, natural selection is the "unmeant meaner." In other words, natural selection has produced people who believe life has meaning. This is not because life really has meaning, but because such belief helps people survive in a truly meaningless world.

A second idea of reductionists is that they have reached their stark conclusions simply by examining the facts and applying the scientific method. The claim is that, unlike religious believers, materialist scientists have no biases that color their interpretation.

Francis Bacon once claimed that the way to do science was to eliminate what he called "idols of the mind," various prejudices that attempt to anticipate how the world must be and which therefore distort the data to fit preconceived ideas. The reductionist believes that religious believers are saddled with idols of the mind that predispose religious people to find meaning and purpose, the true, the good, and the beautiful where there is none. By contrast, reductionists believe themselves to be, of all people, the least prone to illusions and idols of the mind. So they believe that they alone courageously assert the naked truth. The idea that no scientist can avoid presuppositions is downplayed. The idea that all scientists, including unbelievers, are committed by their office to meaning, truth, beauty, and goodness is ignored.

If you could briefly set aside personal notions about meaning, truth, beauty, and goodness, what might life look like? Would such a life be worth living?

Beauty in Science

The idea that matter is most fundamental is not scientific at all. It is a philosophical, indeed a religious, idea. Looking at the apparent design in the natural world, some people assume there is no God and conclude that the design is only apparent. Looking at the same world and believing in God, others see the apparent design as evidence of a designer. In his book *Miracles*, Lewis makes a similar point about people's interpretations of the marvelous. If we are committed to denying God, then no matter what the evidence and even if we cannot explain the marvelous event by any known law of nature, we will say that there must be some unknown natural explanation. We can rationalize away almost anything! Looking at the same event, someone who believes in God is open to the possibility that God intervened in nature to produce the event.

Our prior worldview controls how we interpret facts. For example, the Cartesian mechanists thought that all causation involved the direct contact of material particles. Therefore, they initially dismissed Newton's idea of gravitation as an "occult" force that would have to work across empty space. Newtonians likewise came to see the world as a clockwork machine and were opposed to the idea of random chance, which figures so prominently in quantum mechanics. Reductionists think that everything that occurs can be reduced to the current or prior state of unaided nature.

If someone seemed dead and then alive, then the reductionist would say either that the person was not really dead, or that, although he or she was dead, there was some unknown natural process that brought the dead person back to life. Having dismissed the possibility of miracles, no evidence, however strong, is allowed to substantiate a miracle.

Reductionists do not reach their conclusions because that is where the facts inexorably lead. They assume that nothing other than a reductionist explanation—one that reduces an apparently meaningful feature to an inherently meaningless one—could be a legitimate scientific explanation, and they interpret the data accordingly. The reductionist view is not a conclusion of scientific study but an assumption that some people make before they start science. The idea that believing in God is a bias, while believing in no God is unbiased, is simply a biased definition of biases! There is no neutral ground here, but only competing biases. A fair approach would be to ask which biases are most fruitful and explanatory.

Does believing that one is studying God's handiwork lead to more success in science (the position of Johannes Kepler and Isaac Newton)? Or does believing that one is studying nature's apparent handiwork (the position of reductionists) lead to more success? Motivation is an essential ingredient of success. Cutting God out of science and life will ultimately lead to selfish self-destruction rather than success in any meaningful sense. Science motivated by love for the Creator and one's neighbors will steer science in the direction of responsibility and mutual care.

Philosopher Alvin Plantinga (b. 1932) has raised the worry that if redu tionism is true, then it undermines the idea that scientific practice is rationa and reliable. If reductionists are right about the design in nature being an illusion, how much confidence can we have in reduction scientists' design of theories and experiments?

He raises a good question. It is odd for reductionists to claim both that design does not really exist in nature and that scientists design experiments. The reductionists view scientists as just part of nature, and so if there is no design in nature, there is none in the scientist either. But if scientists do not design experiments, then they are not really in control. They are simply passive puppets controlled by undirected processes in their brains and environment. But if that is so, it seems that science is not rational and there is no ground for expecting that it can find truth (that is, if one can still speak of something called truth). Why suppose that undirected processes that are not even looking for the truth can find it? If scientists really are as reductionism implies they are, surely this is the blind leading the blind.

On the other hand, if reductionists admit that, by some fluke, undesigned processes generated human beings who can really design things, then they are admitting that design can really exist somewhere in nature. But if that is so, why should this be the only place? If design is a legitimate scientific category, because humans design things, then there is no way to exclude the possibility that divine design is operative and detectable in nature as well.

Reductionists are naive to suppose that the ideas of truth, beauty, and goodness can simply be debunked. Reductionists claim to have found the harrowing truth about an indifferent universe, so they are committed to the idea of truth. They think that some ways of doing science are better than others, so they are committed to at least some sort of goodness. And in practice, they prefer scientific theories that are simple, elegant, and coherent instead of a potentially infinite set of alternative theories that are complex, inelegant, and incoherent. So they are committed to beauty not merely because they like it, but because they see it as a guide to reality. The Nobel Prize-winning atheist physicist Steven Weinberg (b. 1933) admits this in his book *Dreams of a Final Theory* (Vintage Books, 1994). He writes that scientists expect to find "beautiful answers" when they study truly fundamental problems. He notes that the beauty in present theories points toward the beauty of the final theory and that a final theory would not be accepted "unless it were beautiful" (p. 165).

If reductionism is true, beauty is an odd luxury, something we happen to like because of the way evolution happened to develop us, but with no objective basis. Reductionism cannot therefore explain the fact, admitted even by atheist scientists like Weinberg, that beauty is an objective sign of truth. Christians can surely suggest that even in a fallen world, God's beauty would ve behind beautiful traces and that we would expect beautiful laws to govern His world.

TRUTH, GOODNESS, AND BEAUTY

When reductionists belittle the true, the good, and the beautiful, they reveal their lack of faith in the source of these qualities. Jesus says, "I am the way, and the truth, and the life" (John 14:6). Truth is real, objective, and personal, not an appearance subjectively generated by impersonal matter. The unbelieving picture of truth as disconnected from God is in fact a deception, a denial of the natural knowledge of God implanted in all human beings.

Paul writes, "The wrath of God is revealed from heaven against all ungodliness and unrighteousness of men, who by their unrighteousness suppress the truth. For what can be known about God is plain to them, because God has shown it to them" (Romans 1:18–19). Likewise, God's objective goodness is revealed to all people because "the law is written on their hearts" (Romans 2:15). And God has the beauty of a perfect love, reflected in the "beautiful" feet of those who bring good news—the messengers of the Gospel (Isaiah 52:7). We also see the beauty of creation: in comparison to "the lilies of the field . . . even Solomon in all his glory was not arrayed like one of these" (Matthew 6:28–29). Since scientists are concerned with objective truth, they should be concerned with the objective truth, goodness, and beauty that emanate from God's nature. The Lutheran Church—Missouri Synod's Commission on Theology and Church Relations publication *The Natural Knowledge of God in Christian Confession and Christian Witness* provides more perspective and context for this.

It is important for Christians who are scientists to defend the ideas of truth, goodness, and beauty in their work. Without the idea of truth, science degenerates into pragmatism. For example, Ptolemy's model of the solar system worked surprisingly well, so scientists could have rested content with it. But they became convinced that it was false and looked for a model that was closer to the truth. Christians who are scientists believe in an author of objective truths that are there for us to discover, and although indeed, as Karl Popper said, "truth is hard to come by," Christians who are scientists should never give up the search for it. Without goodness, science lacks proper direction and again may fall into pragmatism, aiming to please and make a profit, and willing to compromise ethics by treating some humans as "more equal than others." A focus on goodness orients the scientist to honorable research methods aimed at making other people's lives better. Without beauty, scientists can too easily accept ugly but practical solutions and fall away from a higher standard that honors God and respects creation.

Focusing on "higher things" is also good for us, inspiring us to seek truth and meaning and thereby to accomplish good things: "Whatever is true, whatever is honorable, whatever is just, whatever is pure, whatever is lovely, whatever is commendable, if there is any excellence, if there is anything worthy of praise, think about these things" (Philippians 4:8). Johannes Kepler believed that our universe was the product of a "divine geometer" and was therefore inspired to find mathematically beautiful laws to explain the planetary orbits. If Kepler had thought that the universe was fundamentally chaotic and planetary motion ugly and irrational, he would not have expected or sought such laws. Believing that life is ugly is self-fulfilling and leads to negative, nihilistic attitudes and lifestyles. Believing life is beautiful is also self-fulfilling but leads to brilliant discoveries that reveal truth and help others.

A cliché has it that "attitude is everything." An attitude of nihilism (the view that nothing really matters) is very dangerous in scientists because their knowledge can then serve dishonest and evil ends. Focusing on truth, scientists will want to find out even things that many people do not want to hear. For example, some scientists are investigating whether or not there is a connection between abortion and breast cancer. If indeed there is such a link, a scientist who discovered it would demonstrate real love for women, who could then reconsider their options. A focus on beauty will encourage scientists to produce results that will help those who feel ugly because of disabilities to relate effectively to others via technological aids. Such scientists would also seek to explore the natural world without gratuitous disfigurement or depletion of its resources. And because of an orientation to goodness, the work of these scientists would aim to alleviate damage, deficit, and suffering, not to cause these things.

Ultimately, beauty is not in the eye of the beholder. Looking ahead to the crucifixion, Isaiah wrote of the Suffering Servant, Jesus Christ, that many would be "astonished at you—His appearance was so marred, beyond human semblance" (Isaiah 52:14). From a human point of view, Jesus on the cross "had no form or majesty that we should look at Him, and no beauty that we should desire Him" (53:2). Reductionists are right that appearances can be deceiving. But here it is not ugliness that lies behind apparent beauty. Rather, the apparent ugliness of Jesus derives from His bearing our afflictions. The "ugliness" of Jesus is the ugliness of our own sin, which a beautiful Savior took on Himself. For "He was pierced for our transgressions; He was crushed for our iniquities" (v. 5).

Behind all appearances, no matter how ugly, is the beauty of the Word (John 1:1–3), the Creator and Preserver of all, and the underlying rational principle that makes science possible. Behind the ugliness of paralysis, there may be a beautiful mind whose creative potential is revealed when specialized computers allow communication. Friendship, love, and faith that were always there can now be expressed and returned by others. Behind the ugliness of disease are beautiful structures and laws that allow scientists to understand the disease and find a cure.

Beautiful Savior

A world disconnected from God is a horrible world. Sin not only corrupts the natural world around us but also human faculties of perception and judgment. We do not by nature rightly appreciate the true, the good, and the beautiful, even though we know it is there. However, Scripture tells how Jesus brought sight to the blind and light to a world darkened by sin (Isaiah 9:2). Christ saves us and restores the ability to see the truth, goodness, and beauty of God and His world. It is because of Jesus' taking the ugliness of sin on Himself that we are given the righteousness of God. And because we are reconnected with Him, we can see something of the divine reality that we will one day see perfectly: "Now I know in part; then I shall know fully, even as I have been fully known" (1 Corinthians 13:12). Even though we "see in a mirror dimly," what we see reflects God's glory, His eternal truth, His perfect goodness, and the matchless beauty of His holiness.

This biblical picture both discourages the arrogant idea that scientists can know everything about the world and yet encourages the idea that scientists can glimpse objective truth. In this fallen flesh, we can only ever have partial knowledge. Our minds are not powerful enough or clear enough for more than that. But partial knowledge is better than no knowledge. We can say that God is hidden (*Deus absconditus*) and we cannot fully know Him. Yet we can also say that God reveals Himself (*Deus revelatus*) and thereby we can know Him. Likewise with nature, we can know with confidence what God chooses to reveal to us but are spared from the need to know everything about nature. Since God Himself reveals what we can know, we can be confident that it is at least a glimpse of objective truth.

The Gospel reorients us so that we see the beauty of God's love at work even through the ugliness of sin. In the crucifixion, "Upon Him was the chastisement that brought us peace, and with His wounds we are healed" (Isaiah 53:5). It is enormously comforting to see that the beauty that matters is God's, not ours, and that any beauty we have is only a reflection of His glory.

Scientists do not need to be motivated by vanity, seeking praises among people for their brilliant discoveries. Rather, they can search in all humility for what is already beautiful and praiseworthy in God's creation. Then they are set free to say, "To God alone be the glory." Just as this attitude guided the master musician J. S. Bach to produce beautiful music, so it can inspire scientists to discover beautiful truths about the world we live in. There is a readiness to be surprised, a childlike wonder that can marvel in God's majesty. The paradox is that pursuing one's own greatness leads to falsification of reality, but humbling oneself to God's greatness brings one closer to the truth.

If the world exists of itself, disconnected from God, then there is no reason to expect that there are valuable truths to discover, and the wonder and enthusiasm of science is killed. But if the Gospel opens our eyes again to God as the architect, then the universe is His temple, a place full of His marvelous works. This re-creates wonder and draws the mind to look for the higher things of God as evidenced in nature. Openness to truth, goodness, and beauty has led scientists to more accurate, more helpful, and more elegant and simple theories of the universe.

Christians who are scientists see beauty not only in creation but also in their neighbors. In gratitude for their beautiful Savior, such scientists want to help others. And in those others, they can now see Christ (Matthew 25:37–40). They know that whatever they do for "one of the least of these My brothers, you did it to Me [Christ]" (v. 40). To see beyond appearances that all people are beautiful as redeemed by Christ restores a sense of human value. Though sin makes us ugly, it is exchanged for the beautiful white robe of Christ's righteousness. When God the Father looks at us, He does not see the stains and disfigurement of sin but the perfect, beautiful righteousness of His Son. From this perspective, it is impossible to view another human being as a freak of nature, as a misfit with illusions of truth, beauty, and goodness that do not fit reality.

The more scientists succumb to materialism, the more they tend to hold a self-contradictory view, according to which scientists should be exalted for having the specialized knowledge that human life is meaningless. Obviously, if human life is meaningless, this applies to scientists as well, and there is no basis for exalting them.

Seeing oneself and others as redeemed by Christ restores a sense of value for all human beings while denying any exalted value to oneself—even if one is a scientist. Scientists who are Christians see others as beautiful for just the same reason they are, because Christ has honored them by bestowing His righteousness on them. Such scientists are now focused on reflecting that beauty in their treatment of others. The practical result is a more other-centered, sacrificial life.

Points to Ponder

Is beauty in the eye of the beholder, subjective and elusive, or is beauty more fundamental and independent of the beholder? When God finished creation, He proclaimed it good, suggesting an attribute that was quite independent of how humans might feel. Jesus is the way, the truth, and the life, and God is the source of meaning and fulfillment in life. We need to calibrate our values to reflect God's perspective and worship Him in spirit and truth.

WORDS TO REMEMBER

And you, who once were alienated and hostile in mind, doing evil deeds, He has now reconciled in His body of flesh by His death, in order to present you holy and blameless and above reproach before Him. (Colossians 1:21–22)

36

DEFENDING THE FAITH
WITH SCIENCE

Some people think that modern science has disproved the Christian faith. Others allow that faith can continue as a sort of private piety affecting one's moral outlook on life but deny that the truth claims of Christianity have any public, objective validity. In both cases, it is claimed that one cannot be a serious, Bible-believing Christian and also a scientist. The main argument for this view rests on the assumption that modern science has succeeded in showing that the material world is all that can really be known. One can choose to believe in something more if one likes, but this is a private preference that can never be backed up by objective scientific evidence.

Behind this outlook is a post-Enlightenment perspective on what counts as science. As Mark Noll documents in his book *The Scandal of the Evangelical Mind* (Eerdmans, 1994), during the later Enlightenment, universities in both Europe and America underwent secularization. Famous schools such as Brown, Harvard, and Yale began with clergy as presidents and re gents. They emphasized character formation and Christian theology as an overarching frame of meaning for the curriculum. Then there was a major change to an industrialist model, with businessmen running the colleges and a pragmatic orientation to providing "vocational training" (alas, not in the theological sense). When the paradigm of the German research university reached America, theology was displaced by modern, secular science as the final standard of truth.

Events in Germany during the first half of the twentieth century illustrated weaknesses of the modern, secularist approach to education and life. Twentieth-century Germany illustrated many of the worst results of secularization. This was epitomized in the rise of Nazism, which stepped into the spiritual and cultural vacuum created by secularization.

Secular science views nature as an autonomous machine, which has no need for God to sustain its operation. This assumes that rigorous scientific investigation of the material world will look to one state of the natural "machine" to explain another state. In other words, the spiritual state of things would never be considered. In consequence, secular scientists equate empirical science (science based on observation) with materialistic science (science that can only infer material causes).

PROVIDENCE

What is most remarkable about the recent view of science is that the founders of modern science saw things differently. As we saw in our earlier discussion, it was ideas from Christian theology that gave birth to modern science. Great scientists such as Kepler and Newton believed in laws of nature because they believed in providence, that God governed His creation by rational means. Kepler never saw his scientific work as disconnected from God's governance. Indeed, as Peter Barker and Bernard Goldstein have argued, Kepler "believed that he had discovered the part of God's providential plan that embodied the pattern of the cosmos, and the divine laws by which God regulated its moving parts" ("Theological Foundations of Kepler's Astronomy," *Osiris 16* [2001]: 113). In this view, laws of nature are not the autonomous principles of a self-sufficient machine but God's means of governing and sustaining His creation. Newton held a similar view, maintaining that his laws of motion only showed how things moved; the laws were not the ultimate source of motion, which was left to God.

Today's secular understanding of science cannot really justify its assumption that these are "laws of nature." This fundamentally challenges the notions of secular scientists because laws are ordinances that govern how things are done. But of course laws imply the existence of a lawgiver! Laws tell us how things are supposed to go and therefore invite the question "Supposed by whom?" A secular understanding of science excludes a divine lawgiver and so undermines any basis for saying that natural regularities are laws. There is no justification for calling these regularities laws if no one laid them down. The whole idea of a law of nature really derives from the theological doctrine of providence.

It is also false that modern scientists are necessarily driven to compromise their faith. One of the greatest experimental scientists to date was Michael Faraday (1791–1867), director of the Royal Institution in London. Faraday discovered benzene and electromagnetic induction, invented the generator, and was the main architect of the classical field theory of electromagnetism. He also had a robust, orthodox Christian faith. On his deathbed, when asked what new "speculations" he had, he replied, "Speculations, man, I have none! I have certainties. I thank God that I don't rest my dying head upon speculations for 'I know whom I have believed, and I am convinced that He is able to guard until that Day what has been entrusted to me' [2 Timothy 1:12]." Other great scientists who were committed Christians include James Clerk Maxwell (1831–79), who gave the mathematical interpretation of Faraday's concept of electromagnetic field, now known as "Maxwell's equations"; Sir Joseph John ("J. J.") Thomson (1856–1940), discoverer of the electron; and Carolus Linnaeus (1707–78), the father of taxonomy. Francis Collins (b. 1950), director of the National Institutes of Health and former Director of the Human Genome Project, was an unbeliever who was led by some kind people to read C. S. Lewis and the Bible. He is now an evangelical Christian.

Many great scientists, including some atheists, have admitted that science by itself is not enough to make sense of life. Christianity, though, provides meaning and orientation to life that science cannot provide. Science alone does not provide meaning, even at the most basic level of deciding how science should be used. Without the doctrine of vocation, science is just an applied rational activity whose results can be used for any purpose whatever. At a deeper level, science can remedy problems, but it cannot cure sin, conquer death, or save anyone. Christianity gives meaning for this life, directing us to serve others. Ultimately it gives meaning beyond this life in eternal communion with God.

Can one do science without assuming materialism? Phillip Johnson (b. 1940), a retired University of California, Berkeley, law professor, has proposed a "wedge" that can be driven between empirical science and materialistic science. Johnson argues that it is a mistake to equate these two models of science, because a scientist can do rigorous empirical investigation without assuming that only material causes are operative and detectable. He explains that it is possible for science to discover a complex phenomenon that unaided nature would not likely produce. For example, if we see that biological information is too complex and tightly specified to have arisen by chance or by any natural law, we may infer a supernatural mind as the cause.

Given our ability to rationalize, what kind of evidence might convince people that an intelligent agent had intervened in the course of nature? What would convince us that the agent was supernatural and not merely natural?

Suppose you are walking in South Dakota. You see some interesting angular rocks that vaguely resemble a human head but realize that they are not very complex or specific and could have formed either by random wind action (chance) or by a freeze-thaw cycle (natural law). A little while later, however, you see Mount Rushmore, with the faces of American presidents carved in its rock. You can be quite certain that something of this complexity and specificity, matching the appearance of independently identifiable human beings, did not arise from mere chance or natural law. In this case, it is reasonable to conclude that human agents intervened to design a product that unaided nature would not have produced.

Now suppose a scientist discovers that all life contains extremely complex, tightly specified information and can argue rigorously that this cannot have arisen by chance or law and that there were no intelligent, finite agents around to produce it. Then it is reasonable to conclude that the information derived from supernatural agency. The same argument can be made for the simplicity of the fundamental laws of nature and for the fine-tuning of cosmological constants for life.

LOGIC IN CREATION

When secular science investigates nature as if nature is disconnected from its Creator, it embarks on the building of a modern Babel, and its thinking becomes "futile" (Romans 1:21). Science as we know it is possible only because the created world and human beings are rational. We should ask what explains the assumption of rationality that must be made before science can begin. Scripture provides an answer: "In the beginning was the Word, and the Word was with God, and the Word was God. He was in the beginning with God. All things were made through Him, and without Him was not any thing made that was made" (John 1:1–3). Here "Word" is a translation of the Greek word *logos*, which can mean both the Son of God and also a principle of rational order (hence the word *logic*). The apostle Paul states that by Christ "all things were created, in heaven and on earth, visible and invisible, whether thrones or dominions or rulers or authorities—all things were created through Him and for Him. And He is before all things, and in Him all things hold together" (Colossians 1:16–17). Christ is the "reason" involved in the creation of the world and human beings, including their reason.

So how does the Christian idea of Christ as Logos support modern science, and what difficulty does this pose for the non-Christian view of science? Rational order is objectively in the creation through Christ, even behind apparent chaos. Because He shapes our own minds, we are equipped to discern that order. The scientific search for laws of nature is thus on firm ground. For an atheist, however, there is no God and no ground for believing that such rational order exists. What is more, even if it did exist, there is still no warrant for supposing that we are equipped to detect it.

Unbelievers do not accept the authority of Scripture, so unless we can evangelize them first, we can only hope to persuade them of our view through reason. This is the idea of Christian *apologetics.*

Apologetics does not mean apologizing for being a Christian, but derives from the Greek word *apologia*, which means "a reasoned, public defense, appealing to objective evidences," as in a court of law. Some Christians oppose this idea, because they see it as an unscriptural attempt to reason someone into the faith, which is impossible, since faith is the work of the Holy Spirit. However, the true goal of apologetics is not conversion but the removal of obstacles that cause or allow the unbeliever to dismiss the Christian faith without a serious consideration of it. In this sense, apologetics is actually mandated by Scripture: "always being prepared to make a defense to anyone who asks you for a reason for the hope that is in you" (1 Peter 3:15).

Sir John Polkinghorne (b. 1930), a noted physicist and Anglican clergyman, is a strong defender of the Christian faith. Christians who are scientists are given an excellent opportunity to do apologetics. Scientists know how to investigate difficult problems, marshal their evidence, and build convincing arguments and explanations. Christians who are scientists can take these abilities and use them to show how science points to God.

Science can be used to defend the faith in a number of key areas. One can argue like C. S. Lewis (*Miracles*), Angus Menuge (*Agents under Fire* [Rowman & Littlefield, 2004]), Alvin Plantinga (*Warranted Christian Belief* [Oxford University Press, 2000]), and Victor Reppert (*C. S. Lewis's Dangerous Idea* [InterVarsity, 2003]) that the blind, contingent processes of materialistic science cannot explain the goal-directed necessity of the logical thought employed by scientists themselves. One can argue with William Dembski that there are rigorous tests for empirically detecting design in nature (*The Design Inference* [Cambridge University Press, 1998]). One can appeal to the anthropic "coincidences," according to which the universe is very finely tuned to make life as we know it possible (see Larry Witham's *By Design* [Encounter Books, 2003]). One can point out, as has Stephen C. Meyer (*Science and Evidence for Design in the Universe* [Ignatius Press, 2001]), that the information in DNA, which partly specifies how proteins are to be assembled to produce various organs, is like the information in a collection of Shakespeare's sonnets, which nobody supposes arose from undirected causes. Finally, with Michael Behe (*Darwin's Black Box* [Free Press, 1996]) one can call attention to "irreducibly complex" structures in biology, which cannot function if a single part is removed, and so challenge the idea of gradual evolution from simpler precursors.

Sciences such as forensics and archaeology show that we do have empirical methods for detecting design. Forensic pathologists are able to tell whether a death was accidental, the lawful outworking of a medical condition, or the result of an evil plan. Detecting a murder involves eliminating chance (accidental death) or law (natural death) in favor of design. Likewise, archaeologists are trained to discriminate between those pieces of matter that have been altered by human shaping (artifacts) and those that have not. There is no question that scientists can detect human design, and it is only dogmatism that leads some to claim that it must be impossible to detect divine design. Sometimes even theologians claim that divine design would be inscrutable, but not only does this deny the scriptural teaching of the natural knowledge of God, but it also presumes that God would not want to communicate with us.

Paul states that God created the world and the human race so "that they should seek God, and perhaps feel their way toward Him and find Him" (Acts 17:27). Through preachers "He commands all people everywhere to repent" (v. 30). He raised Christ from the dead since "He will judge the world in righteousness by a man [Christ] whom He has appointed" (v. 31). Theologians, can there be any doubt that God wants to communicate with us?

CHRIST, OUR RIGHTEOUSNESS

Apologetics can seem a crushing responsibility to many Christians. There are so many skeptical questions and lines of defense—who can master them all? However, we are not all required to be master apologists. The defense we need is mainly for those we will meet in our vocation. A farmer has a different approach to defending the faith than a theoretical physicist, and this is just as well because their vocations put them in contact with different audiences. Some vocations provide better opportunities for apologetics than others. If a skeptic stumps us, we can recommend someone else whose vocation is better suited to answering the question. Christians as scientists, however, are an asset to the Body of Christ because their training equips them to analyze evidence and present logical explanations to defend the Christian faith.

The doctrine of vocation shows that apologetics is a community matter, not an individual matter. This should be comforting to someone who feels unable to defend the faith effectively. Anyone can be an apologist, even those who are equipped only with their personal confession of faith and not intellectual arguments. For apologists to be really effective, they should learn to defer to the expertise of those who have the relevant vocation. We can be happy to appeal to historians, legal scholars, philosophers, theologians, and scientists when they have the gifts to defend the faith. We are not saved by our defense and do not have to work out all the details on our own. And even if we feel incapable of defending the faith, we can simply point to others in the Body of Christ who are better equipped.

When we have relevant knowledge, we are sometimes afraid to use it. Fortunately, we have a God who enables people to speak out even when they are not "ready." Think of Moses, who claimed he could not speak, and the astonishing performance of Peter, an uneducated fisherman, at Pentecost. In fact, there is comfort for us in the passage immediately preceding the apologist's mandate. Peter's First Epistle was written to Christians suffering persecution, and while today (in North America at least) Christians are no longer tortured or executed, they are sometimes ridiculed or opposed for their faith. Peter advises, "Even if you should suffer for righteousness' sake, you will be blessed. Have no fear of them, nor be troubled, but in your hearts regard Christ the Lord as holy" (1 Peter 3:14–15). Peter explains that even if we suffer, "Christ also suffered once for sins, the righteous for the unrighteous, that He might bring us to God" (v. 18). As a result, there is nothing we really need to be afraid of anymore. With our salvation assured, we should not fear the world's rejection, which ultimately cannot harm us. Furthermore, it is a focus on Christ and the Spirit's work that will enable us to speak. Our focus, too, should not be conquering individuals who disagree with us (this may put them off the faith) but helping our neighbors to see the truth.

Read 1 Peter 3:15–16, and consider why it is important to defend the faith with "gentleness and respect." Although apologetics is not the same as evangelism (presenting the Gospel), the Gospel is the end the apologist should have in view. Master apologist Ravi Zacharias uses an old Indian proverb to make the point that we should not cut off a person's nose and then ask him or her to smell the rose of the Gospel. If we "win" an argument by humiliating someone, we may only alienate that person from Christianity and create a wounded pride that will reject the Gospel. Better than confronting people in this fashion is standing side by side with them and respectfully showing them the grounds for Christian claims. It may take time. But ultimately, it is God, not we, who grants the increase of faith.

Apologetics is never a substitute for faith. At its best, apologetics shows the existence of a designer or a source of reason or a first cause. But this does not establish that this being is the God of Christianity.

Suppose someone has moved into an apartment above yours, but you have never met the person. You hear certain sounds and form an impression of what sort of individual this is. But you do not know the individual. You do not have a personal relationship. Then one day the newcomer comes down to introduce himself. You come to know him personally. Apologetics gets at qualities of God by examining the world. But faith is a personal relationship made possible only because God came down to us in the person of Jesus Christ.

C. S. Lewis once worried that if he was like Hamlet (character) and God was like Shakespeare (author), Lewis could never know God. Yet, according to John 14:8–9, the uniquely Christian claim of the incarnation solves this problem.

If Shakespeare is the author but stays entirely out of the play and does not even include lines that point to him, then a character in the play, such as Hamlet, has no way of knowing the author. Indeed the play may not have an author but may be like improvisational theater, "a tale told by an idiot, full of sound and fury, signifying nothing" (*Macbeth*, act 5, scene 5). If we are like Hamlet in such a play, we cannot know God or be saved from our predicament.

But in the drama of this world written by God, the Author of life also writes Himself in as a character in the play and comes to dwell among us. Just as Alfred Hitchcock often appeared in his own movies, so our God appeared so that we may know Him through the person of Christ. Most scandalously of all, this all happened in the same grimy history that we inhabit. Here Christians have a solid basis for their faith, the likes of which is completely lacking in other religions. Either these other religions have no historical basis at all, or if they do, they provide no grounds for supposing that God has spoken to us and for us. Our God humbled Himself to become man and to die on a cross for our sins for that very purpose.

POINTS TO PONDER

On the whole, science and theology should complement each other. They each investigate certain aspects of God's creation and God's revelation, and they each reflect a God-given curiosity or hunger for knowledge, wisdom, and value. However, they realize their full potential only in service to God. And since the people who do science, theology, and every other kind of study and vocation are all sinners (we are all sinners!), they realize their full value only if redeemed by our Lord and Savior, Jesus Christ. To God be the glory. Amen!

WORDS TO REMEMBER

We destroy arguments and every lofty opinion raised against the knowledge of God, and take every thought captive to obey Christ. (2 Corinthians 10:5)

APPENDIX 1

EVOLUTION

It is often confidently asserted today that large-scale evolution is no longer simply a theory but a fact, so that disagreeing with evolution is like denying that the Earth is round. However, an increasing number of scientists and philosophers argue that these claims go far beyond what the evidence actually warrants and point out that strong evidence points in the opposite direction.

The evolution we can actually observe is so-called microevolution, where there is an increase in the frequency of some members of a species due to a change in environmental conditions. For example, bacteria that are resistant to antibiotics become more predominate than those that are not. Insects respond in a similar way to insecticides. However, when the antibiotics or insecticides are removed, the populations return to normal, with the same distribution of characteristics they had before. And, most important, there is no evidence that these changes in the distribution of characteristics within the population ever produce a new morphology (or body plan), which is required for a new species to form. In other words, microevolution does not provide a plausible account of macroevolution. (For more details, see Michael Denton's *Evolution: A Theory in Crisis* [Adler & Adler, 1985], Phillip Johnson's *Darwin on Trial* [National Book Network, 1991], and Jonathan Wells's *Icons of Evolution* [National Book Network, 2000].)

In addition, Darwin's theory claims that evolutionary change is undirected and the result of chance and therefore can be predicted to be gradual. If this is correct, then, as Darwin himself admitted, there should be innumerable transitional forms in the fossil record. Yet they are not to be found, as even the noted paleontologist and evolutionist Stephen Jay Gould admitted.

Finally, in his book *Darwin's Black Box* (Free Press, 1996), Michael Behe has argued that there is a good reason why a gradual Darwinian path cannot explain certain biological structures: they are irreducibly complex. What this means is that like the common household mousetrap, many biological structures have a number of well-matched parts, the removal of any one of which would prevent the system from functioning. It is hard to see how such structures could develop gradually, since the simpler precursor systems do not work and so would not be selected. Darwinists have proposed "indirect scenarios" to overcome this difficulty, but these do not work either (see William Dembski, *No Free Lunch* [Rowman & Littlefield, 2002], ch. 5, and Angus Menuge, *Agents under Fire* [Rowman & Littlefield, 2004], ch. 4).

In cases of legitimate controversy, scientists should claim only that they have a working hypothesis that covers the data in a limited domain (micro-evolution) and allow the evidence for and against any larger claims to be freely debated. They also should not assert that it is science that establishes philosophical views when in fact these views were really adopted prior to scientific investigation.

APPENDIX 2

ENVIRONMENTALISM, SCIENCE, AND CHRISTIAN STEWARDSHIP

Publication of Rachel Carson's book *Silent Spring* in 1963 began the dramatic growth of what we call the environmental movement. Conservationists, preservationists, and environmentalists had voiced concern about environmental issues for decades, but it was this general-audience book rather than a peer-reviewed scientific paper that caught public attention. In the years since, then environmentalism has risen to a prominence that influences national policies and impacts personal choices and lifestyles. It has become a pervasive political cause with adherents worldwide in the green movement.

Over the last two centuries, we have acquired a mastery over the planet Earth never before seen in history. That mastery, fueled by the scientific and technological revolutions, has brought about dramatic improvements in human health and well-being but has often come with a cost to the environment. The environmental movement has drawn attention to the way in which our domination has diminished the beauty of God's earth, damaged the health of its ecosystems, and pushed many creatures to the brink of extinction. The environmental movement has also called for action by alarming people with doom-and-gloom scenarios predicted to take place if we do not act to avert them. And for many people, environmentalism has provided a spiritual kind of fulfillment as they commit their time, energy, and other resources to the green movement.

The Lutheran Church—Missouri Synod's Commission on Theology and Church Relations publication *Together with All Creatures: Caring for God's Living Earth* (expanded version) provides a brief history of the evolving relationship between the environmental movement and Christianity. While many members of the environmental movement include other priorities among their personal values, and some are devout Christians, other members are devoted to the cause with an almost religious fervor. Although they may not realize the implications, they deny other priorities, put environmental issues above everything else, and even in some sense begin to worship the creature rather than the Creator, as Paul described in Romans 1:25. This breaks the First Commandment; it can also devalue human life when it denies that children are a blessing (Psalm 127:3) and instead claims that "people are the problem."

We need to be circumspect about the claims of the movement in at least two ways. First, if love for the environment begins to rival love for God, we must recall Christ's admonition that it is impossible to serve two masters (Matthew 6:24). It is fitting and quite appropriate for us to love God's world as He loves the world, but God and His love come first. Second, if the environmental movement claims support from scientists but tries to silence questions, data, or alternative analyses, then it is not following the scientific method and its claims of scientific support are not authentic.

We should be appropriately careful of the environmental movement as we should be careful of any other movement that demands our first love. However, this caution does not relieve us of our responsibilities as stewards of the world that God has entrusted to us. Even if some elements of the environmental movement go off the rails into their own form of spiritualism, we need to realize that Christian stewardship of the earth did not end when Adam and Eve were evicted from the Garden of Eden. Our response to or participation in the environmental movement must revolve around two principles: God's ownership, and our stewardship. So, with these principles in mind, what is our role in caring for the earth?

Drawing key thoughts from the CTCR report mentioned above, our role in caring for the earth first involves recognizing where we fit in God's creation. The fact is, we are part of His creation and we are His creatures. However, even though we have much in common with the other creatures in His world, we are different and special: we are made in God's image, and we have a soul. And we all share a calling as stewards of the earth, indeed, the whole life He gives us. Next, we see that we can and should delight in God's creation, just as He delights in what He has created. We recognize that we serve as stewards of the earth and everything in it, serving with humility and kindness, and with accountability to God. Finally, we thank and glorify God for the beauty, power, and majesty revealed through His creation.

APPENDIX 3

BIBLICAL TERMS FOR HEAVEN AND HELL

(adapted from *Christian Cyclopedia,* Concordia Publishing House, © 1984)

Abyssos, Abyss. *Abyssos* is a Greek word meaning "bottomless, unbounded." It means (1) the "deep," or primeval waters (Genesis 1:2); (2) the depths of the earth as a symbol of great distress and anguish of soul (Psalm 71:20); (3) the abode of the dead (Romans 10:7); and (4) hell, as Apollyon's abode over evil spirits (Revelation 9:1–2, 11; 11:7; 17:8; 20:1, 3).

Gehenna. Gehenna is the Greek name of a deep, narrow valley, which runs southwest alongside Jerusalem and wraps around its south end. In this valley, wicked Israelites sacrificed children to the Canaanite idol Molech ("Valley of . . . Hinnom" in 2 Kings 23:10). Later, the valley was used for burning refuse. Because of its sordid past, *Gehenna* came to refer to the abode of the wicked after death (Matthew 5:22, 29; 10:28; Mark 9:43, 45; Luke 12:5; James 3:6).

Hades. *Hades* may come from the Greek word for "unseen." In nonbiblical Greek literature, it means the realm of the dead. In the Greek translation of the Old Testament (Septuagint), *Hades* is used almost exclusively for *Sheol;* in the New Testament, it means "realm of the dead" (Acts 2:27, 31; Revelation 20:13–14) or a place where unbelievers, like the rich man, suffer (Luke 16:23).

Heaven. Heaven is (1) the sky with everything in it (Hebrews 1:10; Matthew 16:2); (2) outer space (Hebrews 11:12); (3) the dwelling place of God, Christ, and the angels, and our heavenly home (Matthew 5:12; 5:34; 18:10; 23:22; 24:36; Acts 1:9–11; 7:49; 1 Peter 1:4).

Paradise. *Paradise,* perhaps a Persian word, can mean (1) a garden or park, for example, the Garden of Eden (Genesis 2:8–17); (2) the heavenly paradise, home of God's saints (Luke 23:43; 2 Corinthians 12:3; Revelation 2:7).

Sheol. *Sheol* occurs sixty-five times in the Hebrew Old Testament. Scholars still struggle to understand it. Martin Luther translated it as "hell" in all places except Genesis 37:35; 42:38; 44:29, 31. In these passages he translated it as "grave." The King James translators used "grave," "hell," and "pit." Since the origin of the word is uncertain, the context must determine the meaning in each case.

Sheol may mean the resting place of man's mortal remains (Job 17:16; Isaiah 38:10) or the "realm of the dead" (e.g., Genesis 37:35; Job 7:9; Psalm 16:10; 31:17; 89:48). In this sense *sheol* is very much like the English expressions "the hereafter" or "the beyond." Going "down to Sheol" means "to die, to depart from the land of the living." But it should be noted that when the righteous are said to descend into Sheol, their fate beyond is never taken into account. The hope of the pious in the Old Testament is expressed differently (e.g., Psalm 73:24).

Sheol may also mean the place where evildoers face God's judgment. Sheol receives people taken away in God's anger, such as Korah's rebel band (Numbers

16:30, 33) and harlots (Proverbs 5:5). The Lord's anger burns to the depths of Sheol (Deuteronomy 32:22). According to Psalm 49, all people die physically, righteous as well as ungodly (v. 10). But there is a difference in their existence in the hereafter. The psalmist confidently expresses, "Their form shall be consumed in Sheol, with no place to dwell. But God will ransom my soul from the power of Sheol, for He will receive me" (Psalm 49:14–15). Clearly there is a sharp contrast between the doom of the ungodly and the glorious hope of the believer, who hopes to rest securely in the hands of God. (See also Psalm 73.)

Tartaros. The Greek word *Tartaros* is not in the Bible, but a related verb form occurs in 2 Peter 2:4. In Greek mythology, Tartaros is an underground prison, regarded as the abode of the wicked dead where they suffer punishment for their evil deeds; it corresponds to **Gehenna** as a name for hell.

APPENDIX 4

COMPARATIVE VIEWS ON LIFE AFTER DEATH

Faith Group	Death	Body	Soul	Resurrection	Heaven & Hell
Lutheran	Temporal and spiritual death results from the fall. Temporal death separates soul from body.	The body is an important part of God's creation. It is laid to rest until the resurrection on the Last Day.	Souls of believers immediately go to heaven. Souls of unbelievers immediately go to hell.	The souls of all the dead will be rejoined with their earthly bodies at the resurrection on the Last Day.	Believers spend eternity in a new heaven and earth. Unbelievers spend eternity in the torments of hell.
Conservative Protestant	Temporal and spiritual death results from the fall. Temporal death separates soul from body.	The body is an important part of God's creation. It is laid to rest until the resurrection.	Souls of believers immediately go to heaven. Souls of unbelievers immediately go to hell.	The souls of all the dead will be rejoined with their earthly bodies at the resurrection (or resurrections).	Believers spend eternity in a new heaven and earth. Unbelievers spend eternity in the torments of hell.
Eastern Orthodox	Temporal death and spiritual impairment results from the fall. Soul and body separate at death.	The body is an important part of God's creation. It is laid to rest until the resurrection on the Last Day.	Souls of believers doing good works go to heaven. Other souls go to hell.	The souls of all the dead will be rejoined with their earthly bodies at the resurrection on the Last Day.	Believers doing good works go to the new heaven. Others, separated from God, go to the new earth.
Roman Catholic	Temporal death and spiritual impairment results from the fall. Soul and body separate at death.	The body is an important part of God's creation. It is laid to rest until the resurrection on the Last Day.	Perfect souls go to heaven. Imperfect souls spend time in purgatory. Souls in mortal sin go to hell.	The souls of all the dead will be rejoined with their earthly bodies at the resurrection on the Last Day.	Those doing good works spend eternity in a new heaven and earth. Those in mortal sin go to hell.

Faith Group	Death	Body	Soul	Resurrection	Heaven & Hell
Liberal Protestant	Death occurs naturally as a part of physical existence. An afterlife may or may not exist.	The human body holds value only in so far as it supports painless, productive human existence.	The "soul" is a person's cognitive and emotive abilities and/ or spiritual aspirations.	The "resurrection" is best expressed as improving human life through Jesus' ethical teachings.	All people will be "saved," if only through their memories being preserved by their loved ones.
Jewish	Range from end of bodily life and entrance into "the world to come," to an end of all existence.	The body is an important part of God's creation.	We are made in God's image with the capacity to choose good or evil.	Wide range of beliefs including bodily resurrection.	Orthodox: reward or punishment in heaven or hell. Liberal: denial of afterlife.
Mormon	The fall opened the way for Gospel and ordinances. Death separates soul from body.	Procreation is encouraged because God's pre-existent spirit children need earthly bodies.	Pre-existent children of God; gods-in-embryo with the potential of achieving godhood.	Teaches a general, bodily resurrection for all the dead.	Only the best Mormons go to the Celestial Kingdom. Only the worst sinners go to the Outer Darkness.
Jehovah's Witness	Cessation of both soul and bodily life.	The body is an important part of God's creation.	Created in Jehovah's image, although the soul is not immortal.	No literal resurrection, but at the end Jehovah will re-create all but the most wicked.	144,000 "elect" Witnesses go to heaven; others go to paradise on earth. Those rejecting Jehovah face annihilation.
Muslim	Death separates soul from body	The body is an important part of Allah's creation. It is laid to rest until the resurrection.	Humans created basically pure, although fallible and in need of Allah's guidance. Soul immortal.	Teaches a general, bodily resurrection for all the dead.	Faithful Muslims go to Paradise. Non-Muslims and those who commit shirk (apostasy) go to a fiery hell.

Faith Group	Death	Body	Soul	Resurrection	Heaven & Hell
Hindu	Basic human condition is samsara, the cycle of birth and death.	Physical body has little worth.	The soul is immortal, part of Brahman. People unaware that they themselves are "God."	No resurrection. Goal of life is to obtain final release, or moksha, from reincarnation.	Cycles of reincarnation (birth, death) until one is absorbed into Brahman, the Ultimate Reality.
Buddhist	Human condition is suffering, caused by the attachment and desire for material things.	Attachment to the physical body is actually a hindrance to achieving nirvana.	Denies existence of the "self" apart from physical and mental attributes.	No resurrection. Goal of life is nirvana (negation of suffering), achieved only by eliminating desire.	May pass through a series of heavens and hells on the way to achieving nirvana.
Secular Humanist	Man is part of nature. Death is a natural process in which man participates.	Body serves no purpose after death.	The "soul" ceases to exist at bodily death.	No resurrection.	"Heaven" can only mean the improvement of man's condition through science and technology.

GLOSSARY

adult stem cells (ASC). Cells found in adult tissues, such as bone marrow, lung, pancreas, brain, breast, fat, and skin (also in umbilical cord and placenta), that contain cells that will develop into tissues or organs.

agnosticism. A philosophical view that any knowledge of the supernatural—God, creation, the afterlife—is incomplete, or has not been reached. Agnosticism does not reject the possibility that a deity may indeed exist.

allegorical interpretation. The interpretation of things or events as symbols for higher realities or truths. Allegory often denies or ignores the literal meaning of a text or a subject of study.

amoral science. The view that scientific investigation should not be obstructed by moral considerations.

annihilationism. The belief that God will annihilate—cause to cease to exist—the souls of the unrighteous after death. This unbiblical view is taught by the "Christian" cult, the Jehovah's Witnesses.

anthropic principle. The observation that Earth is especially well suited for life, which implies that it was created to host and sustain life.

apologetics. From the Greek word for "defense." The reasonable defense of one's beliefs.

artificial insemination. The introduction of sperm into the vagina other than by coitus.

assisted reproductive technology (ART). Technological or medical procedures that assist a man and a woman in reproducing a child other than by coitus.

atheism. The belief that no supreme being exists outside of the physical universe. Ironically, because atheism is dogmatic (insistent that its beliefs are absolutely true), it may be considered a "religion."

aura. An energy field, which some believe emanates from a living being.

autonomy. The ability to govern or control one's self.

autoscopic hallucinations. When one projects an image of self into visual space in a third-person perspective (e.g., meeting one's double on the street).

beauty. A quality or union of qualities, such as symmetry and balance, that brings pleasure to the senses.

Big Bang. The cosmological theory that matter and the universe emerged from an explosion of dense energy billions of years ago.

biological determinism. The theory that chemical processes naturally and necessarily led to the evolution of life.

calling. See *vocation*.

cloning. The asexual production of an organism that has an identical genetic constitution to its "parent."

contact. An encounter between extraterrestrial and human life.

contrition. To feel sorry for one's sin.

cosmology. From the Greek word for "world" or "universe." The study of the origin and nature of the universe.

cultural mandate. God's command to Adam and Eve to cultivate and care for the Garden of Eden and all creation (Genesis 1:28; 2:15).

demonologist. Literally, "one who studies demons"; moreover, one who studies the nature and acts of demonic beings and other paranormal phenomena from a Christian perspective to help both Christians and non-Christians deal with their presence and occurrences in a healthy manner.

determinism. The belief that everything happens because of causes outside of an individual. In other words, people do not have the will to make choices. What they do is caused by God, nature, society, or some other force.

direct egg sperm injection. Introduction by injection of one sperm into one egg.

embryo. The developing human from fertilization through the eighth week.

embryonic stem cells (ESC). The inner cell mass of a five- to seven-day-old embryonic human being that is harvested, thereby destroying the embryo's life.

empirical. Based on the senses: sight, hearing, touch, taste, and smell.

enlightened. Full of spiritual insight.

eschatology. Literally, "the study of last things," referring to the end of the world. In theology, eschatology deals with the topics of death, the reappearing of Christ, judgment, and eternal life.

ethical science. The view that scientific investigation should be subject to and limited by moral considerations.

eugenics. A science that seeks to improve the hereditary traits of a race or breed.

evolution. Literally, "unrolling." A process of change. In biology, evolution refers to (1) the changes in a species of organism through the process of reproduction or (2) the naturalistic theory that life developed through chemical and biological processes such as mutation and natural selection.

ex nihilo. Latin for "from nothing." In theology, the term means that God created the universe from nothing rather than from preexisting matter.

extraterrestrial life. A term for a life form that is not from planet Earth.

gamete intrafallopian transfer. The placement of one to three eggs and sperm in a woman's fallopian tubes, attempting to mimic the normal physiological process.

Gnosticism. An early heresy (whose teachings are promoted by some modern "Christian" cults), which disparaged the created material world. Gnosticism denied that Jesus had a physical body. John refers to Gnostic teachers as "antichrists" (1 John 2:18; 4:3).

Gospel. The message of Christ's death and resurrection for the forgiveness of sins. The Holy Spirit works through the Gospel to create faith and convert people.

Gospel principle. Using the Gospel to discern the spiritual value of an event or teaching (see 1 John 4:1–3).

heat death. The ultimate exhaustion of energy in the universe, as described by the second law of thermodynamics.

hyper-spiritualism, hyper-spirituality. In this study, excessive interest in or focus on the spiritual world to the depreciation, if not exclusion, of the material world.

Hyper-spirituality may deny the incarnation of the Son of God in human flesh or His bodily resurrection, pit personal religious "revelation" or "experience" against the concrete Means of Grace (Word and Sacraments), stress God's miracles at the expense of God's regular work in the created order, or de-emphasize (or reject) the bodily resurrection of the dead while promoting post-death "spiritual" existence. See *Gnosticism*.

hypothesis. A proposed explanation. In science, the truthfulness of a hypothesis is tested by experimentation or observation. If the hypothesis holds up, it is regarded as a viable theory.

immediate revelation. The direct revelation of truth from God in the hearing or in the mind of an individual.

incarnation. From the Latin "in the flesh." It refers to the conception of Jesus, God the Son, in the womb of the Virgin Mary by the Holy Spirit. Do not confuse *incarnation* with *reincarnation*, a Hindu doctrine.

intermediate state of souls. The Roman Catholic Church teaches that when people die, their souls may go to places other than heaven or hell. Instead, they may go to limbo (unbaptized infants) or purgatory (those who have not attained perfection in this life). Other denominations have held that the soul of a dead person does not go to heaven, but rests in the ground with the body until the resurrection ("soul sleep").

in vitro fertilization. The process by which an egg and a sperm are combined in a petri dish in an effort to induce fertilization.

Law. God's will that shows people how they should live (e.g., the Ten Commandments) and condemns their failure. The preaching of the Law is the cause of contrition (genuine sorrow over sin).

law. In science, an established fact or principle. In theology, the Law is God's will, which shows people how they should live (e.g., the Ten Commandments) and condemns their failure.

laws of nature. The consistent behaviors of natural things, discovered by observation or experimentation (e.g., the law of gravity).

literal interpretation. A nonsymbolic interpretation of events or things according to natural meaning (e.g., a lamb is a lamb and not a symbol of something else).

logos. A Greek term for an idea, word, or reason. The apostle John uses this term to describe Jesus as the reason or logic of God's created order (John 1:1–18).

masks of God. Persons, institutions, or things through which God works in order to accomplish His purposes.

materialistic. Based on consideration of material reality, excluding spiritual realities.

means. In theology, an object through which God reveals His teaching or blessing or works something, such as the Bible, a Sacrament, a person, and so forth. The object stands as an intermediary for God's presence.

Means of Grace. The means by which God gives us forgiveness, life, and salvation, won by the life, death, and resurrection of Jesus Christ: the Gospel and the Sacraments. See also *sacrament*.

mediate revelation. See *means*.

medium. A person who claims the ability to communicate with the dead.

metaphysics. Philosophical teaching that addresses the nature, origin, and understanding of reality.

methodological naturalism. To investigate things or events without considering supernatural causes.

monism. The belief that everything that exists has one substance or ultimate reality (e.g., no distinction between mind and matter).

naturalism. Philosophical worldview maintaining that nothing exists beyond the world of nature and material realities.

natural knowledge of God. An understanding of God's characteristics through study of nature as His creation.

natural law. In science, the regular course of events occurring in nature at-large such as gravity or energy loss in the atmosphere; description of events in the realm of nature that are seen as usually occurring as opposed to necessarily occurring.

natural selection. The teaching that animals or people who are most fit to survive will most likely survive. This is also called "survival of the fittest."

New Age. The eclectic blend of religious and cultural beliefs, customs, and attitudes arising in the twentieth century and later that emphasizes reincarnation, alternative spiritualities, and health.

nihilism. From the Latin, *nihilo* (nothing); a philosophical worldview denying the existence of an afterlife and/or any ultimate accountability such as God.

original righteousness. The state of sinless perfection into which God created Adam and Eve (Genesis 1:31; 2:25).

original sin. The biblical teaching that each person inherits sin and guilt from his or her parents, back to the first sin committed by Adam and Eve (Genesis 3).

oscillating-universe theory. The universe will not endlessly expand. In the future, gravity may cause it to contract.

out-of-body experience. The feeling of being outside your body, usually accompanied by the sense that you can see your body from an external perspective.

palliative care. Proactive, intensive comfort care.

panspermia hypothesis. The idea that life on Earth came from other planets.

pantheism. The philosophical position that everything that exists is god.

paranormal. Events or experiences that surpass normal sensory experience, such as ESP, telekinesis, and psychic ability.

phenomenon. An object or event known through the senses.

polytheism. Belief in multiple gods.

priesthood of all believers. The belief that every Christian is called to serve God, pray to God directly, and speak God's Word (1 Peter 2:9–10).

"priests . . . in . . . the book of nature." A name given to scientists by the astronomer and mathematician Johannes Kepler. Kepler held that scientists were God's servants (priests) studying God's creation (the book of nature).

primary creation. God's act of creating something or someone from nothing, as in Genesis 1. See also *secondary creation* and *tertiary creation*.

providence. The belief that God created and continues to provide for the existence of the universe.

psychic. A person sensitive to nonphysical forces such as thoughts, feelings, or spirits.

psychosomatic. Bodily condition(s) caused by the mind, such as worrying yourself sick.

redeem. To buy back; to set a captive free by paying a ransom. Christ paid the price for our sins and so redeemed us.

reductionism, materialist. The belief that the material universe has no inherent meaning; truth, goodness, and beauty are values humans impose on the material universe in their quest for meaning.

reincarnation. The Hindu teaching that after death the life force, or soul, of the deceased transmigrates to other bodies, including human, plant, or animal. The cycle of birth, death, and rebirth occurs until the soul merges with Brahman, the Ultimate Reality. Many New Age beliefs are based on Hindu teachings.

repentance. Sorrow for sin brought about by the goodness of God. Sometimes repentance is used in a broad way to describe all of conversion, including faith in God's mercy.

reproductive cloning. Using cloning technology to produce a full-gestational-term cloned human being at birth.

Rituale Romanum. Roman Catholic liturgical book, first published in 1614. The services were significantly altered following the Second Vatican Council (1962–65).

Sacrament. Literally, something sacred. In the Lutheran Church, a Sacrament is a sacred act that (1) was instituted by Christ, (2) has a visible, earthly element, and (3) offers the forgiveness of sins earned by Christ. The Sacraments include Holy Baptism, Holy Communion, and Holy Absolution.

Santeria. Occult beliefs and rituals in which Roman Catholic saints represent gods from Yoruba, a West African religion. Santeria originated in Cuba and involves ritual sacrifice.

Scholasticism. From the Greek word for "school." A theological and philosophical school of late medieval Europe. Scholastics sought to prove their beliefs through logic, based on the methods of the Greek philosopher Aristotle and the citation of ancient authoritative documents such as the Bible and the Church Fathers.

secondary (sub) creation. The act of creating something from existing materials. See also *primary creation* and *tertiary creation*.

secularization. The process of eliminating theological beliefs as a basis for life and understanding.

secular salvation. The idea that science saves us by relieving us from the effects of the fall into sin (Genesis 3:15–19).

sentience. Awareness of one's surroundings; capable of sensation.

social Darwinism. A sociological theory based on Charles Darwin's theory of evolution, holding that certain races have biological superiority and will naturally dominate other races.

spiritist. One who regularly seeks to contact the dead or claims to communicate with spirits.

spirituality. Personal religious interest or sensitivity; recognizing that more than the material world exists.

steady-state theory. The cosmological theory that matter and the universe have always existed.

stem cells. Cells that have the ability to divide indefinitely and to give rise to specialized cells (bone marrow, pancreas, skin, muscle, etc.) as well as to produce new stem cells with identical potential.

stewardship. To act as a steward; to manage something or someone.

stigmata. An event whereby a person receives a copy or duplication of the five wounds of Christ upon his or her own body.

stigmatic. One who has claimed to have received the five wounds of the stigmata.

supernaturalism. A philosophical worldview asserting that there is existence "above" nature such as spiritual or divine beings.

tertiary creation. The act of creating something by machine through programming (e.g., a computer programmed to manufacture products without direct human control). See also *primary creation* and *secondary creation*.

therapeutic cloning. Using cloning technology to recover cloned embryonic stem cells. One of the main purposes of this approach is to avoid tissue and organ rejection.

thermodynamics. An area of physics dealing with the properties of heat.

transcendent. The teaching that God is beyond and completely separate from earthly, material reality.

utopia. An imaginary, ideal place.

vocation. The Latin word for "calling." The teaching that God calls people to certain kinds of life and work (1 Corinthians 7:17).

worldview. How one looks at the universe and his or her place in it, so that one can make moral decisions.

zygote. A cell that results from the union of an oocyte (egg) and a sperm. According to K. L. Moore and T. V. N. Persaud in *The Developing Human: Clinically Oriented Embryology* (1998), "A zygote is the beginning of a new human being."